New Frontiers
in Popular Romance

ALSO EDITED BY SUSAN FANETTI

Bonds of Brotherhood in Sons of Anarchy: *Essays on Masculinity in the FX Series* (McFarland, 2018)

New Frontiers in Popular Romance

Essays on the Genre in the 21st Century

Edited by SUSAN FANETTI

McFarland & Company, Inc., Publishers
Jefferson, North Carolina

This book has undergone peer review.

LIBRARY OF CONGRESS CATALOGUING-IN-PUBLICATION DATA

Names: Fanetti, Susan, editor.
Title: New frontiers in popular romance : essays on the genre in the 21st century / edited by Susan Fanetti.
Description: Jefferson, North Carolina : McFarland & Company, Inc., Publishers, 2022 | Includes bibliographical references and index.
Identifiers: LCCN 2022022392 | ISBN 9781476682464 (paperback : acid free paper) ♾
ISBN 9781476646220 (ebook)
Subjects: LCSH: Romance fiction—History and criticism. | Popular literature—21st century—History and criticism. | BISAC: LITERARY CRITICISM / Gothic & Romance | LCGFT: Literary criticism. | Essays.
Classification: LCC PN3448.L67 N49 2022 | DDC 823/.08509092—dc23/eng/20220531
LC record available at https://lccn.loc.gov/2022022392

BRITISH LIBRARY CATALOGUING DATA ARE AVAILABLE

ISBN (print) 978-1-4766-8246-4
ISBN (ebook) 978-1-4766-4622-0

© 2022 Susan Fanetti. All rights reserved

No part of this book may be reproduced or transmitted in any form or by any means, electronic or mechanical, including photocopying or recording, or by any information storage and retrieval system, without permission in writing from the publisher.

Front cover image © 2022 YagudinaTatyana/Shutterstock

Printed in the United States of America

*McFarland & Company, Inc., Publishers
Box 611, Jefferson, North Carolina 28640
www.mcfarlandpub.com*

Table of Contents

*Introduction—Popular Romance in the 21st Century:
Time to Claim Its Due*
    SUSAN FANETTI   1

Part One: Problematic Masculinities

Healing Toxic Masculinity in *Sweatpants Season*
by Danielle Allen
    JONATHAN A. ALLAN   17

From Darcy to Dickheads: Why Do Women Love
the Bad Boy?
    ASHLEIGH TAYLOR SULLIVAN   31

Part Two: Navigating Consent After #MeToo

Tingles and Shivers: First Kisses and Intimate Civility
in Eliza Redgold's Historical Harlequin Romances
Pre- and Post-#MeToo
    DEBRA DUDEK, ELIZABETH REID BOYD, MADALENA
    GROBBELAAR, *and* ROSE WILLIAMS   47

I Thought You'd Never Ask: Consent in Contemporary
Romance
    COURTNEY WATSON   62

Part Three: History and Historicity

"Say, could that lass be I?" *Outlander*, Transmedial Time-
Travel, and Women's Historical Fantasy
    ASHLEY ELIZABETH CHRISTENSEN   79

"Place the glass before you, and draw in chalk your own
picture": The Recasting of *Jane Eyre*
    Lucy Sheerman   97

Part Four: Representation Matters

"The Realness" in Jasmine Guillory's Sista Lit Rom Com Novels
    Camille S. Alexander   121

Eating Disorders and Romance
    Ellen Carter   136

The "Grandly and Inhospitably Strange" World of
Autistic Heroines in Romance Fiction
    Wendy Wagner   150

Part Five: Romance Tropes and Social Status

Women Policing Whiteness: Deviance and Surveillance
in Contemporary Police Procedural Romance
    Nattie Golubov   167

"I'm a *mehfil*, I'm a gathering to which everyone is invited":
Reading "Outcast" Romances in Arundhati Roy's Fiction
    Lucky Issar   187

Part Six: Romance Tropes in Online Spaces

The System That Loves Me: The State of Human Existence
in Web-Based Romantic Fiction from Post-Socialist China
    Jin Feng   201

Original Slash, Romance, and C.S. Pacat's *Captive Prince*
    Maria Alberto   216

About the Contributors   233

Index   237

Introduction

*Popular Romance in the 21st Century:
Time to Claim Its Due*

Susan Fanetti

As a field of scholarly inquiry, popular romance has long been such an ignored (at best) and maligned (at worst) genre that seemingly every scholarly work on it opens with a lengthy defense of, first, the genre itself, and, second, its value for academic study. This remains true even as the field expands and the body of research and analysis focused on popular romance steadily grows. I will make the same defense here, because we're not yet at the point where respect can be assumed. But each new essay, each collection, each monograph is a step forward. In the 21st century, the genre has gained an academic association—the International Association for the Study of Popular Romance, founded in 2009—and with it a conference and a journal—the *Journal of Popular Romance Studies*—devoted to the study of romance. I anticipate the day in the not-so-distant future when a defense of the very idea of studying popular romance no longer feels necessary.

Today is not that day, alas. Even among genre fiction, every aspect of which, from science fiction to detective stories, has struggled for respect under the weighty shadow of "literary fiction," popular romance has been the bastard stepchild in cultural commentary and scholarly analysis alike. Writing in 1996, Stephen Brown notes that romance novels are dismissed as "mass produced fantasies that are atrociously written, mindlessly consumed, and concocted according to the same tired and tiresome recipe" (qtd. in Johnson 55), which denigrates the entire genre and all its participants in a single patronizing sweep. This attitude was the rule 25 years ago, and it holds tenaciously in many corners today, even as popular culture studies in general has grown as a discipline and the genres clustered beneath that large umbrella gain respect and attention.

Even the early scholarly works that took the genre seriously—Tania

2 Introduction

Modleski's *Loving with a Vengeance: Mass-Produced Fantasies for Women* (originally 1982), Janice A. Radway's *Reading the Romance: Women, Patriarchy, and Popular Literature* (1984), and Pamela Regis's *A Natural History of the Romance Novel* (1993)—all approach the genre in ways that, while primarily respectful, and certainly without the disdain Stephen Brown describes, make sweeping generalizations about popular romance, its texts, and its readers.

All three are still considered important and "seminal" texts for study and generally considered the points from which romance scholarship must launch—and they were, indeed, revolutionary for simply taking romance seriously. Yet they have not held up especially well to the tests of time. Modleski and Radway now have revised editions of their texts, which seek to update and account for faulty assumptions or aging ideas; in her new introduction, Modleski apologizes for being "too categorical" with some of her language choices (*Vengeance*).

Mary Bly, an academic as well as a consistently best-selling romance novelist, writing under the pseudonym Eloisa James, asserts that existing scholarship—including particularly Modleski and Radway—is "theoretically naïve, depending on essentialized versions of both gender and genre" (60). Linda Lee concurs:

> Popular romance novels are often interpreted as providing insight into the way women negotiate fantasy lives within patriarchal culture. Most scholarship on romance novels falls into one of two polarized camps that view these novels as conservative forms that uphold the existing patriarchal structure, or as subversive, resistant forms that challenge the existing structure [54].

Bly challenges this "pattern of a duel between feminism and the patriarchy, applicable to each and every romance novel" that was "set" by Radway and Modleski and notes that "[t]ellingly, both consider culture, rather than individual authors, as generative of romance fiction" (61). In other words, Radway and Modleski, planting the seeds for scholarly inquiry into popular romance in the 1980s, established the frame of that study through an exclusively cultural lens and set up the genre as a field on which a duel between feminism and patriarchy played out.

This seems to have had the effect of locking romance into a solely cultural conversation, where individual novels and their writers and readers are little more than cogs in a cultural machine. This is merely the other side of the coin that declares romance to be "mass-produced," each title churned out as if on an assembly line and conforming to a "tired and tiresome recipe." Radway and Modleski made a case for the significance of the genre but not for its texts.

A decade later, Pamela Regis's *A Natural History of the Romance Novel* improves on Radway and Modleski with a more nuanced consideration of the genre, and the influences of patriarchy and feminism on it. But still, she essentializes the texts within the genre to assert a fixed definition of romance:

> All romance novels contain eight narrative elements: a *definition of society*, always corrupt, that the romance novel will reform; the *meeting* between the heroine and hero; an account of their *attraction* for each other; the *barrier* between them; the *point of ritual death*; the *recognition* that fells the barrier; the *declaration* of heroine and hero that they love each other; and their *betrothal* [13, emphasis original].

Such a detailed definition is necessarily constraining, but that's not the main problem, at least not when it's read in 2021. The hero's journey is a similarly detailed definition of a type of fantasy novel, and that hasn't slowed fantasy writers down any. The main problem with Regis's definition of what "all" romance novels "always" do is that it's just *wrong*—or, at least, badly outdated. *A Natural History of the Romance Novel* remains an important, relevant work in many ways—and is cited frequently in the essays of this collection—but that absolutist definition does not hold up. As Bly argues, "there is no one romance novel" (61).

Never has that been more true than in the current moment. The 21st century brought a perfect storm of culture and technology that ignited an explosion in genre literature—especially in romance. In the digital age there are myriad new ways of writing, publishing, reading, and sharing romance, from discussion boards and fanfiction sites, to e-readers and a whole new world of self-publishing options. Those who want to write romance can, and they might find an audience whether or not an agent or editor thinks their work is "marketable." Those who want to read romance can do so and collect as many sexy covers in their digital libraries as they wish without incurring derision. Those who wish to talk about the books they love and hate can find global communities waiting for them in a cornucopia of social media options.

Social media is key. The days of J.D. Salinger eschewing his public are over. Now, parasocial relationships—connections between people who don't really know each other, especially connections between celebrities/creatives and their fans—are the rule. It's practically, and sometimes literally, a requirement for authors to be present and accessible to their readers online. Now authors and readers can connect in real time, as well as observe robust conversations happening around—and about—them. Readers who aren't interested in the convention of marriage and would love to read a romance that ends in an HEA (happily ever after) but not a betrothal or the suggestion that one is coming can tweet that wish out and find other readers who feel the same. Readers who would like to read about couples who don't want children. Readers who want to read an asexual romance.

4 Introduction

Or a polygamous romance. Readers who want to see romantic leads of different shapes and sizes. Readers who hate couples breaking up over misunderstandings. Readers who want the "barrier" to be external, something the couple fights together. Readers who would like to read about normally endowed men. Or "BBW" (big beautiful women) heroines and heroes with "dad bods." Social media allows them all to put that desire into the world and, in real time, find people who share it—and authors can do the same.

When enough people share such ideas on the widely visible platforms of social media, movements arise and become influential. Though these stories might not fit the canonical conventions of the genre, though they might thus not gain traction with agents and editors, self-publishing circumvents those concerns and connects authors and readers directly. Books that might never have seen the light of day through the portal of traditional publishing can find readerships—and if a readership is large enough, the industry takes notice. And so Regis's rigid definition of what "all" romance novels "always" do limps to the sidelines, its moment over.

The reception of books and the ways we measure success are changing as well. Book reviews are written and published not only by professional critics but by everyday readers—and those reviews have sway. A whole industry of review-bloggers has arisen that participates fully in the popular romance ecosystem. Bloggers, from those with no formal qualifications beyond an interest in romance novels and access to a free Wordpress site to high-profile, professionally managed sites like *Smart Bitches, Trashy Books*, are now collectively powerful enough to make or break a new release. The instant feedback and constant conversation on social media are changing popular literature at its very core.

Again, the surge of self-publishing, and the increasing respect it has garnered as its market share grows, is an integral part of this dynamic. No longer is self-publishing an expensive "vanity project." It is now a valid, and potentially lucrative, professional publishing option, particularly in the digital realm. Independently published novels routinely hit the same major bestseller lists traditionally published authors do, and the most successful indie authors regularly earn five or six figures a month (Haysom), while keeping the bulk of the royalties for themselves.

The blossoming of self-publishing into a viable alternative for serious, savvy, and talented authors has put pressure on the genre as a whole. The RWA began actively recognizing self-publishing as a valid option in 2014 (Gold), literary agents have begun to offer "subrights" services for indie authors (Brower), major traditional publishers have launched "digital-only" imprints (Markert 272) to try to compete with indie authors publishing via Kindle Direct Publishing, or Smashwords, or other rising platforms serving indie authors.

A cottage support industry has risen right alongside indie publishing. An indie author can contract for all the same services a traditionally published author receives: editing, formatting, cover design, cover model photography, publicity and advertising, and more. Professional freelancers and small businesses have flourished with independent publishing, and the works being published independently are, increasingly, of a quality indistinguishable from traditionally published works, from "Big 5" houses or from small presses.

These new frontiers in publishing and parasocial relationships are changing the industry as a whole. In her essay included here, Ashleigh Taylor Sullivan notes the "transgressive potential of the indie publishing market." Claire Parnell describes the "contemporary digital publishing sphere" as one of "hybridity, convergence, and messiness" ("Models of Publishing"). At the heart of all that chaos is potential—and that is perhaps most apparent in popular romance, which has been at the vanguard of this digital surge from the start.

Today, authors can write and publish what they want. In some cases, sure, it means that someone can put up for sale a poorly written, unedited story, but that story might yet resonate with readers enough to shape the market. It also means that elegantly written, thematically complex stories with vividly rendered characters and worlds find an audience even when they buck tradition or challenge industry conceptions of commerciality. BIPOC writers and characters, neurodivergent writers and characters, LGBTQ+ writers and characters, and more have found a place in the market that had been denied them by mainstream traditional publishing for years (Liu).[1] Their success puts pressure on the industry to adapt.

The rise in self-publishing has also impelled an eruption of new subgenres. Though the traditional historical romance, with 18th- and 19th-century lords and ladies in elegant silks, remains a significant presence in the genre, and Harlequin-style "category" romances (which do, in fact, have rigid formula requirements) remain significant as well, other kinds of stories are finding large readerships through self-publishing, even if they would be considered too "niche-y" or controversial for traditional, market-focused outlets. Subgenres such as dark romance (which can include BDSM and "taboo" storylines like incest, "non-con" and "dub-con" [sexual situations without consent or with so-called dubious consent], and other such "edgy" tropes), and violent genres like biker and motorcycle club romance and Mafia romance, for example, have become wildly popular, and the industry is taking note and beginning to offer those authors, whose stories tend to be outside the bounds of traditional romance, traditional publishing contracts. In her examination of the way romance—especially the indie-driven "New Adult" subgenre (college-age protagonists)—is evolving, Jodi McAlister discusses several best-selling indie authors, including stars Colleen Hoover and Jennifer L. Armentrout, whose self-published works were snapped up by traditional publishers and repackaged ("Defining and Redefining").

Of course, this was exactly what happened with E.L. James and *Fifty Shades of Grey*. The story is well known enough by now to have become publishing legend: the text began as *Twilight* fanfiction called "Master of the Universe," became extremely popular on fanfiction.net; James "filed off the serial numbers" (removed identifying elements such as character and place names) and self-published through The Writers' Coffeeshop, where it continued to be extremely popular, and she eventually sold the trilogy to Vintage Books in 2012—and it became the cultural behemoth we know it to be (Spatz). James thereby virtually singlehandedly brought BDSM and "dark romance" into the mainstream of popular romance fiction.

It is not an exaggeration to say that James' success changed the face of romance, and it's important to recognize that it began as fanfiction, because that writing experience—the interplay between author and readers while a text is being written, the ways reader reaction acts on such texts, shapes and changes them, the particular kinds of expectations and assumptions fic readers have that don't entirely align with traditional book readers—factors into the writing of James' text and the response to it. In the same way it's not an exaggeration to say that James' success changed romance, neither is it an exaggeration to say that fanfiction and its culture changed romance.

Fifty Shades of Grey, and other successful fic-to-original works, brought new subgenres into the fold, and it normalized not only descriptive sex but *frankly* descriptive sex, largely forgoing the euphemistic language that had been a defining feature of romance. In 2008, Linda Lee noted that romance novels "typically include numerous examples of various sexual acts that are usually described in an explicit manner, albeit using a highly coded language" such as "velvet knobs" and "fiery sheaths" to refer to genitalia (55). These days, a reader of romance, especially of contemporary romance, is as likely, if not more, to read about "pussies" and "cocks" as they are to find a "turgid sword."

Even perhaps the most sacred element of romance is beginning to soften of late. The HEA or at least an HFN (happy for now) ending has, from the time that romance has been recognized as a genre, been a pro forma requirement of any romance. The Romance Writers of America (RWA), with a far more accommodating definition of romance than Pamela Regis's, lists only two defining elements: a "central love story" and an "optimistic ending," with the lovers "rewarded with emotional justice and unconditional love" ("The Basics"). This is widely interpreted as either an HEA or an HFN (and most readers expect an HFN to really mean "the HEA isn't here yet, but it's on its way"). The HEA rules all.

Despite its recent troubles,[2] the RWA is the primary trade organization in the United States, so we can take their definition as controlling. Certainly, the readers who will fight to the death to keep the HEA sacrosanct are legion—and vocal. At this point, the happy ending is a requirement of popular romance, as it has always been.

However. As indie authors publish their work their way, and assign BISAC codes that identify their work as romance, and as readers are able to commune with each other online in large numbers and find likeminded fellow readers, a conversation—some might call it a conflict—has begun within the community of genre stakeholders focused on the question: must a love story end happily to be considered a romance? So far, most in the community say yes. Emphatically. But the very existence of that conversation, and of novels categorized as romance that bend, or outright flout, the HEA, suggests that there might someday be room for change on even this point (Barron)—and that would be a sea change of tsunami magnitude.

Sadly, all this "hybridity, convergence, and messiness," all this change and potential, all this cultural relevancy, has not much softened the general cultural disdain for romance. Writing for *JSTOR Daily* in 2019, Farah Mohammed asserts that "the romance genre has a decided lack of cultural clout" ("Business")—this despite, as Mohammed notes, romance being a "wildly successful genre." Lee, to a degree, blames this frustrating tension between respect and popularity on the infamous mass-market paperback covers of the 1970s–1990s: "Such 'bodice-rippers' came to stand for the entire genre and were used to justify dismissing this 'trivial' form of women's fiction as naturalizing sexual violence against passive, naïve women through rape fantasies and other sexual brutalities" (55). Jayashree Kamblé goes even further, coining a term to define the cultural narrative of contempt for popular romance fiction as "its own genre—the 'Media Romance,' a fantastic combination of sexual comedy and literary tragedy" (269). Invoking Roland Barthes, Kamblé blames "bodice ripper" covers and the media's intransigent refusal to read past them:

> Their dependence on the clichéd novel covers as forensic evidence of silly plots and overblown prose creates the parodic Media Romance. It is a maneuver through which the cover, a paratextual sign that means carnal and emotional love to romance readers, is mythologized into a new sign: intellectual vapidity and infantilized sexual desire.... Media romance mythologies appropriate what genre insiders receive as the sign for love and equitable partnerships (alongside other marketing elements, such as a subgenre indicator) and turn it into a signifier of porn, erasing its pre-existing life as a sign to make room for a new one [269].

In other words, romance-genre insiders—readers, writers, publishers—see sexy covers, be they old-school bodice-rippers, new-school headless oiled abs, or any other variation that codes a cover as "romance," and read that sign as an indication of the deep and complex relationship that holds the heart of the story. Outsiders see the same cover, erase all that interpersonal depth and complexity, and read "porn." They are, quite literally, judging books by their covers—without sufficient experience to decode their signs.

There is nothing wrong with (consensual) porn. There is nothing wrong with erotica. But romance is neither, even when the sex is detailed and descriptive. The story inside a romance-coded cover is that of a *relationship* that grows into deep and abiding love. The sex in a romance novel is not its own end, merely a means to titillate the reader, but a crucial element of character and relationship development. To note the presence of a genre-defined narrative arc that highlights the development of that relationship, when a genre-defined arc is present in virtually every genre of storytelling—and call it a "tired and tiresome recipe" is, frankly, to suggest that one doesn't understand storytelling very well. I wonder if such critics would call the hero's journey a "tired and tiresome recipe."

Moreover, to suggest that all romance is "atrociously written" and "mindlessly consumed" is to expose a very great chasm in one's understanding of the genre. The writers in the genre are as talented as any other, and the readers as sophisticated. This version of the romance genre that cultural gadflies so emphatically deride simply does not exist. As Kamblé succinctly puts it: "The Media Romance ... is a myth" (269). Kamblé is writing in 2020, by the way, for a book published in 2021. More than thirty-five years after Radway, romance is still fighting for its due.

This is perhaps particularly frustrating because romance is by far the most popular and lucrative genre in publishing, a juggernaut consistently earning more than most other genres combined, and for the past decade or more earning well over a billion dollars a year (Herold). Citing statistics now at least fifteen years old and largely predating the massive surge of digital reading and independent publishing, not to mention the phenomenon of *Fifty Shades of Grey*, all of which added substantially to the genre's industry dominance, Linda Lee calls the industry statistics for romance "staggering":

> Alternately dismissed as "trash," "smut," or "women's pornography" popular romance novels—and their readers—are often criticized, marginalized, and mocked. These novels, however, are the most popular of all genres of fiction. The statistics are staggering. According to the Romance Writers of America (RWA), romance fiction had $1.37 billion in sales in 2006 and held a 26.4 percent share of the consumer book market. More than 64 million Americans read at least one romance novel in 2004, and 42 percent of these readers hold at least a bachelors' degree (Romance Writers of America). Studies of romance readers suggest that a third of all women who read, read romance novels [52].

Considering its large market share, and its substantial influence on the publishing industry and on culture, why does romance bear the brunt of disdain for genre texts? The most common, and the most reasonable, answer among those who've asked and studied the question is the most obvious: because romance is the only genre dominated by women, in all aspects of its creation and production, and misogyny abides (Markert 3).

Immense popularity and profit make romance the back on which all other publishing genres stand. But this common aspect of the defense of popular romance—its profitability and the way it funds the publishing industry as a whole—is problematic, because at the same time it asserts the power of the genre to support and shape a whole industry and beyond, it also buys into the culture's dismissal of the genre as a pre-packaged, mass-produced commodity rather than as literature (Kamblé 271). I also want to move on from arguing, as a primary thesis, that canonical popular romance can withstand and reward critical analysis. I want to take these—marketability and literary merit—as givens and consider the texts. What influences the stories in the genre and what do those stories influence? I want to highlight what writers and their stories are doing in the texts—what those texts have to say. I want to think about where popular romance is now and where it might be going.

Because popular romance in the 21st century is going places.

This collection examines the genre as it has arrived in this moment—powerful, imperfect, fractious, significant, and evolving with the times. The essays here, by scholars from a range of disciplines and locations across the globe, discuss traditionally published and independently published works without privileging one form of publication over another. They discuss wildly popular works and works with much more modest readerships, and a wide range of types of texts, from canonical literature to amateur fics. They reach out to other genres and consider the influence of romance on other kinds of stories and the use of romantic tropes to deepen their themes.

In the same way that popular romance itself is evolving, its conventions and genres expanding and adapting to new modes of discourse and ways of making meaning, so is academic discourse, and this collection reflects that. The approaches these scholars take range from conventional academic writing to a more casual rhetorical style and diction. In her essay included here, Courtney Watson welcomes an evolution in modes of academic scholarship and recognizes a "hybrid" kind of scholarship, especially in genre studies: "Much of the writing being done across multiple platforms, particularly online, does not fit the traditional definitions of scholarship so much as informed public discourse, but maybe it should"—some scholars are turning from gatekeeping jargon and expensive, exclusive traditional academic publications in favor of open-access spaces and accessible language. The essays here embrace many facets of diversity, including in discourse itself.

This collection is organized in six parts. Part One, "Problematic Masculinities," includes two essays that take one of the most common critiques of the genre head-on and consider the continuing presence and substantial popularity of masculine characters and tropes we have come to recognize as toxic. Jonathan A. Allan, in "Healing Toxic Masculinity in *Sweatpants Season* by Danielle Allen," showcases the ways in which romance authors are confronting and "healing" the trope and focuses particularly on one novel's attempt to remediate its male lead's toxic behaviors. In her essay "From Darcy to Dickheads: Why Do Women Love the Bad Boy?" Ashleigh Taylor Sullivan considers these "alphahole" romantic "heroes" through the lens of #MeToo and other evolutions in cultural perception of gendered roles and asks why the trope of the Bad Boy remains popular in the genre, even among women who recognize its toxicity.

Part Two, "Navigating Consent After #MeToo," continues in a similar vein, with two essays focused specifically on consent. In their essay, "Tingles and Shivers: First Kisses and Intimate Civility in Eliza Redgold's Historical Harlequin Romances Pre- and Post-#MeToo," the group of scholars Debra Dudek, Elizabeth Reid Boyd, Madalena Grobbelaar, and Rose Williams, examine—from various perspectives, including the author's—Redgold's novels' response to changing mores around consent. Eliza Redgold is Boyd's penname. Courtney Watson considers the evolution of ideas of consent in the romance genre and the larger culture in the second essay here: "I Thought You'd Never Ask: Consent in Contemporary Romance."

The two essays that make up Part Three, "History and Historicity," travel through time to consider historical dimensions of influence on and of two major texts. Ashley Elizabeth Christensen examines the weight of history and the gendered tension among past, present, and future in the hugely popular *Outlander* series, books and television both, in "'Say, could that lass be I?' *Outlander*, Transmedial Time-Travel, and Women's Historical Fantasy." And Lucy Sheerman examines the dark and snarled legacy of Charlotte Brontë's most famous work for genre romance in her essay, "'Place the glass before you, and draw in chalk your own picture': The Recasting of *Jane Eyre*."

Part Four shifts the lens to another issue in the genre, one which has always been problematic but has only recently been widely acknowledged as such, and even more recently showing signs of remediation: representation. Thanks to social media movements like #ownvoices, romance as a genre, particularly its traditional-publishing arm, is beginning to recognize long-entrenched disparities in representation of race, ethnicity, gender, orientation, neurodiversity, mental health, and more. Readers are certainly vocal about such things, and publishers are finally beginning to take notice, now that those readers have the megaphone of social media, and now that self-publishing is demonstrating that diversity sells. The three essays here each examine works that take on characters and stories that diverge from stereotypical romance pairings (i.e., white, cishet, neurotypical) and worlds built around them by apparently white, cishet, neurotypical authors. Camille S. Alexander studies Jasmine Guillory's bestselling romantic comedies featuring Black female leads, and often males leads of color as well, in "'The Realness' in Jasmine Guillory's Sista Lit Rom Com Novels." Ellen Carter looks at an aspect of mental health representation in "Eating Disorders and Romance." And Wendy Wagner considers the emerging popularity of lead characters with autism in "The 'Grandly and Inhospitably Strange' World of Autistic Heroines in Romance Fiction."

Romance does more than reflect its own moment, of course. Influences on the genre extend in every direction and touch every aspect of history, society, and culture. Moreover, its tropes exert influences of their own, extending beyond the bounds of the genre. The two essays that make up Part Five: "Romance Tropes and Social Status" examine these types of influence on and of romance. In "Women Policing Whiteness: Deviance and Surveillance in Contemporary Police Procedural Romance," Nattie Golubov takes a hard look at race, class, and the related themes of this subgenre. Lucky Issar, in "'I'm a *mehfil*, I'm a gathering to which everyone is invited': Reading 'Outcast' Romances in Arundhati Roy's Fiction," uses romance and its tropes as a lens through which to view Roy's work and finds a strong shaping hand of genre romance there.

Part Six, "Romance Tropes in Online Spaces," where our project ends, considers the ways in which authors use online spaces to tell their stories, how they use tropes of popular romance and the conventions of their online communities, and how these evolving and overlapping forms of publication, and increasing reader influence, is cross-pollinating and shaping the genre itself. In the powerfully topical "The System That Loves Me: The State of Human Existence in Web-Based Romantic Fiction from Post-Socialist China," Jin Feng explores amateur Chinese web fiction, specifically romances, and the political and cultural discourse occurring within those love stories. "Original Slash, Romance, and C.S. Pacat's *Captive Prince*," Maria Alberto's essay, concluding the collection, considers the heretofore unusual but increasingly common course of publication of that bestselling series, from LiveJournal posts to more formal self-publishing, eventually to prestige traditional publishing. Alberto in particular examines the ways the story grew from the highly interactive seeds of fanfiction and its own "slash" genre—and how the sometimes conflicting expectations of romance and "slash" readers jostle.

The scholars here are not cynics of romance. Each one comes to the study with an open mind and an honest respect. Indeed, many of the contributors to this project are scholar-fans studying the genre from a place of affection as well as deep knowledge and experience. Elizabeth Reid Boyd and I are ourselves romance novelists as well; Boyd publishes traditionally under a pseudonym, and I publish independently under my own name. Here you will find an honest examination of a wide range of current issues in and elements of the genre, its cultural and historical influences, its community, and the ways it is continuing to adapt in a constantly changing world.

Notes

1. Since 2016, Leah and Bea Koch, owner-proprietors of The Ripped Bodice, an independent bookstore in the Los Angeles area that specializes in romance novels, have compiled "The State of Racial Diversity in Romance Report," which is generally regarded as the first of its kind and has provided statistical evidence for what members of "Romancelandia" (the self-assigned moniker for the community) have long known: that BIPOC authors are grossly underrepresented. The 2020 report found that for "every 100 books published by the leading romance publishers in 2020, 12 were written by BIPOC." There has been some pointed challenge to the Kochs' methods of compiling and aggregating the data, but it remains an important document—and one that is putting pressure on publishers to do better.

2. In 2019, the very same year that it awarded its highest honor—the RITA for best "Contemporary Romance: Long"—to a Black writer for the first time ever (the indie author Kennedy Ryan, for her novel *Long Shot*), the RWA was rocked and almost undone by a scandal rooted in racism and failures of representation and inclusion (Ryan, Claire). Courtney Milan—a member of the RWA board, a popular and highly influential romance author (both traditionally and independently published) and a woman of Chinese heritage who is outspoken on issues of racism and representation in Romancelandia, was disciplined for calling out racism in another member's work. In the board's initial ruling on an ethics complaint against her, Milan was removed from the board, barred for life from holding future leadership positions, and suspended from membership for one year. The ensuing storm of outrage on Milan's behalf, and the infighting between writers of color and their allies in the community on one side, and the so-called "Nice White Ladies" who wished everyone would just be nice and not bring up uncomfortable things on the other, threatened the very existence of the RWA—the leading industry organization in the United States. There was a substantial membership exodus, and most members of the board resigned or were pushed out as well. The newly reconfigured board and organization has spent the time since rebuilding and, one hopes, reflecting on and correcting its mistakes.

Works Cited

Barron, Kaelyn. "The Great HEA Debate: Can Romance Be Romance Without a Happily Ever After?" *TCK Publishing*, https://www.tckpublishing.com/the-hea-debate/. Accessed 18 Dec. 2020.

"The Basics." Romance Writers of America, https://www.rwa.org/Online/Romance_Genre/About_Romance_Genre.aspx#The_Basics. Accessed 15 Dec. 2020.

Bly, Mary. "On Popular Romance, J.R. Ward, and the Limits of Genre Study." Frantz and Selinger, pp. 60–72

Brower Literary Management. "Subrights Management." https://browerliterary.com/submissions/subrightsmgmt/. Accessed 15 Dec. 2020.

Frantz, Sarah S.G., and Eric Murphy Selinger, editors. *New Approaches to Popular Romance Fiction: Critical Essays*. MacFarland, 2012.

Gold, Jami. "The Future Is Here: Self-Publishing and RWA." 31 July 2014, https://jamigold.com/2014/07/the-future-is-here-self-publishing-and-rwa/. Accessed 18 Dec. 2020.

Haysom, Sam. "These Self-Published Authors Are Actually Making a Living. Here's How." *Mashable*, 24 Feb. 2020. https://mashable.com/article/self-published-authors-making-a-living/. Accessed 18 Dec. 2020.

Herold, Thomas. "Book Publishing Market Overview for Authors—Statistics & Facts." *Book Ad Report*, https://bookadreport.com/book-market-overview-authors-statistics-facts/. Accessed 15 Dec. 2020.

Johnson, Naomi R. "Consuming Desires: Consumption, Romance, and Sexuality in Best-selling Teen Romance Novels." *Women's Studies in Communication*, vol. 33, 2010, pp. 54–73.

Kamblé, Jayashree. "Romance in the Media." *The Routledge Research Companion to Popular Romance Fiction*, edited by Jayashree Kamblé, Eric Murphy Selinger, and Hsu-Ming Teo. Routledge, 2021, pp. 269–293.

Koch, Leah, and Bea Koch. "The State of Racial Diversity in Romance Publishing." *The Ripped Bodice*. https://www.therippedbodicela.com/sites/therippedbodicela.d7.indiebound.com/files/2020%20Diversity%20Report%20MASTER_0.pdf. Accessed 21 June 2021.

Lee, Linda J. "Guilty Pleasures: Reading Romance Novels as Reworked Fairy Tales." *Marvels & Tales: Journal of Fairy-Tale Studies*, vol. 22, no. 1, 2008, pp. 52–66.

Liu, Sydney. "How Self-Publishing Is Diversifying the Book World." *Thrive Global*, 11 Mar. 2018, https://thriveglobal.com/stories/how-self-publishing-is-diversifying-the-book-world/. Accessed. 18 Dec. 2020.

Markert, John. *Publishing Romance: The History of an Industry, 1940s to the Present*. MacFarland, 2016.

McAlister, Jodi. "Defining and Redefining Popular Genres: The Evolution of 'New Adult' Fiction." *Australian Literary Studies*, vol. 33, no. 4, 2018, MLA International Bibliography, DOI: 10.20314/als.0fd566d109. Accessed 17 Jun 2021.

Modleski, Tania. *Loving with a Vengeance: Mass-Produced Fantasies for Women*. (1982) 2nd ed., e-book ed., Routledge, 2008.

Mohammed, Farah. "The Business of the Romance Novel." *JSTOR Daily*, 11 Feb. 2019. https://daily.jstor.org/the-business-of-the-romance-novel/. Accessed 21 June 2021.

Parnell, Claire. "Models of Publishing and Opportunities for Change: Representations in Harlequin, Montlake, and Self-Published Romance Novels." *Australian Literary Studies*, vol. 33, no. 4, 2018, MLA International Bibliography, DOI: 10.20314/als.1cd73e2f68. Accessed 17 June 2021.

Radway, Janice A. *Reading the Romance: Women, Patriarchy, and Popular Literature* (1982). U of North Carolina P, 1991.

Regis, Pamela. *A Natural History of the Romance Novel*. U of Pennsylvania P, 2003.

Ryan, Claire. "The Implosion of the RWA." 27 Dec. 2020, https://claireryanauthor.com/blog/2019/12/27/the-implosion-of-the-rwa/. Accessed 18 Dec. 2020.

Spatz, Steven. "What Indie Authors Can Learn from E.L. James' Self-Publishing Success." *The Writers' Collective*, 2 Aug. 2018. https://writingcooperative.com/what-indie-authors-can-learn-from-e-l-james-self-publishing-success-242236d8635d. Accessed 21 June 2021.

PART ONE

Problematic Masculinities

Healing Toxic Masculinity in *Sweatpants Season* by Danielle Allen

Jonathan A. Allan

I want to begin this essay with a fairly obvious assertion yet one that needs to be repeated: romance novelists, like their novels and like their readers, are not dumb, simple, or banal—let's move beyond this lousy and lazy stereotype. This claim is obvious to a reader of romance novels, but to a popular culture that thrives on deriding the romance, this may be less obvious. It is important that we begin with a recognition that the popular romance novel is literature. I say this because scholars of popular romance continue to face questions about the "value" of their study of these novels. There are very few courses across university campuses devoted to the study of popular romance, and yet, as readers will tell you, romance novels are *doing* a lot—there is much that happens before the happily ever after.

Romance novels attend to many cultural dilemmas and concerns. Since the 1980s and the HIV/AIDS crisis, safer sex practices are common in popular romance novels. Romance novels can reflect the diversity of relationships, for instance, the rise of the male/male popular romance as one example, but, of course, the genre is exploring sexuality writ large from romances about trans characters to BDSM romances, and recently asexual romances, as well as varying degrees of sexuality and explicitness. In terms of gender and sex, women are no longer virginal secretaries as a stereotype of the genre might hold (truth be told, they were never only virginal secretaries, and even though the genre has grown, virginal secretaries might still be found!), but they can be CEOs, just as men can be nannies and stay-at-home dads. The world of romance reflects the world in which it is written.

In this essay, I wish to focus on the shifting nature of masculinity in the popular romance novel, and in particular, I seek to consider, once more and again,[1] Eva Illouz's question, "why is traditional masculinity pleasurable in fantasy?" (58). I agree with the assumptions that underlie her question and I continue to be fascinated by how traditional masculinity *works* in the genre, for instance, how masculinity is represented. That being said, I also recognize and insist that the popular romance novel is thinking deeply about the nature, expression, performance, and expectations of gender. That is, as much as the genre may be interested in so-called traditional masculinity, I cannot help but see the ways in which masculinity is also challenged and reimagined. In this essay, then, I am interested in a very specific manifestation of masculinity, namely, "toxic masculinity," which has become a media and popular phenomenon that has, unsurprisingly, made its way into the world of romance.

Before moving further, it might do well to ask: what is toxic masculinity? The term is thrown around throughout the media, but, truth be told, few scholars have set out to define it. My approach to this term is from the starting point of critical studies of men and masculinities, a subfield of gender studies, wherein scholars tend to think of this kind of masculinity as hegemonic, which is to say, "a set of ideas about what men should and should not do, authorized by a gender order" (Donovan 817–818). In some ways, toxic masculinity is a bit like pornography: "I know it when I see it," as Justice Potter Stewart quipped. We tend to think of toxic masculinity as an exaggerated performance of traditional masculinity: at times, the masculinity might be violent or aggressive.

Previously, toxic masculinity was understood as hypermasculinity whereby the performance of masculinity was excessive; but the toxic seems to be doing more work in terms of framing masculinity as either "healthy" or "toxic" (see Waling 2019). That is, toxic masculinity becomes a health crisis, a site for repair, rather than a site for moderation. We would do well to reflect here, however briefly, on the history of the term. It would seem that "toxic masculinity" is a relatively new term, a term of the #MeToo era, coming into prominence in the 2010s. But toxic masculinity as a term begins earlier, likely in the 1980s and 1990s, when it was used by Promise Keepers, to refer to the ways masculinity "poisons through means such as neglect, abuse, and violence," and thus, many mythopoetic groups, for instance, opted for "deep masculine" as a kind of "generative, earthy, nurturing, playful, forceful, and zany" kind of masculinity (Bliss qtd. in Ferber 36). For Aaron R. Kipnis, who aligns with the Jungian-inspired mythopoetic movements, "alcoholism, drug abuse, and crimes related to their use are diseases exacerbated by the health-neglecting, toxic male role model in our culture," and Kipnis further explains that "many of these behaviors can be viewed as unconscious forms of social protest against a cultural ethic that systematically degrades and damages men's bodies and souls" (37).

In Kipnis's rendering, what makes masculinity toxic comes not from within, so much as it is a foreign influence on men's bodies and souls. Likewise, Tracy Karner develops the use of "toxic masculinity" in "Fathers, Sons, and Vietnam: Masculinity and Betrayal in the Life Narratives of Vietnam Veterans with Post Traumatic Stress Disorder," writing,

> They found themselves stranded somewhere between who they once were and who, after Vietnam, they could never be. They lived in a nebulous state of unfulfilled manhood, where traditional means of attainment had been invalidated and their strivings to regain this loss were manifested in forms that I characterize as "toxic masculinity" [66].

Karner notes the presence of "excessive drinking, almost compulsive fighting, and violent competition with other men and male authority figures, dangerous thrill seeking, and reliving or reenacting combat behavior in their stateside environments" as part of the toxic masculinity (77).

I have to admit that I am not entirely comfortable with conflating the mythopoetic men's movement with Promise Keepers; after all, the latter had a clear and discernible ideological, or rather, theological framework that informed their work.[2] I am noting this here because it seems very easy to slip all these masculinities into a unified notion of "toxic masculinity" or "hegemonic masculinity." We need to treat these masculinities as unique and distinct, even if they have similarities amongst them.

Karner's toxic masculinity seems to be a result of post-traumatic stress disorder. In another example, as Don E. Eberly explains,

> A society of too few mature fathers ends up with what Dr. Frank Pittman calls "toxic masculinity," where essentially weak, insecure, and poorly fathered men chase after a socially destructive masculine mystique. This mystique robs men of the capacity to be close to their fathers and denies them the freedom to talk about masculinity and its roots. It instead glorifies masculinity and subjects men to "impossibly unachievable myths of masculine heroics" [32].

In this example, then, toxic masculinity is a failure of fathers to help their sons become real men; instead, boys idolize "impossibly unachievable myths of masculine heroics," a kind of masculinity found in Karner's study. Elsewhere, I have suggested that this is part of a "cruel optimism" that underpins so much of masculinity today ("Masculinity as Cruel Optimism"). Indeed, this is one of the challenges of toxic masculinity: it reduces masculinity to either healthy/toxic, and all masculinities that are not "healthy," if we accept a binary, then become "toxic."[3]

But surely there must be levels to toxicity? That is, some masculinities might be more or less toxic than other masculinities. As toxic masculinity is framed today, it is a zero-sum game. And even amongst these definitions the origins or etiology of toxic masculinity is different. Accordingly, one risk of toxic masculinity is that, paradoxically though originating in a post-structural climate, the term essentializes masculinity. Moreover, this risk lends itself to another risk, namely, that "the toxic/healthy dichotomy doesn't resonate for many men." It is not something about which most men speak, but rather it is imposed upon them in a kind of clinical diagnosis (Kimmel and Wade 237).

In a kind of reparative gesture, Matthew Gutmann proposes that "the whole point of talking about toxic masculinity is, or should be, to critique a form of noxiousness that employs masculinity to make its point and enforce its rule" (238). For Gutmann, then, the labeling of toxicity is not quite the point, but rather, the point is to "critique a form of noxiousness." Indeed, Gutmann will suggest that we might do well to move beyond gender categories, for instance, "by buying into the idea that alternative, non-toxic masculinities should emphasize cooperation over domination, we are essentially arguing that men, because they are men, have to act in masculine ways" (239).

While I agree with Gutmann in theoretical terms, in real and lived terms I am less inclined to agree because I still think masculinity is important—it is important because it matters to a range of diverse people for a variety of reasons from self-actualization to how we conceptualize desire. And romance novels are one of these spaces in which gender is *essential* to the genre, as Illouz notes, "few genres are more clearly gendered than the romance novel" and further, "the numbers reveal a genre that has perfected the art of offering to its (mostly) female readers what nourishes their fantasies" (13).[4] In my own work on romance, I have witnessed an expansion of gender performance, without ever surrendering masculinity; for example, we now regularly see active fathers as heroes, or we see the virgin hero. These examples defy the normative expectations, and at no point do these men become "less masculine." Instead, they are expanding the expectations of what masculinity could be and should be.

To be certain, I do not believe it is a stretch of the imagination to see some heroes of masculinity not only as paragons of what Janice Radway called "spectacular masculinity," (128) but also as examples of toxic masculinity. Writing for the website Fondlist, Gauri Pandit asks, "why is equality so rare in romance?" and suggests that "we need to stop romanticizing characters that don't understand the concept of equality" ("Fifty Shades of Toxic Masculinity"). Truth be told, Pandit is not alone in this assertion. During the rise of The Twilight Saga, numerous critics lamented Edward Cullen's paternalistic and patriarchal tendencies. *Fifty Shades of*

Grey brought those discussions to a climax, with critics lamenting the "mommy porn," which almost perfectly embodied Germaine Greer's claim that readers of romance are "cherishing the chains of their bondage" (202). Likewise, shortly after the election of Donald Trump, Sarah MacLean published an op-ed in *The Washington Post* titled "How Trump killed off my romantic lead," in which MacLean wrote about having crafted a hero who was "toxic," a hero she imagined "would have voted for Donald Trump," and thus had to abandon him. But this kind of hero is almost essential to the genre, the alpha hero is a kind of "essential covenant" between readers and authors in which "the impenetrable alpha is always heroic" (MacLean). To be clear, however, I am not creating a universal truth here that all heroes are toxic or alpha, but rather that this kind of hero has a rather important role in the history of the genre. Of course, over the history of the genre, the hero of the romance also changes, grows, transgresses, regresses, progresses, and so on. For instance, there is much to be said about alternative masculinities in popular romance which challenge the expectations of normative masculinity, I think here, for instance, of the male virgin, or the widower as examples that defy those expectations (Allan 2011, "Mourning," 2020; "And he absolutely fascinated me," 2020). As well, male/male romance novels have sought to show different ways of doing masculinity—even if one of those ways is or may be perceived to be toxic. Simply, I would suggest, as I have elsewhere, that the popular romance novel provides a rich archive for the critical study of men and masculinities (Allan 2021).

It is against this backdrop that I wish to think through toxic masculinity and popular romance fiction, and more particularly, how the popular romance novel seeks to *cure* or *heal* the toxic hero. In her work, Pamela Regis has noted that there are two types of heroes in popular romance, namely, the alpha male and the sentimental hero. The heroes that I am interested in exploring are a kind of amalgamation of these two; that is, the heroines meet them as alpha males and come to see them as sentimental heroes; for some, these heroes might be "gamma male" heroes. The heroes, thus, complete both of the actions that Regis speaks of; for instance, the heroine "forces [the alpha hero] to acknowledge power as a woman," as Krentz writes ("Introduction" 5), and in the case of the sentimental hero, "the heroine must heal him" (Regis 113). Admittedly, Krentz is less interested in the sentimental hero, who, in a sense, is dismissed as being "a sensitive, understanding, right-thinking, 'modern' man who is part therapist, part best friend," and as such, "you don't get much of a challenge for [the heroine] from a neurotic wimp or a good-natured gentleman-saint who never reveals a core of steel" ("Trying to Tame the Romance" 109). The heroes that I am interested in exploring are complicated and complex.

Even though romance novels exist in the realm of archetypes and stereotypes, they are doing complicated work with regards to gender. These novels respond and react to shifting paradigms, shifting gendered expectations.

In this essay, then, I am interested in exploring a novel called *Sweatpants Season* (2018) by Danielle Allen. This novel is explicitly feminist; the heroine identifies as feminist. The author dedicates the book "to everyone who knows there is no compromise between right and wrong. And to Tarana Burke," who, of course, is the founder of the #MeToo movement. The story is, in some ways, fairly straightforward. Akila Bishara meets Carlos Richmond and their story develops with a number of hurdles along the way, on the one hand, as the back cover reads,

> I don't view men as objects of my affection rather than complex people with feelings, wants, and needs of their own. I don't treat men the way society often treats women. I treat men the way I want to be treated as a woman—with respect! [Allen]

Meanwhile, as readers learn over the course of the novel, Carlos Richmond is part of a radio program called "Date Night with the Lost Boys." These "Lost Boys" are not necessarily the lost boys of J.M. Barrie's Neverland—though they share some affinities—but those of Michael Kimmel's "guyland," which is

> both a stage of life, a liminal undefined time space between adolescence and adulthood that can often stretch a decade or more, and a place, or rather, a bunch of places where guys gather to be guys with each other, unhassled by the demands of parents, girlfriends, jobs, kids, and other nuisances of adult life [4].

Guyland, then, is a homosocial space—like the radio show—where the guys can be guys. In this space there is also a culture of entitlement, an idea that Kimmel will call a sense of "aggrieved entitlement," which refers to a "sense of entitlement that can no longer be assumed and that is unlikely to be fulfilled. It's about rear guard actions, of bitterness and rage, about fingers shoved in the crumbling dikes, trying, futilely, to hold back the surging tide of gender equality and greater justice" (*Angry White Men* xiv). If we look, then, at the content of the Lost Boys, we find a melding together of guyland and aggrieved entitlement:

> All women who wear lowcut shirts are doing it so that we can check out the fun bags! They want us to look.... So, VanDamn645, you are not wrong for looking at your classmate's cleavage. She has them out for a reason [Allen 5].

This book is one in which opposites attract. Akila is a feminist, she does not objectify men, she believes people should be treated with respect. Carlos, by way of contrast, is part of a program that objectifies women; this program is a kind of homosocial space, one marked by "dominance bonding" (Messner 114).[5] Akila will only learn of Carlos being a member of the Lost Boys after an initial attraction has been established. In the language of romance, then, this becomes "the barrier," which Regis defines as

> A series of scenes often scattered throughout the novel establishes for the reader the reasons that this heroine and hero cannot marry. The romance novel's conflict often consists entirely of this barrier between the heroine and hero. The elements of the barrier can be external, a circumstance that exists outside of a heroine or hero's mind, or internal, a circumstance that comes from within either or both [32].

For Regis, then, "the barrier drives the novel," (32) and so the hero and the heroine will need to overcome this barrier if they are to achieve the ultimately teleological goal of happily ever after.

What is so interesting to me, as a reader, is that this book almost seems to be actively responding to Eva Illouz's question, "why is traditional masculinity pleasurable in fantasy?" (58). In *Sweatpants Season*, once Akila realizes she is lusting after a Lost Boy, Alex asks her, "How did you end up falling for a Lost Boy?" (Allen 52). This question seemingly responds to Illouz's, or asks it in another fashion. Akila responds, "I didn't fall for him […] I—I had a mild interest, but clearly, that was a mistake, and the interest subsided" (Allen 52). Of course, as readers of the romance will know, this is hardly the end of the relationship: "It didn't make any sense that someone who was so captivating and appealing to me was somehow also a supporter of misogyny and fuckboy-ish ways" (Allen 53). It is as if Akila is trying to answer Illouz's question—a question, I admit, that fascinates me because it hits at the heart of romance. How could one fall in love with someone who is so fundamentally opposed to what one is or imagines oneself to be?

Perhaps the "tell" as it were is the use of "ish," as if Carlos is only partway to reprehensible. Maybe we need to make excuses, at least momentarily, for the object of affection, in hopes of understanding that person. Truth be told, many of us do this in our pursuit of love. For Laura Kipnis, this is the domestic gulag, where love is no longer an emotion but a kind of labor (*Against Love*). In the romance novel, then, the heroine might speculate that there is a reason the hero is the way he is, and that the hero can be "healed" or "cured" of these habits, as is common with the sentimental hero. As much as this might be an example of "nice guys finish last," it is also an invocation to look beneath the surface; maybe there really is something more to Carlos, unlike the "nice" guy that Akila went out with. But as Akila insists, "He's a Lost Boy, and I'm a grown ass woman. There's nothing magical about that combination" (Allen 54).

24   Part One: Problematic Masculinities

Over the course of the book, Akila learns as much about Carlos as she does about herself; for instance, in this book, we have the objectification of men.

> "Do you think I objectify women? Did you think it was me who said that?"
> I shrugged. "I know that it came from a show you're on, so even if you didn't say it, you support it."
> "No." He stood. "You're not going to lump me in a...."
> *Holy shit.*
> I was eye level with the most impressive dick print I'd ever seen in my life.
> My heart thumped against my chest with reckless abandon and my face felt flushed. A desire deep within my core stirred dangerously as I saw the outline of his dick against his grey sweatpants [Allen 63–64].

Said "dick print" is prominently featured on the cover of *Sweatpants Season*; readers are encouraged to think carefully about what objectification might and might not look like. There is a political risk here in doing this work because it may, in some ways, discount or diminish what the Lost Boys are doing on their program, but at the same time, it may well show the ways in which desire works. It is worth recalling that Janice Radway speaks of the hero in terms of "spectacular masculinity" (128). He is a spectacle to be watched, observed, desired, and consumed.[6]

It is, perhaps, worth pausing here to note that Radway is part of an earlier generation of scholars on popular romance novels, and many have found her work less than satisfying in recent years; however, as I have argued elsewhere (Allan 2020), Radway's work is the most widely read in the field and remains valuable in spite of its apparent flaws. Some have critiqued her method, and others have critiqued her conclusions. I am not accepting the totality of her work; rather, I am interested in a very specific part of her work, the treatment of the hero, and more particularly, her evocative phrase, "spectacular masculinity" (128). And this spectacular masculinity is precisely what is happening in *Sweatpants Season*.

The challenge with this scene is that while it reverses the objectification, it runs the risk of normalizing objectification. But that, of course, is not the goal here; instead, the goal here is to humanize, to some degree, Carlos. If Akila can be guilty of objectification, then maybe she can understand why the Lost Boys believe women who show their cleavage are asking men to look (Allen 5).

Throughout *Sweatpants Season* there is an attempt to understand and to recognize who Carlos is or is not. Akila cannot understand how he can be part of the Lost Boys, especially since "he's a sexy, educated, creative, passionate man who gave [her] butterflies and called [her] beautiful" (Allen 50). His being a part of the Lost Boys is "his one fatal flaw" (Allen 67). Over and over again, readers see Akila struggle with who Carlos is:

Healing Toxic Masculinity in Sweatpants Season (Allan)   25

> His energy, his passion, his wit captured me first. His eyes, his smile, and his determination captured me next. His protectiveness, his intelligence, and his physical attractiveness sealed the deal. But from the moment I learned that he was one of The Lost Boys, everything changed [Allen 89].

She struggles, then, to make sense of the attraction. How can she be attracted to someone who represents what she politically opposes? After all, she had written a damning review of the Lost Boys, whom she calls "peddlers of toxic masculinity" (Allen 79). As we learn, Carlos was less than pleased with the review (Allen 82). In the language of romance, all of this is essential to the genre; it speaks to the barrier or the conflict that keeps the narrative in motion, recalling that "it is the barrier that drives the romance novel" (Regis 32). The barrier is important because, as Regis notes:

> Removal of the barrier usually involves the heroine's freedom from society, civic, or even religious strictures that prevented the union between the her and the hero. This release is an important source of happiness in the romance novel's happy ending. The barrier's fall is a liberation for the heroine. It is a moment of rejoicing for the reader, whose response to the heroine's freedom is joy [33].

The removal of the barrier is important and it is not epiphanic, per se; rather it is a long and meandering process that aligns the popular romance novel with the tradition of the quest romance. Over the course of *Sweatpants Season*, Carlos will be recognized bit by bit by Akila, who will chip away at his veneer. For Northrop Frye, "the adventure pattern of so many romances is the quest for light, the wandering in the wilderness of the dark world" (155). In this case, Akila is wandering through a seemingly dark world of toxic masculinity in hopes of finding a good man.

Thus, as Akila wanders in this dark world, we see moments in which she hopes to find the light. For instance, when her friend tells her, "Even though birds of a feather flock together, we have to admit that there's a slim possibility that he isn't like his friends" (Allen 101). Slowly but surely, Akila begins to parse the personality dynamics found in The Lost Boys, for instance:

> It was clear that City Boy was the biggest jackass. Country Boy was a slightly less ridiculous version of City Boy, but he still agreed with most of City Boy's antics. Carlos, better known as Los Cabos, was the voice of reason [Allen 102].

This moment leads to a rather lengthy scene in which the Lost Boys discuss some writing by Akila:

> "Apparently A. Bishara is blaming our show because she can't get a date," City Boy yelled, causing Country Boy to laugh. "We said something that offended her delicate sensibilities, and now she's writing columns about how we are what's

wrong with the modern man. KillerMiller1 attached the article, and he wants to know our thoughts on her calling us, and the men who listen to us, toxic, misguided and communication deficient. Those were her exact words. She said that we feed bad advice to susceptible men!"

"Oh god, here we go," Country Boy muttered as he laughed. "Here we go!"

"Well, A. Bishara, we are not going to apologize that you can't get a date. That's not our issue. Maybe you have a stick up your ass and that's the problem. So, sure ... we aren't always the most politically correct, and I already issued an apology for my unfortunate comments. But come on ... don't make us the scapegoat for your personal problems, sweetheart."

"So, you think her issue with us is her lack of a man in her life?" Country Boy asked. "Because this doesn't sound like the complaints from last week."

"It's not. Those were complaints of the offended. This is the ramblings of a basic looking spinster chick—probably a three—who is lonely and is looking for someone to blame for her spinster lifestyle!" City Boy roared, riling himself up. "So, KillerMiller1, to answer your question, my response to A. Bishara is for her to get a life. I have more to say, but I'm going to just leave it there. Los Cabos is shaking his head and mouthing for me to stop."

"Los Cabos. Always the diplomat," Country Boy teased.

"What's the problem?" City Boy asked. "We are answering a listener's question about an article that talks about us. It's fair game" [Allen 102–103].

I highlight this passage at some length because it gives a real sense of the discursive nature of aggrieved entitlement of which Kimmel speaks. For instance, "these young men feel entitled to a sense of belonging, of holding unchallenged moral authority over women and children, and of feeling that they count in the world and that their lives matter" (*Healing from Hate* 10). These men are infuriated that Akila is speaking back to the presumed "unchallenged moral authority of men." These men, thus, "believe that power and authority were what they were entitled to, by birth" (*Angry White Men* 14). They are challenging the idea that Akila is entitled to anything because whatever she is seemingly entitled to is something that they have, in turn, lost. After this debate amongst the Lost Boys, Carlos speaks, and we read:

> the official Lost Boys response is that A. Bishara is entitled to her opinion— albeit wrong, she's entitled to it." He paused before continuing, "I mean, look, we don't always agree with one another and some of the responses to listeners may toe the line, but we aren't peddling toxic masculinity. This show is for entertainment purposes only. That is our statement" [Allen 103].

This is an important moment in the romance novel because Carlos proves that while "birds of a feather flock together," he is that "slim possibility." That is, he is different from his friends. Akila is able to begin to realize how different Carlos is from the other Lost Boys. Indeed, Carlos is beginning to develop a kind of feminist consciousness, to recognize that Akila is entitled to an opinion. This is also a moment when Carlos becomes desirable; his toxic masculinity is crumbling.

In many ways, these moments over the course of the novel are the breaking down of toxic masculinity that the Lost Boys peddle; that is, Carlos becomes less and less toxic as he comes to understand Akila. In the case of this particular episode, Akila has been listening, and she is able to witness his transformation—he is becoming more and more sensitive.

Carlos reveals himself thus to be a kind of sentimental hero, recalling that Regis has argued "the heroine must heal him" (113). In the case of Carlos, he is being healed of his toxic masculinity, and with each interaction, each conflict, the toxic masculinity becomes less toxic, and the relationship becomes more and more in sync. Unsurprisingly, Akila will, as readers expect, fall in love with Carlos—moving from the instant attraction to a genuine love, from lust to love. Perhaps nowhere is this more obvious than when Carlos speaks about Akila's artistic output. Throughout the novel, they have been working together as part of a photography class. Her final project is called "Sweatpants Season," which consists of a number of men wearing sweatpants, revealing a bulge. This project objectifies men, particularly the bulge in their pants that seemingly reveals their manhood and their virility. When Carlos is asked about the project, he responds, "Akila is doing a role-reversal, objectifying men to the degree that women are objectified" (Allen 251). In a sense, he has seemingly come full circle from the initial objectification of women and their "fun bags" (Allen 5), to understanding how this feels when the shoe is on the other foot as it were.

But there is more to this than just overcoming toxic masculinity and becoming Akila's lover; he also becomes an ally for her. Shaun Wiley and Christine Dunne, quoting bell hooks, note that "male allies play an important role in the feminist movement due to their position as '…the primary agents maintaining and supporting sexism and sexist oppression'" (656). Likewise, Michael Messner, Max A. Greenberg, and Tal Peretz observe that, "men, because of their privileged social positions as men, are more likely than women to be listened to when they speak in opposition to violence against women" (136). As Wiley and Dunne further note, "to be a 'good ally' […] men must offer support in a way that resists the gender hierarchy. Calling oneself a feminist is only a start" (662). When Carlos speaks up on the podcast, and then when he seemingly endorses Akila's "Sweatpants Season," he is doing the work of an ally. It is important to note here that being an ally is not a "once and done" kind of identity, but rather is a continual process. His work of being an ally to Akila leads to the moment all romance readers crave, the moment when it becomes clear that love has been achieved:

"You know I'll protect you, right?" he asked with unquestionable sincerity.
"From toxic masculinity?"
"From everything. Anything you can't handle, give it to me." He kissed me. "I want you" [Allen 255].

Undoubtedly, at this point, the novel has reached its apotheosis, but it is also an important reminder that the role of an ally, like the role of a hero, is not to overwhelm, but to support. His responsibility is not that of a caregiver; he is not to take on a role of parent, but rather, his role is to support his partner. And this is what we are led to believe will ensure their happily ever after.

Sweatpants Season is one of many romance novels that are openly tackling the question of toxic masculinity, which for some critics is at the core of popular romance novels. Eva Illouz rightly, to my mind, asks, "why is traditional masculinity pleasurable in fantasy?" (58) and what she means by traditional masculinity is often what we mean by toxic masculinity. The term itself is popular more than it is theoretical or scholarly (Waling 363), but it gives us a sense of masculinity that needs reform. In her critique of the term "toxic masculinity," Andrea Waling notes that "in using a term such as 'toxic masculinity,' we continue to position men as victims of a broader vague entity, rather than highlighting their agency in the reproduction of masculinity." And in *Sweatpants Season*, we see that agency on full display. Carlos is able to willingly leave behind toxic masculinity. He is not a victim, but rather has enough agency to realize that he can do better—while not surrendering his masculinity either. The romance novel always, regardless of the hero, celebrates masculinity—there is no desire to get rid of masculinity, but there is a desire for a loving, caring, harmonious masculinity that is relationally defined. He becomes a better man, as it were; he is healed of his toxic masculinity, because he has fallen in love and learned about himself.[7] As a novel, then, *Sweatpants Season* does important work in the study not only of feminism and the popular romance novel, but also, as romance novels have so often done, reminded us that gender is relational.

Notes

1. Jonathan A. Allan, *Men, Masculinities, and Popular Romance* (Routledge, 2020).
2. Admittedly, their theologies are different; for instance, in accounting for the accountability groups, John P. Bartkowski (2000) notes that "these groups aim to build bridges across different Christian (though mostly Protestant) denominations—e.g. Methodist, Baptist, Assembly of God" (40).
3. I am deeply affected by Andrea Waling's discussion of this binary, which she sees not as destabilizing gender binaries, but actually reinforcing them. Accordingly, for Waling, as for a growing number of scholars in critical studies of men and masculinities, it is necessary to challenge the simplicity of toxic masculinity. See: Andrea Waling, "Problematising 'Toxic'

and 'Healthy' Masculinity for Addressing Gender Inequalities," *Australian Feminist Studies*, 34, 2019, pp. 362–375.

4. To be certain, the suggestion here that the gender is essential to the genre does not mean and should not be read as meaning that this is about a binary gender system of masculinity and femininity; quite the contrary, the genre is richly exploring the diversity of gender and its expressions and performances. Thus, readers can find nonbinary characters, as well as agender, genderqueer, and genderfluid characters.

5. Dominance Bonding as an idea is developed by Kathryn Ann Farr, see: Kathryn Ann Farr, "Dominance Bonding Through the Good Old Boys Sociability Group." *Sex Roles*, vol. 18, no. 5–6, pp. 259–77.

6. For a valuable discussion of "spectacular masculinity" and "masculinity as spectacle," especially in cinema and film theory, see Steve Neale, "Masculinity as Spectacle: Reflection on Men and Mainstream Cinema," *Screening the Male: Exploring Masculinities in Hollywood Cinema*, Eds. Steve Cohan and Ina Rae Hark (Routledge, 1993), pp. 9–21.

7. When I speak of "healing," I do not mean to draw on ideas of so-called "healthy masculinities," because I agree with Waling that "there is no consensus as to what a 'healthy masculinity' is or how multiple facets of identity can complicate this concept" (368). Instead, I am drawing on the language of Regis, wherein the hero, as a fictional character, is healed of some past trauma and thus becomes whole. In so doing, he also is able to love the heroine fully.

Works Cited

Allan, Jonathan A. "'And He Absolutely Fascinated Me': Masculinity and Virginity in Sherilee Gray's *Breaking Him*." *Journal of Popular Romance Studies*, vol 9, 2020.

——. "Gender and Sexuality in Popular Romance Fiction." *The Routledge Research Companion to Popular Romance Fiction*, edited by Jayashree Kamblé, Eric Murphy Selinger, and Hsu-Ming Teo. Routledge, 2021, pp. 428–453.

——. "Masculinity as Cruel Optimism." *NORMA: International Journal for Masculinity Studies*, vol. 13, no. 3–4, 2018, pp. 175–190.

——. *Men, Masculinities, and Popular Romance*. Routledge, 2020.

——. "Mourning and Sentimental Heroism in Maureen Child's *Lost in Sensation*." *The Journal of Popular Culture*, vol. 53, no. 5, pp. 1160–1178.

——. "Theorising Male Virginity in Popular Romance Novels," *Journal of Popular Romance Studies*, vol. 2, no. 1, 2011. http://jprstudies.org/2011/10/theorising-male-virginity/.

Allen, Danielle. *Sweatpants Season*. Self-Published, 2018.

Bartkowski, John P. "Breaking Walls, Raising Fences: Masculinity, Intimacy, and Accountability Among the Promise Keepers." *Sociology of Religion*, vol. 61, no. 1, 2000, pp. 33–53.

Donovan, Brian. "Political Consequences of Private Authority: Promise Keepers and the Transformation of Hegemonic Masculinity." *Theory and Society*, vol. 27, 1998, pp. 817–843.

Eberly, Don E. "Making Great Men and Fathers." *The Faith Factor in Fatherhood: Renewing the Sacred Vocation of Fathering*, edited by David Blankenhorn. Lexington Books, 1999, pp. 21–38.

Farr, Kathryn Ann. "Dominance Bonding Through the Good Old Boys Sociability Group." *Sex Roles*, vol. 18, no. 5–6, 1988, pp. 259–277.

Ferber, Abby L. "Racial Warriors and Weekend Warriors: The Construction of Masculinity in Mythopoetic and White Supremacist Discourse." *Men and Masculinities*, vol. 3, no. 1, 2000, pp. 30–56.

Frye, Northrop. *Northrop Frye's Notebooks on Romance*, edited by Michael Dolzani. Vol. 18 of *Collected Works of Northrop Frye*. University of Toronto Press, 2004.

Greer, Germaine. *The Female Eunuch*. HarperCollins, 2003.

Gutmann, Matthew. *Are Men Animals? How Modern Masculinity Sells Men Short*. Basic Books, 2019.

Illouz, Eva. *Hard-Core Romance: Fifty Shades of Grey, Best-Sellers, and Society*. University of Chicago Press, 2014.

Karner, Tracy. "Fathers, Sons, and Vietnam: Masculinity and Betrayal in the Life Narratives of Vietnam Veterans with Post Traumatic Stress Disorder." *American Studies*, vol. 37, no. 1, 1996, pp. 63–94.

Kimmel, Michael. *Angry White Men: American Masculinity at the End of an Era*. Nation Books, 2013.

_____. *Guyland: The Perilous World Where Boys Become Men, Understanding the Critical Years Between 16 and 26*. Harper, 2008.

_____. *Healing from Hate: How Young Men Get Into—And Out Of—Violent Extremism*. University of California Press, 2018.

Kimmel, Michael, and Lisa Wade. "Ask a Feminist: Michael Kimmel and Lisa Wade Discuss Toxic Masculinity." *Signs: Journal of Women in Culture and Society*, vol. 44, no. 1, 2018, pp. 233–254.

Kipnis, Aaron R. *Knights Without Armor: A Guide to the Inner Lives of Men*. Indigo Phoenix Books, 2004.

Kipnis, Laura. *Against Love: A Polemic*. Vintage, 2003.

Krentz, Jayne Ann. Introduction. *Dangerous Men and Adventurous Women: Romance Writers on the Appeal of the Romance*, edited by Jayne Ann Krentz. University of Pennsylvania Press, 1992, pp. 1–9.

_____. "Trying to Tame the Romance: Critics and Correctness." *Dangerous Men and Adventurous Women: Romance Writers on the Appeal of the Romance*, edited by Jayne Ann Krentz. University of Pennsylvania Press, 1992, pp. 107–114.

MacLean, Sarah. "How Trump Killed Off My Romantic Lead." *The Washington Post*, August 8, 2017.

Messner, Michael A. *Out of Play: Critical Essays on Gender and Sport*. SUNY Press, 2007.

Messner, Michael A., Max A. Greenberg, and Tal Peretz. *Some Men: Feminist Allies & the Movement to End Violence Against Women*. Oxford University Press, 2015.

Neale, Steve. "Masculinity as Spectacle: Reflections on Men and Mainstream Cinema." *Screening the Male Exploring Masculinities in Hollywood Cinema*. Edited by Steve Cohan and Ina Rae Hark. Routledge, 1993, pp. 9–21.

Pandit, Gauri. "Fifty Shades of Toxic Masculinity: Why is Equality So Rare in Romance?" fondlist Online. http://fondlist.com/fifty-shades-of-toxic-masculinity-why-is-equality-so-rare-in-romance/.

Radway, Janice. *Reading the Romance: Women, Patriarchy, and Popular Literature*. University of North Carolina Press, 1991.

Regis, Pamela. *A Natural History of the Romance Novel*. University of Pennsylvania Press, 2003.

Waling, Andrea. "Problematising 'Toxic' and 'Healthy' Masculinity for Addressing Gender Inequalities." *Australian Feminist Studies*, vol. 34, 2019, pp. 362–375.

Wiley, Shaun, and Christine Dunne. "Comrades in the Struggle? Feminist Women Prefer Male Allies Who Offer Autonomy- Not Dependency-Oriented Help." *Sex Roles*, vol. 80, 2019, pp. 656–666.

From Darcy to Dickheads
Why Do Women Love the Bad Boy?

Ashleigh Taylor Sullivan

The Gothic villain, the Byronic hero, the rake, the antihero, the player, the alpha male, the bad boy, no matter his guise, this arsehole has long dominated the romance genre.[1] Although he may have risen from the dubious depths of castle dungeons to plush penthouses overlooking the city he now owns, his behavior remains remarkably unchanged despite women calling Time's Up.[2] If anything, his appeal has only grown, spawning a whole host of subgenres in which he reigns supreme, like enemies to lovers, Mafia or MC romances. There is no denying there has been a marked rise in the popularity of dark/taboo subgenres that exploit and eroticize patterns of abuse including, but not limited to, violence, manipulative and coercive behavior, dubious consent and abuses of power, with authors (and filmmakers) operating within a decidedly grey area.

With the advent of platforms like Kindle Unlimited, independent (indie) publishing has begun to dominate the romance market, arguably overtaking the likes of Mills and Boon and Harlequin. The ability to instantly download eBooks to your phone or tablet has helped remove some of the stigma surrounding the genre that has prevented readers from purchasing their favorite brand of literary kink in the past.[3] Through online publishers like Kindle, Apple Books, Kobo and Eden,[4] readers have unlimited access to titles they are unlikely to find (or unwilling to buy) at their local bookstore. With readily available apps, filthier eBooks can be purchased from the comfort and safety of your own sofa, sequestered away from prying eyes. The transgressive potential of the indie publishing market has subsequently seen its outputs grow increasingly darker, featuring storylines with significant age gaps, borderline incest, contracted sex slaves, stalker/capture fantasies and rape play. The romance genre shows no signs of slowing or backing down, with these novels frequently ranking top ten

32   Part One: Problematic Masculinities

on Amazon Kindle downloads and even reaching mainstream bestseller lists like the *New York Times*, *The Wall Street Journal* and *USA Today*.

However, this is arguably nothing new. Canonized texts like Jane Austen's *Pride and Prejudice* (1813), Charlotte Brontë's *Jane Eyre* (1847) and Emily Brontë's *Wuthering Heights* (1847) have helped create and perpetuate the questionable tropes that continue to persist within contemporary culture.[5] The likes of E.L. James' Christian Grey (*Fifty Shades* trilogy, 2011), Penelope Douglas' Michael Crist (*Devil's Night* series, 2015), L.J. Shen's Vicious (*Sinners of a Saint* series, 2016), and Jade West's Brandon Grant (*Sixty Days* trilogy, 2019),[6] have merely inherited the legacy of their highly esteemed, but ironically more reputable ancestors. Do not be fooled, though, Mr. Darcy, Mr. Rochester and Heathcliff proudly wore the dickhead crown long before they did.[7] So why have women (the genre's main consumers) fallen for characters who have since been found wanting in the wake of the #MeToo movement?

Founded by Tarana Burke in 2006, the #MeToo movement sought to help survivors of sexual violence, particularly Black women and girls, by "address[ing] both the dearth in resources for survivors [...] and to build a community of advocates [...], who [would] be at the forefront of creating solutions to interrupt sexual violence in their communities" (History and Vision). In less than six months, the MeToo hashtag had gone viral, opening up global discussions about issues surrounding sexual violence, such as consent, rape culture and toxic masculinity. The ever-growing popularity of darker romance subgenres therefore seems at odds with recent and ongoing conversations about women's experience with sexual harassment and violence. As a result, the bad boy/alpha male archetype has become difficult to reconcile within today's cultural climate. This essay does not seek to judge or demonize these trends but examines the rising tensions within the romance subgenres to consider why the age-old adage "girls love a bad boy" still applies today.

Being a self-proclaimed feminist, budding academic and avid fan of the romance genre, I have long questioned why the bad boy/alpha male figure appeals to me. He is quite obviously flawed, with issues that would make even the most experienced psychiatrist shudder and consider calling the police. In reality, I would not condone his behavior, so why does the alpha feature so prominently on my bookshelves and in my fantasies? The trope's popularity proves I am not the only woman who finds her thoughts occupied by douchebags. Women across the world find themselves bending to the darker, sometimes sadistic impulses of the bad boy while still expounding women's rights and struggles. Author groups and fan accounts across social media platforms often share memes that attempt to dismiss these growing concerns: "'but why do you ship a hero with the villain??!

It's so problema–' for the angst and attempted murder 3 times before they fuck jessica [sic] it's not that deep" (@kyloslo). Yet even as I find myself wanting to agree, I am ultimately deciding to ignore attempted murder, and this opens another philosophical debate: what are we ready to overlook and accept in exchange for the ultimate fantasy—which, more often than not, is a gazillionaire with washboard abs and a fantastically tailored suit. Plus, "if authors don't want us to fall for the villains[,] why do they give them messy hair[,] sharp jawlines[,] pretty eyes and tragic backstories, i'm [sic] not that strong" (@willjem).

When I raised the question of why the bad boy/alpha male archetype is so popular to Alessandra Torre's[8] writing group *Inkers*,[9] the responses were varied. Many emphasized the safety of exploring fantasies through fiction and the thrill to be found in escapism. In a follow-up chat with member and fellow academic Danielle Marie, she wrote:

> I struggle quite a bit with enjoying this genre, because I'd like very much to believe I'm an ardent feminist who doesn't buy into this "trash." So I've thought quite a bit about why I value it [...]. Subconsciously the draw of the alpha male comes from being really tired of having to constantly fight for everything—for career stuff, life stuff, rights [...]. It would be nice to let someone else especially a very toned and delicious male who knows what a clitoris is for, take care of me for once.

The allure of "giving up control" was a recurring theme in my conversations surrounding the myth of the bad boy. As women we are so often told that we can "have it all," but balancing a career, husband/partner, children and an active social life is incredibly difficult, sometimes showing little in the way of reward. It seems only natural that women would fantasize about breaking free, or perhaps being abducted from, the burden of responsibility. There is decidedly less guilt involved when the decision to leave is taken out of your hands by a mysteriously sexy stranger.

While Danielle Marie is not a fan of the kidnapped-to-lovers trope, which is currently enjoying media attention with the release of the Polish erotic film *365 days* to Netflix,[10] she gets "why some women [are] turned on by that":

> Please. God. Steal me from my life where I'm picking up my husband's underwear from the floor [...]. It's fine if you murder people and tie me up and fuck me—just give me some excitement [a storyline which is played out in the film]. No one thinks those things are okay or wanted, but escape? A little danger? Lamenting the adventures you gave up for a normal life? Okay. For an hour.

After all, the melodramatic storylines of the commanding bad boy are a powerful distraction from the stresses of everyday life.

Other members of the group questioned the standard to which the romance genre is held, and why the distinction between fantasy and reality must be explained. Amongst the genre's critics there is a general assumption that authors and readers who enjoy writing and reading novels about extremely kinky alpha male heroes must secretly want that in real life. Of course, some authors and readers will espouse the BDSM lifestyle or partake in rough sex, but most are simply indulging in fantasy; readers are not necessarily looking for an instruction manual, nor are authors claiming to write one. As Doreen Owens Malek explains in her response as a writer to the appeal of the romance genre for the edited collection *Dangerous Men and Adventurous Women*, "nobody" is "confused" about what they are reading, they take "the fantasy for what it [is], an intoxicating illusion" (74). Besides, as new adult, romantic suspense author Ashley Claudy commented, why should "women have to read about romance they desire in real life? That would be boring." For the most part, I agree. It is more exciting to read books about mob bosses who know their way round a g-spot, but it is difficult to ignore the context in which these books are written and read.

In this cultural moment Western society has never been more aware of issues relating to sexual harassment and violence, yet the female protagonists of this type of novel often endure what precariously borders on abuse for 50–80 percent of the book (depending on how slow the burn is) before she is allowed to bask in the afterglow of her multiple orgasms (which are, at times, mercilessly withheld). So, can fiction really just be fiction when it reinforces dangerous attitudes (misogyny) and gendered stereotypes (toxic masculinity/submissive femininity)? The romance genre has arguably built its reputation around the concept of access, recognizing there is a market for all types of books which readers should not be ashamed to enjoy. In discussing the need to prioritize the readers' desires in an interview with Bustle, paranormal queer romance author Michele Osgood proposes that "the question is less [about] whether or not the characters consent, but whether or not the reader consents to the content" (Colyard). The overwhelming popularity of the bad boy trope suggests that readers consent to the content, despite the (sometimes) lack of consent within the genre. Yet Osgood maintains that fantasies involving force "serve a valuable purpose for particular readers, who need the safe space of fiction to explore what they want and need" (Colyard). Many authors and readers contend that dark/taboo romance novels allow them to explore their fantasies and trauma without shame. I am therefore inclined to agree with new adult, sport/college romance author Kat Kenyon's suggestion that "bad boys allow us to explore the darker issues we have with society," but this is often overshadowed by the pull of the happy ending.

Pride and Prejudice, *Jane Eyre*, and *Wuthering Heights* have long been recognized as great literary works, persistently challenging new generations of readers to discuss themes of morality, social class, imperialism, and gender inequality. Yet amongst these lofty debates is a firm belief that these are some of the best love stories ever written. Readers extol the growing tension, the push/pull, love/hate dynamic of the protagonists, their all-consuming passion, and many think fondly of the scene in which Colin Firth dives into the lake in the BBC adaptation of Jane Austen's much beloved book. You can buy "Talk Darcy to Me" pins and go on Brontë Experiences where you tramp across the moors pretending to be Cathy (perhaps while listening to Kate Bush as you do). How quickly our dear readers forget that Mr. Darcy thought Elizabeth was beneath him, Mr. Rochester locked his first wife in an attic and attempted to commit bigamy, while Heathcliff pretty much tortured Cathy to death, but as the saying goes, "treat them mean, keep them keen," right?

Although Mr. Darcy's pride and conceit has certainly contributed to the bad boy's swagger, the contemporary "fuckboy" has much more in common with Rochester and Heathcliff. Unlike Mr. Darcy, these dangerous demon lovers possess a deep-rooted darkness that seemingly drives women wild. Interestingly, *Jane Eyre* and *Wuthering Heights* belong to a subgenre of the Gothic novel which has undeniably influenced modern-day dark romances. In fact, the publication of *Jane Eyre* ensured that a complicated or forbidden love story became the genre-defining plot structure of what we now refer to as Gothic romance, a tag that has since been adopted by vendors like Kindle Unlimited to describe dark Mafia or omega/shifter romances. Moving into the 20th century, Daphne du Maurier's *Rebecca* (1938) reinvigorated public interest in Gothic romance, with the figure of "Rochester revivified" as "Max de Winter" (Lutz 14). The popularity of these novels has subsequently led Joanna Russ to submit that "Modern Gothics [and perhaps by association, dark romances,] resemble […] a crossbreed of *Jane Eyre* and […] *Rebecca*" (660). The Byronic heroes of the 19th and 20th century thus codified the bad boy/alpha male archetype: mysteriously brooding, rich and arrogant, a "sardonic *Super-Male*" (Russ 668, original emphasis), who is emotionally scarred or unavailable, with dark secrets and a dysfunctional family.

Although castle ruins and ancestral estates have since been upgraded to luxurious mansions with walk-in closets and infinity pools, the trappings of the Gothic still linger. As Deborah Lutz writes, "not only do we find gothic demon lovers in contemporary romance, a certain gothic air settles over much of the literature" (17). Dark furnishings, sprawling interiors, dim lighting and wrought-iron finishes all decorate the alpha's territory, a prime example being the family home of one Baron "Vicious" Spencer:

> Black choked out every pleasant feeling you might possibly have as soon as you walked through the big iron-studded doors. The interior designer must've been a medieval vampire, judging from the cold, lifeless colors and the giant iron chandeliers hanging from the ceilings. Even the floor was so dark that it looked

like I was hovering over an abyss, a fraction of a second from falling into nothingness [Shen 2].

L.J. Shen's ominous description of the Spencers' home strategically invokes the Gothic tradition through references to the "medieval" and "vampires." The atmosphere is oppressive, filled with the possibility of violence as it threatens to "choke" or drain the life right out of you. Michael Crist's family home is described in similarly menacing terms:

> I often saw a coat of paint that you apply when you're trying to cover up rotting wood. There were dark deeds and bad seeds, but who cared if the house was falling apart as long as it was pretty, right? [Douglas 12]

Despite its extensive renovations, remnants of the Gothic seep through the glamorous façade of the house to reveal the decay that remains just beneath surface. This "darkness" extends to Michael's dimly lit penthouse (decorated in mostly "black" and "gray") strategically located within one of the buildings his family owns (Douglas 154). Christian Grey and Brandon Grant actively conceal Bluebeard-esque chambers in which they dominate and punish women, albeit with their written consent. Much like his home, the bad boy's handsome exterior conceals his own corruption; underneath it all, he is rotten. The "dark deeds" these men have collectively committed range from invasion of privacy, manipulation, theft, procuring (the facilitation of prostitution), stalking, abduction, torture, and murder. The bad boy's domain is thus rendered a physical extension of his character, a symbolic representation of his power, which is precariously built upon secrets and lies.

However, the darkness that surrounds these men, from the spaces they occupy, right down to the very clothes they wear (all black everything), signifies the "abyss" from which they are always trying to escape: their terrible past. For it is a truth universally acknowledged that an alpha in possession of a good fortune and an unhealthy relationship with women has suffered emotional and/or physical trauma, a plot device that can be traced back to some of our classic heroes: Mr. Rochester was forced into an arranged marriage with an unstable woman, while Heathcliff was an orphan who suffered further neglect and abuse at the hands of the Earnshaws. Our contemporary heroes have equally been found suffering: Christian Grey was neglected by his "crack whore" mother, beaten by her pimp and later groomed by "Mrs. Robinson," Michael Crist's father was a controlling, serial adulterer who exploited those around him,[11] Vicious was abused by the step-uncle who murdered his disabled mother on the orders of his father and wicked stepmother,[12] and Brandon Grant's father was murdered by the best friend who then raised him to become a glorified prostitute. In her analysis of Gothic hauntings, Christine Berthin aptly writes that "unstated secrets from the past [...] haunt younger generations [...] warp[ing] the course of their existence" (5). The bad boy's "unstated secret," his trauma, thus remains like a spectral presence within the text, "warping" his understanding of the world. The bad boy fashions an "armor of indifference" (Shen 67) to protect himself from the pain he has endured. Many readers see the bad boy's past as a sign of his inherent vulnerability, but it is ultimately the source of his power. He creates his own moral code that enables him to circumvent societal expectations or even break the law which failed to protect him. The bad boy's trauma acts as his very own "get out of jail free card," allowing him to operate outside of the accepted structures within society.

If he so chooses, the bad boy can center his entire world around the heroine. In doing so he will be ready to destroy anything or anyone that stands in his way, a level of devotion women rarely experience in real life. To protect their love, the bad boy will go to any lengths, an extreme reaction that tends to go down well with his fans. As Hannah hilariously attests, "yeah sex is great[,] but have you ever witnessed a fictional character snapping and going absolutely feral because the person that they love is in danger" (@darlingtcn). Somewhat like a modern-day Helen of Troy, the heroine is the face that lost thousands of dollars. For instance, Vicious sells a large percentage of his company to remain in New York with Emilia, while Brandon Grant dismantles the sixty-day enterprise (whereby girls are contracted to sixty days of total submission for the pleasure of online subscribers) to save Paige (his latest recruit), from the sinister senior management team and their dubious clientele (although it can be argued he just didn't want to share).

Still, no matter how noble his intentions or the moral justifications for his actions, the bad boy's trauma is used to negate the pain he inflicts on others, especially the woman he loves. Yet in spite of this, the heroine continues to "prop up" the bad boy's character "where [she] sees damage" (Dyhouse 103). Her inherent goodness, innocence and apparent insignificance serve as the perfect foil to the bad boy's character. As Vicious perfectly illustrates: "she didn't do revenge. Was never cruel or selfish or any of the things that were the essence of my being" (Shen 41). In setting up a direct contrast between these characters, the reader is forced to see the couple as an oppositional pairing, somewhat typical of the traditional gender binary.

The heroine's ongoing rationalization for their relationship seemingly relates to the gendered stereotype that if a boy bullies you, he must like you. Within the genre, this is played out to varying degrees, from the obvious bully-to-lover romances to more complicated Dom/sub relationships or sadomasochistic fantasies. L.J. Shen introduces this premise at the outset of her novel: "Grandmama once told me that love and hate are the same feelings experienced under different circumstances. The passion is the same" (1). This quote reinforces the idea that the mistreatment of women is acceptable if there is a promise of love. The heroine's continuing interest in the bad boy thus stems from within a misogynistic assumption that has been instilled in women for generations. For the bad boy's love, the heroine is "belittled" (Shen 2), "humiliated" (Shen 12) and "terrorized" (Douglas 339), but contrary to popular belief, she is not powerless.

Carol Dyhouse argues that "investing the hero with a hidden history of hurt, of crediting him with having endured a miserable childhood of abuse, or the trauma of an exploitative relationship, can serve the same function" as "the levelling down in power through imaginary violence" seen in classic romances like *Jane Eyre* (160–161). It is only once Rochester loses his estate and eyesight to a fire that the happily ever after can take place. The heroine consequently holds all the power over the narrative because she is integral to the bad boy's redemption. Her love is the catalyst for his transformation, which cannot take place without her. Helen Taylor thus proposes that "women are never just someone's daughter, wife, or mother. Instead, they are the central drivers" of the plot ("Unexpectedly Subversive"). The bad boy ultimately turns good when the fear of losing the heroine outweighs everything else and he experiences what essentially amounts to an existential crisis. In effect, the heroine forces the bad boy to process his trauma and recognize his own toxic masculinity. As Emilia explains to Vicious, "you're not my villain. You're your own villain" (Shen 235). Robyn Donald therefore contends that "[the hero's] strength is a measure of [the heroine's] power. For it is she who must conquer him" (81). Hence, the dramatic irony of these stories is that the bad boy believes he is "taming" the heroine when she is, in fact, domesticating him (Shen 85). In this way, romance novels dramatize "a battle of the sexes in which the woman always wins"; "the more obdurate the hero, the sweeter the triumph when the heroine brings him to his knees" (Owens Malek 75). L.J. Shen comically refers to this as "behavioral boot camp" within her text (194).

With that being said, the heroine's power is still dependent on a man. As she almost submissively waits for the bad boy's future character development, he gets away with murder. Christian Grey runs extensive background checks on Ana and tracks her every movement, Michael Crist plans an elaborate revenge plot which involves stealing Rika's assets and abducting her mother before physically intimidating Rika into a submissive relationship with all four Horsemen, while Vicious and Brandon Grant take advantage of Emilia and Paige's vulnerability. Both women have financial and familial obligations that arguably force them to accept (very different) contractual agreements.

While there is no denying the bad boy's actions are problematic, the genre is not blind to its own shortcomings. L.J. Shen almost self-consciously warns the reader that Vicious' story is "littered with red flags" (50), a metafictional awareness that can be traced back to the likes of Emily Brontë's *Wuthering Heights*. Through Heathcliff's own words Brontë almost explicitly warns the reader not to fall in love with him when he refers scornfully to Isabella, "picturing in me a hero of romance, and expecting unlimited indulgences from my chivalrous devotion. I can hardly regard her in the light of a rational creature" (109). It can therefore be argued that the romance genre uses what Luce Irigaray terms "mimicry" by imitating the societal expectations of gender to convert a form of subordination into affirmation, by subverting the relationship of power from within (795).

When examined closely, these novels offer interesting examples of how dark/taboo subgenres sometimes further the very conversations critics claim they are at odds with. For one, these men are obsessed with consent even when the sex borders on non-consensual. There are so many contracts: contracts to outline limits, contracts to state there are none, even Penelope Douglas' Horsemen have a verbal contract which stresses that Rika must "agree" to their terms before they can take their revenge (305). Brandon Grant's entire sixty-day operation is an exercise in consent. The sixty-day girls and the website's patrons are subject to contracts.

The subscribers must also follow strict community "guidelines" that are enforced by "compulsory understand buttons." Those who break the rules can have their accounts "suspended" or be forced to take a "refresher" course on the website's terms of use (West 32–33). Where there are no contracts, there are vehement declarations that affirm the heroine has to want or even "beg" for sex (West).[13] There are also non-verbal cues like body language which the bad boy is adept at reading: "Emilia LeBlanc wanted to fuck me as much as I wanted to fuck her. It was written all over her body" (Shen 159). Nothing is ever really taken by force. As Jade West explains in an interview for this essay, "there isn't any disrespect or confusion about what the heroines are seeking from [the male heroes]. If anything, I'd like to think my heroines are very self-assured in what they want, and how they are taking it." One of the examples West provides to illustrate her point is her novel *Bait* (2017), a story which centers around rape play. West writes: "Abigail wanted Leo in that way. She knew what was coming and was very clear that she wanted him in that form." It seems the traditional convention of reluctant heroines being overpowered by dominant men is slowly being dismantled by women claiming ownership of their sexual preferences and fantasies.

The bad boy's appeal may thus lie in the freedom he grants women to explore their sexuality. As Taylor suggests, with "women's increasing knowledge about their bodies and sexual potential, it's not surprising that readers are turned on by narratives of male characters who understand and know how to excite and satisfy women's bodies" ("Unexpectedly Subversive"). This is especially true of West's character Paige, who begins the series ashamed of the "disturbing thrill" (West 37) she gets from the prospect of sixty days of total submission:

> It was a horrible, strange little ache, hurting deep. And underneath it was an excitement. A weird relief at the crazy prospect of relinquishing control [...]. Yes, it may be beyond my worst nightmares. But I'd be free. Free in the most perversely bizarre way imaginable [West 36].

Here Paige echoes the same sentiments raised in Alessandra Torre's writing group, the "relief" to be found in "relinquishing control," but her "excitement" is overshadowed by the fear that what she desires is somehow wrong or "perverse." Throughout the series, Paige consequently uses her sister's troubling situation as an excuse to give in to her darker impulses; she has no "choice" but to help her sister. By having her hands metaphorically and physically tied, Paige can disassociate from the shame society places on "deviant" sexualities and ultimately "frees" herself from judgment. After so many "years [of] trying to destroy this side of [herself]" (West 48), Paige finds love and acceptance within the very community society would have her believe is a "nightmare."

In her novel *Corrupt*, Penelope Douglas explores similar themes of acceptance. When Michael discovers Rika's kink is fear, he plays out her fantasies, instead of standing in judgment. Throughout the narrative the reader is led to believe that Michael is teaching Rika to "push boundaries" (274) and not be ashamed of her impulses, but Douglas subtly shifts the dynamic of power within their relationship when Michael openly admits he has "never role-played, worn [his] mask, played games, or anything like that with anyone" else (264). Michael's inexperience with kink combined with his willingness to experiment, consigns control to Rika's desires. However, Douglas takes this further by suggesting Rika held the power within their relationship all along. In a narrative time-flip, we witness a conversation between the two, revealing the moment Michael was "corrupted" by Rika (454):

> The rules, the restraints, the expectation, and what was considered acceptable were things that held me back, but they were all things of other people's design [...]. And they were all an illusion. They only exist when I let them. She's absolutely right [453].

In a society that restricts female expression, Douglas is able to subvert our gendered expectations of the genre from within the very structures that are used to "keep [women, and I would also argue, men,] in a box" (Douglas 88). The bad-boy trope, but more broadly erotica, gives women permission to explore their sexualities.[14]

The same can be said for men within the genre. Before the bad boy meets the heroine, he is sexually jaded. He still enjoys sex, but all the emotion has been removed. Christian Grey, for example, cannot comprehend a relationship outside of BDSM, or how that dynamic can include love. Brandon Grant sees sex as nothing more than an occupation: "My actions were increasingly for the pleasure of the patrons behind their private login screens and not for my own" (West 27). Meeting the heroine subsequently brings about a sexual and emotional awakening whereby the alpha is shown to be not merely a sex machine in an expensive three-piece suit, but a person with his own hang-ups and insecurities. Christian learns to love, Vicious allows himself to be vulnerable, Michael embraces his kink and finds his equal, while Brandon finally loses himself in the moment. The bad boy archetype thus offers a more multidimensional concept of masculinity than it is perhaps given credit for.

Although the trope can be applauded for its open and positive portrayals of sex, it is somewhat counterproductive for "deviant" or different sexualities to be almost exclusively represented within dark/taboo subgenres. As Jade West notes, "a lot of the dirtier novels in the genre [are] contained within dark romance. Sitting on the edge of non-con [non-consensual] […]. It [is] almost like a lot of the time that darkness [can] be an excuse for filth. For edgier, rougher sex." Unfortunately, society has often othered that which it does not understand, pushing those who are different to the fringes. Much like the Gothic tradition, dark/taboo subgenres attempt to carve out a crucial space for different identities and sexualities to exist, constructing an alternative narrative to the dominant fiction. In his seminal work *Queer Gothic*, George E. Haggerty (2006) contends that Gothic fiction "challenges the status quo with the taboo […]. [F]orms of extreme and excessive desire, violent sexuality, victimization, and erotic submission […] [do not] merely contribute to the sexual status quo, […] they militate strenuously against it" (19). The same can be said of dark/taboo subgenres, for within their pages "desire is expressed as the exercise of [and resistance to] power" (2) and "no matter how tidy, no marriage at the close," ever "entirely dispel[s] the thrilling dys–(or different) functionality at the heart" of these texts, to borrow Haggerty's words (3).

Despite his obvious flaws, the bad boy/alpha male archetype is evolving. From within the very conventions critics condemn, romance authors are beginning to deconstruct our gendered expectations of the genre. Both the heroine and the hero are thus enabled to explore their sexuality and find acceptance within a society that would otherwise repress their desires. Yet the most enticing thing about the bad boy is seemingly his female counterpart, the woman who usurps power and control over the narrative to become dominant in their relationship, even when she is the submissive. The trope is consequently becoming less about why girls love the bad boy and more about how women are learning to love and embrace themselves.

The affinity between the Gothic and dark/taboo romance subgenres is something that requires further exploration, and with increasing academic interest in the romance genre more generally, I look forward to seeing how this develops. Whatever your stance, the bad boy myth is still incredibly hot.

Notes

1. There is some contention within the romance community about the distinction between the bad boy and the alpha male. The use of the word "bad" implies there is something socially unacceptable or even criminal about the "bad" boy which more firmly aligns him with darker romance subgenres. Whereas the alpha male is widely considered a better, more protective figure despite continuing debates surrounding the concept in the fields of gender studies. Most authors and readers agree that bad boys can be alphas and I will use the terms interchangeably throughout this essay.

2. Founded in 2018 by over 300 women in Hollywood in response to the Weinstein effect following the #MeToo movement, the Time's Up movement focuses "on the premise that everyone, every human being, deserves a right to earn a living, to take care of themselves, to take care of their families, free of the impediments of harassment and sexual assault and discrimination" (Langone). The movement specifically targets workplace inequality through changes in policy and legislation.

3. This was largely due to the conspicuous and overly sexualised cover designs that were normally housed on the bottom shelf. The phenomenon of E.L. James' *Fifty Shades* trilogy has immensely improved public perception of romance subgenres, particularly erotic romance, and this type of book can now be found in window displays.

4. Eden often publishes books that Amazon attempts to ban or place in what indie authors call the "dungeon."

5. This is not, by any means, an exhaustive list of texts key to the development of the romance genre but are arguably the most popular and widely known amongst authors and readers. It is worth noting that Samuel Richardson's earlier novel *Pamela: Or Virtue Rewarded* (1740) has been declared foundational to modern romance (see Pamela Regis, *A Natural History of the Romance Novel*), offering one of the earliest examples of the threatening romantic hero archetype.

6. These texts were chosen to cover a spectrum of darker romance subgenres, from enemies to lovers to hardcore BDSM erotica. Both Penelope Douglas and Jade West's novels are specifically advertised as dark romance and are prefaced with suitability/trigger warnings on Amazon.

7. Although some readers will argue that Mr Wickham is more deserving of this title, Mr. Darcy's disdainful demeanour and later redemption has undoubtedly fed into the characterization of the modern-day bad boy. Deborah Lutz aptly contends that Mr. Darcy "influenced the creation of many later dangerous lover figures in his powerfully aloof stance as the rich misanthrope who stands apart, sneering at the vanity and silly folly of those around him." "While Darcy's only violence lies in his reserve, his resentfulness, on some level he becomes a rake who must be reformed" (43).

8. Alessandra Torre is a *New York Times* bestselling romance author who has published books with Harlequin, Hachette and Mills and Boon, but found her greatest success self-publishing. Torre has written contemporary, new adult, and erotic romances that often feature alpha male protagonists.

9. *Inkers* currently has over sixteen thousand members some of whom are highly successful indie romance authors from across a range of subgenres including dark/taboo romance, alongside popular book bloggers and "street teams." The group is highly regarded amongst the indie community, providing inspiration and guidance to aspiring and established authors.

10. The film is based on Blanka Lipinska's book *365 Dni* which has yet to be translated to English. Petitions are currently circling the internet calling for the film to be removed from the popular streaming service because some viewers believe it "glorif[ies] sex trafficking" and "facilitate[s] sexual aggression towards women" (Venables).

11. The three remaining Horsemen in Penelope Douglas' *Devil's Night* series are newly released from prison for crimes they have compelling reasons for committing, such as beating up the abusive brother of one of their respective love interests.

12. Almost all of the leading men in L.J. Shen's *Sinners of a Saint* series are troubled. Dean is a functioning alcoholic who grapples with the fact he is the result of an extramarital affair (*Ruckus*, 2017), Trent carries enormous guilt for his daughter's trauma (she was abandoned by her mother, a former prostitute, and left mute) (*Scandalous*, 2017) and Bane was born of his mother's rape (*Bane*, 2018).

13. Different variations of the word "beg" ("begging"/ "begged") are used throughout West's *Sixty Days* trilogy. In the majority of these instances women, including Paige, are shown "begging for more" (676).

14. This is especially true of the *Fifty Shades* trilogy. While it has been widely criticised for its portrayal of BDSM relationships, it did inspire a whole host of readers to experiment sexually. At the height of the books popularity, *Ann Summers* reported a boom in the sales of blindfolds, whips, handcuffs and jiggly balls (Urquhart). For this reason, Dr Hilda Hutcherson maintains that "*Fifty Shades of Grey* is an important book" (109).

WORKS CITED

Austen, Jane. *Pride and Prejudice*, 1813.
Berthin, Christine. *Gothic Hauntings: Melancholy Crypts and Textual Ghosts*, Palgrave Macmillan, 2010.
Brontë, Charlotte. *Jane Eyre*, 1847.
Brontë, Emily. *Wuthering Heights*. Wordsworth Editions, 1992.
Claudy, Ashley. Comment on Alessandra Torre Inkers, 29 June 2020, https://www.facebook.com/groups/torreink.
Colyard, K.W. "Has #MeToo Changed Romance Novel Publishing? Authors & Editors Say the Changes Began Before the Movement." *Bustle*, 3 April 2019, https://www.bustle.com/p/-has-metoo-changed-romance-novel-publishing-authors-editors-say-the-changes-began-before-the-movement-16096558. Accessed June 2020.
@darlingtcn. "Yeah sex is great but have you ever witnessed a fictional character snapping and going absolutely feral because the person that they love is in danger." Facebook, https://www.facebook.com/photo?fbid=10157222110096761&set=g.81395395205128439539 52051284. Accessed June 2020.
Donald, Robyn. "Mean, Moody and Magnificent: The Hero in Romance Literature." *Dangerous Men and Adventurous Women Romance Writers on the Appeal of Romance*, edited by Jane Anne Krentz, University of Pennsylvania Press, 1992, pp. 81–84.
Douglas, Penelope. *Corrupt*, Kindle ed. Amazon Media, 2015.
Du Maurier, Daphne. *Rebecca*, 1938.
Dyhouse, Carol. *Heartthrobs: A History of Women and Desire*, Oxford University Press, 2017.
Haggerty, George E. *Queer Gothic*, University of Illinois Press, 2006.
"History and Vision." *Me Too*, https://metoomvmt.org/about/. Access June 2020.
Hutcherson, Hilda. "Fifty Ways of Looking at Sex in Fifty Shades." *Fifty Writers on Fifty Shades of Grey*, edited by Lori Perkins, Smart Pop, 2012, pp. 109–113.
Irigaray, Luce. "The Power of Discourse and the Subordination of the Feminine." *Literary Theory: An Anthology*, edited by Julie Rivkin and Michael Ryan, Blackwell Publishing, 1998, pp. 795–798.
Kenyon, Kat. Comment on Alessandra Torre Inkers, 29 June 2020, https://www.facebook.com/groups/torreink.
@kyloslo. "'but why do you ship a hero with the villain??! It's so problema-' for the angst and

attempted murder 3 times before they fuck jessica it's not that deep.'" *Facebook*, https://www.facebook.com/photo?fbid=10158286838743158&set=g.813953952051284. Accessed May 2020.

Langone, Alix. "#MeToo and Time's Up Founders Explain the Difference Between the 2 Movements—And How They're Alike." Time, 22 March 2018, https://time.com/5189945/whats-the-difference-between-the-metoo-and-times-up-movements/. Accessed May 2020.

Lutz, Deborah. The Dangerous Lover: Gothic Villains, Byronism, and the Nineteenth-Century Seduction Narrative, The Ohio State University Press, 2006.

Marie, Danielle. Comment on Alessandra Torre Inkers, 29 June 2020, https://www.facebook.com/groups/torreink.

_____. Personal Interview. 30 July 2020.

Owens Malek, Doreen. "Mad, Bad and Dangerous to Know: The Hero as Challenge." Dangerous Men and Adventurous Women: Romance Writers on the Appeal of Romance, edited by Jane Anne Krentz, University of Pennsylvania Press, 1992, pp. 73–80.

Rebecca. Directed by Alfred Hitchcock, Selznick International Pictures, 1940.

Regis, Pamela. *A Natural History of the Romance Novel*, University of Pennsylvania Press, 2003.

Richardson, Samuel. *Pamela: Or Virtue Rewarded*, 1740.

Russ, Joanna. "Somebody Is Trying to Kill Me and I Think It's My Husband: The Modern Gothic." *The Journal of Popular Culture*, vol. 6, issue 4, Spring 1973, pp. 660–691.

Shen, L.J. *Vicious*, Kindle ed., Amazon Media, 2016.

Taylor, Helen, "The Unexpectedly Subversive World of Romance Novels." *Literary Hub*, 16 March 2020, https://lithub.com/the-unexpectedly-subversive-world-of-romance-novels/. Accessed May 2020.

356 days. Directed by Barbara Bialowas and Tomasz Mandes, Next Films, 2020.

Urquhart, Conal. "Shades of Grey Success Brings Sex Toy Shoppers out in Force." *The Guardian*, 1 July 2012, https://www.theguardian.com/lifeandstyle/2012/jul/01/sex-toys-ann-summers-boom. Accessed June 2020.

Venable, Sophie. "Netflix: Remove '365 days' for Glorifying Human Trafficking and Stockholm Syndrome." Change.org, https://www.change.org/p/netflix-netflix-remove-365-days-for-glorifying-human-trafficking-and-stockholm-syndrome?recruiter=352383452&recruited_by_id=67bb8fa0-3635-11e5-a674-9fe9f52eafe2&utm_source=share_petition&utm_medium=copylink&utm_campaign=psf_combo_share_initial. Accessed June 2020.

West, Jade. *Bait*, Amazon Media, 2017.

_____. *Sixty Days Box Set*, Kindle ed., Amazon Media, 2019.

_____. Personal Interview. 16 April 2020.

@willjem. "if authors don't want us to fall for the villains why do they give them messy hair sharp jawlines pretty eyes and tragic backstories, i'm not that strong." Pinterest, https://www.pinterest.co.uk/pin/744571750877073330/. Accessed June 2020.

Part Two

Navigating Consent After #MeToo

Tingles and Shivers

First Kisses and Intimate Civility in Eliza Redgold's Historical Harlequin Romances Pre- and Post-#MeToo

DEBRA DUDEK, ELIZABETH REID BOYD,
MADALENA GROBBELAAR, *and* ROSE WILLIAMS

Post #MeToo, issues of consent have come to the forefront in everyday life—and in the romance genre. In this essay, we analyze four Historical Harlequin romance novels written by Eliza Redgold—two published before and two published after #MeToo—and argue that these four novels can serve as a case study for how #MeToo informs the representation of desire between lovers. In particular, we analyze these relationships via the intertwined concepts of consensuality and Intimate Civility. We approach this essay from an interdisciplinary perspective, bringing together academics from the following four areas: literary studies; social science; psychology (psychosexual therapy); and creative arts psychotherapy.

Our essay is structured around three sections. In the first section, Elizabeth Reid Boyd, who writes Historical Harlequin romances under the name Eliza Redgold, discusses her inspiration to return to writing Harlequin romances post #MeToo and its effect upon her creative process. In the second section, Elizabeth Reid Boyd, Madalena Grobbelaar, and Rose Williams parse their impetus for constructing the Decalogue of Intimate Civility. In the third section, Debra Dudek composes a close analysis of first-kiss scenes in Redgold's four novels and argues that while each of these novels represents Intimate Civility, the two post-#MeToo novels position the female subject in a more active role as a being of desire.

Part One: Making Do with Romance

It was the best of reviews; it was the worst of reviews.

In 2019, I saw there was a review of *The Scandalous Suffragette* on the U.S. website *Smart Bitches, Trashy Books*. I was eager to see what they had made of my latest publication with Harlequin Mills and Boon.

My stomach lurched.

"The strengths of this book are the time period and subject matter," wrote reviewer Carrie S., "as well as the lovely friendship between Violet and Adam. I love seeing a romantic couple who, in addition to mad lust, also enjoys an easy friendship and even partnership." However, the reviewer "was so stressed out about Adam discovering what Violet was planning to do … they were getting along so well, and I just COULD NOT EVEN with this stupid conflict that was so contrived but which also filled me with dread."

It was not what I had hoped for. I muttered "thesis, anti-thesis, synthesis," yet Hegel didn't help my dilemma. It would take a different kind of thinking: a philosophy in the making.

But this is near the end of the story. Back to the beginning.

You Can't Fake a Mills and Boon

After more than a decade as a researcher and teaching Gender Studies at tertiary level, I investigated a new direction. In 2013, I published my first romance novel with Harlequin Escape, Australia, and in 2013–14 I took some time off from university work and submitted the manuscript of a Victorian historical romance that would become *Enticing Benedict Cole* to the London office of Mills and Boon. A year later, I received a call from Harlequin UK; they wanted to published *Enticing Benedict Cole* and offer a contract for another book. By the end of 2015, I'd produced *Playing the Duke's Mistress*. Harlequin offered me an ongoing contract, but because I was back teaching and researching, I turned it down.

Then, in early 2017, the academic commentary website *The Conversation* suggested I write a defense of the romance genre.

It wasn't only my stomach that lurched. My heart sank. While I'd not hidden my romance writing, I wasn't especially public about it. I couldn't argue it was a political act if I lacked the courage to respond in good faith.

"And the kind of courage?" asks Hélène Cixous in *La Venue*. "We have to not defend ourselves."

My essay, "To the Mattresses: a Defence of Romance Fiction," appeared on Valentine's Day in *The Conversation*, and was picked up by *The Guardian*. In my essay, I argue, "There are many things a woman can fake, but you can't fake a Mills and Boon…." It wasn't possible to pretend I wrote a romance "by accident, mistake, in irony, or to put it down to research." It forced me to confront

> my own freedoms, limitations, inconsistencies and desires, in the confines of my life and the page…. In a world where women's rights are under attack, it may seem that romance novels might be slapped again with a warning label. In a sea of pink pussy hats, does purple prose have a female part? Freedom is created when we are liberated from oppressive thought. This is the most powerful freedom of all. It allows us to create new ways of thinking, being knowing, speaking, writing, and belonging, of loving, and new kinds of relationships. Every act of bravery encourages another, whether it's made standing up, marching, sitting-in, or lying down.

The response was heartening. "I wanted to stand up and cheer," wrote a Twitter commentator. At this cheering point, it might have been easier to end the tale. But there is a further chapter—and another start.

Beyond Defense: The Scandalous Suffragette

Me too.

Two words changed by a hashtag.

For me, as for many, the #MeToo movement was liberating and life-changing, giving voice to the silent suffering of generations of women. I welcomed the new, predominantly American lexicon, although aware of French feminist philosophical criticisms that sexual freedom would not be achieved by making more rules.

In 2018, I read on the Harlequin email list that #MeToo was reshaping publication around sexual consent. I contacted Harlequin in London (by then part of Harper Collins) to ask them to consider publishing *The Scandalous Suffragette*. In 2015 I'd submitted a synopsis and three chapters, but Harlequin rejected it. This time they agreed and offered either a one or two book deal. I took the latter.

I also became aware of some masculinist takes on romance. In *Feminism and the Creation of a Female Aristocracy*, a book with a Pre-Raphaelite cover of a man kneeling at a woman's feet to be knighted, Peter Wright, a men's rights activist, and creator and founder of gynocentrism.com[1] had concluded his argument against feminism by quoting "the words of an academic feminist, one not so coy about identifying courtly love with the project of feminism" from my 2014 paper "Romancing Feminism":

> Romance calls on us constantly to recreate a language of love. Romance is thoughtful, a philosophy of love, an ethical code of living. Its language is the not yet said, not yet imagined relationship between and among women and men, the unspoken forms of a love in the process of being born. How do we create

this language? We turn to each other with respect. We reconsider the codes we live and love by. We revise. We try something old, something new. Together, we rewrite romance. Like the courtiers of the Middle Ages, we continue to study romantic traditions. We philosophize, we ponder, we laugh, we discuss, we converse, we explore. We know our bodies, we divine our souls. We turn to art, as love's expression. We express love, as an art. This love asks of us. And love will answer [270].

I did hope romance could be imagined beyond oppression swapping.

I discussed with Rose Williams some issues *The Scandalous Suffragette* raised for me, especially around consent. I can't "future feminist-proof" the book, she wrote in a pre-publication critique, but she thought the sexual consent scene captured some of what I had hoped to achieve. She raised more issues around privilege in the story of Violet Coombes, who secretly joins the Women's Social and Political Movement founded by Emmeline Pankhurst in 1903. In the historical notes to the novel I included:

> "**Activists and Militants**. In the early 20th century, frustrated by their lack of progress, the women's movement splintered into various groups with competing means to achieve the goal of suffrage, including those who used radical and militant means, from civil disobedience to property damage, arrest and even arson. Some suffragettes supported these activities, others thought they harmed the Cause. Violet's story represents this turbulent period."

The suffragist (activist)/suffragette (militant) dynamic captures the liberal versus radical political debate played out in feminism and elsewhere, whether to make change from within or from without: to renovate, or to burn down the house. Rather than considering these two positions to be concrete and oppositional, they seem, like so many other positions, to be more usefully understood as dialectical and relational.

In her introduction to *Women and Power: A Manifesto* Mary Beard writes, "If I was starting this book again from scratch, I would find more space to defend *women's right to be wrong*" (i). In Jacqueline Rose's review of Beard's book, entitled "We Need a Bold, Scandalous Feminism," Rose concludes, "Today more than ever, we need a politics that makes space and time for human fallibility (and not just for women). The question I finally take from this brilliant book is: what would such power—no rape, no guns, no shutting up of women—look like?" In her 2014 book *Women in Dark Times*, Rose proposes,

> Let feminism, then, be the place in our culture that asks everyone, women and men, to recognise the failure of the present dispensation—its stiff-backed control, its ruthless belief in its own mastery, its doomed attempt to bring the uncertainty of the world to heel. Let feminism be the place where the most painful aspects of our inner world do not have to hide from the light, but are ushered forth as handmaidens to our protest. The feminism I am calling for would have

the courage of its contradictions. It would assert the rights of women, boldly and brashly, but without turning its own conviction into a false identity or ethic. It would make its demands with a clarity that brooks no argument, but without being seduced by its own rhetoric. The last thing it would do is claim sexuality as prize possession or commodity. This is a feminism aware that it moves, that it has to move, through the sexual undercurrents of our lives where all certainties come to grief [268].

Such a forgiving feminism does not make us unanswerable. It makes us understandable. Embarrassment—fear and shame over error, or inadequacy—comes from the word *imbarrare*, to bar in. It traps us in a prison of our own making. The tension Carrie S. described reviewing *The Scandalous Suffragette* reflected mine, as I tried both too hard and not hard enough to find solid ground in the shifting sands of the post-#MeToo romance genre.

The Master's New Governess and the Master's Tools

In 2019, I completed the second book due to Harlequin. I hoped to title it *The Fairytale Governess*, since romance evolved from fairy tales, or *The Ruined*[2] *Governess*, as the label seemed ripe for reclamation, but Harlequin had the final say to publish it in 2020 as *The Master's New Governess*.

I had become more self-conscious about writing in and about the genre, aware of my limitations (the ones I could see, anyway) as a writer, a thinker, a human being. Was romance only making do with what Audre Lorde called the master's tools, that would, must, never rebuild the master's house? I believed in romance, with its centuries-old herstory, as a potential form of Cixous's women's writing, as Irigaray's female imaginary (something held in reserve, a flourishing still to come) and in the possibilities it presented.

"Love heals," writes Amber Belldene in her 2014 "Creed of Romance." I, too, had become interested in the genre's spiritual elements. In 2016, I delivered a paper on *mystique courtoise*, courtly mysticism, a phrase coined by feminist theologian Barbara Newman to describe the spiritual language created by medieval women[3] at around the same time as *amour courtoise*, courtly love and chivalric romance. In French feminist philosopher and novelist Julia Kristeva's imagined life of St. Teresa of Avila—one of the medieval evocators of *mystique courtoise*—Kristeva discerns a "new humanism, interaction with others—all the others—socially marginalized, racially discriminated, politically, sexually, biologically or psychically persecuted others" (64). We take this new humanism[4] to be a tenet of Intimate Civility.

Kristeva suggests going further: "to discover the frontier where that otherness dawns in me, to nurture and respect it … to approach these others as beings of desire, rather than objects of need" (64). Such freedom of desire provides both fluidity and solidity, singularity and plurality, certainty and uncertainty. It confronts us with choices, taking us beyond making and/or breaking rules, to the place—the sacred space—where being bad (making mistakes) in good faith is better than doing good (forgiving) in bad faith. The romance genre is a creative crucible, of love, imagination, and desire. Its forgiving future is bright with opportunity to see what we are made of.

Part Two: *Consensuality and Feeling Together*

The concept of Intimate Civility—developed by Elizabeth Reid Boyd, Madalena Grobbelaar, Eyal Gringart, Alise Bender, and Rose Williams—argues for an interpersonal ethics that can resituate men and women as working together within the frame of gender ethics in navigating intimate relationships. From an Intimate Civility perspective, sexual consent is one of the many areas of gender dynamics that requires repurposing and rethinking from a past time, recognizing that civility "does not traditionally 'belong' in our most intimate relationships. Rather, it's been presumed, even idealized, that intimacy in our personal lives transcends the need for public values to govern relationships between/among men and women (i.e., that romantic love is all you need). Civility developed as a public, gendered concept" (n.p.).

One of the benefits of the #MeToo social project has been the movement toward a broader recognition of the socially constructed basis of ideas about consent. The #MeToo movement raises awareness of how consent is generated between people in intimate life and the impacts of social and power relations on their capacity to do so. Simultaneously, it raises questions regarding how consent is navigated in the intimate sphere of individual people's lives and represented within the broader social imagination. What constitutes and who determines the definition of a sexual act? What are the internal, personal, moral or other practical intentions of sexual actors when these physical actions are taking place and how does this change the frame for understanding these actions? What is the context around a sexual interaction and how does this change the effects of or interpretations about what is taking place? These questions emphasize the legal, political, and personal conditions under which judgments about what is "consensual" or "non-consensual" are made.

As the above discussion suggests, the #MeToo movement has highlighted how the public imagination changes its response to issues of consent, applying evolving social coding to issues of sexual difference and diversity in order to differentiate between an act of sex and an act of power. Ultimately, #MeToo allows us to focus on what we have already known: the intimate space of this negotiation is profoundly political; sex and power are indivisible. The notion of Intimate Civility requires us to stay open to the complexity of the postmodern, social constructionist, and post-structural turns on this issue, considering a plurality of experience around issues of consent. It is not good enough for us to conceptualize consent as a single binary yes/no answer to a straightforward question about an overt sexual act. Instead, it is an ongoing ethical negotiation by intimate partners about how to be with each other in a message-saturated world, a world which makes it all too clear that their intimate experience has connections to a heavily contested evocative process of social change in gender relations, which is recoding our collective moral imaginations regarding sexuality and desire.

Consensuality is a term coined by Donald Melzer to describe the imaginative play of a child and his observation that their imaginative absorption, combined with the sensory stimulation of and concentration on the play, allowed the child to hold their "senses together in consensuality" (12–13). Melzer observed this combination of sensory and imaginative focus and attention within the play as providing the child with the opportunity to experience themselves as contained and held together within themselves. He proposed that imagination coalescing with play and focus had created a psychic opportunity for the child's development of a contained self, which could be elicited through their own action and interaction with their sensory and imaginal worlds.

French psychoanalyst Didier Anzieu, interested in the concept of self-analysis and also ego-containment functions, took this concept further and used the term *consensuality* to define the fifth function of what he described as the skin-ego. Working from Melzer's observations, he points to the skin as the site within which this sensory convergence and experience of self-containment could occur. Anzieu's adaptation of Melzer's consensuality came at a period in his analytic work where he was defining the concept of skin as a psychic container that allows for five key psychic functions. Firstly, skin operates as a psychic membrane within which a subject experiences herself as a self, and secondly, and simultaneously, as separate to an other. Specifically, the skin of the baby operates as a sensory membrane, which both surrounds and contains her and separates her from the other (Segal 47–48).

Anzieu also proposes that the skin acts as the organ through which touch and the sensorium are gathered and situated. In Anzieu's schema of embodiment, touch operates as the method through which sensory experiences are transferred to the body, entering into the body's sensory reservoirs through the senses. Touch incorporates non-literal experiences, such as an aesthetic experience, as well as internal sensation by which the senses are touched by experiences, such as smell or being emotionally moved by a person. The sensorium relates to these reservoirs of sensory experience, which are consciously registered through interior and exterior connections through the senses. Skin performs a coordinating and mediating function for these sensory experiences. Anzieu identifies that sensory information is a primary means through which the subject coordinates their understanding of what/that they are feeling, and so the skin mediates this potential for psychic growth. Skin, and its capacity specifically to register touch, is an organizing membrane for the subject's experience of self and other as indivisible. It establishes the self as an intersubjective being at all times, while also announcing her separation from others (Segal 48).

Touch allows for an always double experience; when one is touching, one is also touched. Consensuality as a term allowed Anzieu to express the way in which he understood the skin, through touch, to be the place in which the sensorium coalesces. Skin acts as both a psychic and sensory membrane that allows the subject self to experience herself as able to both be, as constructed through sensory experience, and to be contained. He describes the subject self as first and always being engaged through the sensorium—and feeling together with an other that excites the sensorium. Skin establishes a psychic understanding for the subject of herself as always related through the sensorium to the other, while also as a self.

Consensuality, in this frame, is useful as a concept when considering gender ethics because it can bring together the building blocks of a psychology of consent that is simultaneously embodied, sensual, imaginal, and relational. As Segal writes, "If the intelligence of the body is the basis of both sense and consent, the question of consensuality is also to do with human relations based on the sense of touch, most particularly the mother-child couple and the relation of desire" (Segal 6). Segal proposes that it is not skin but the skin touched, and touchable, that allows us to recognize a continuous and ongoing psychic reality of being intersubjective with all things and beings at all times.

Consensuality is an approach that complements the concept of Intimate Civility, which calls for a reconnection with moral imagination and reclaims the space of the imaginal as the space in which moral development can be explored and brought forward. It holds with Irigaray's and Cixous's urging that the feminist project is one in which we can and must redefine subject-object relations at the point of differences between us, within the context of relationship, and through the methodology of touch and desire and its representations (Irigaray 1990; Cixous 1980, 1997). We propose consensuality as a core aspect of Intimate Civility that provides the capacity for intimate partners to enter into intersubjective negotiation using their bodies, imaginations, and sensorium to feel together to explore desires that arise through relating. It is this capacity to feel together we propose as a core ethical relational skill in navigating sexual consent. By re-engaging with these aspects of human experience as methodologies for research into intimate life, we stand to gain deeper insight into how and in what ways our intimate partnerships can be ethically navigated and to uncover the gendered ways in which intimate partnerships, and thereby gender relations, become constructed.

Part Three: Beings of Desire

We put this concept of Intimate Civility to work by analyzing the creations of Eliza Redgold's moral imagination as represented in her four Harlequin Historical romances: *Enticing Benedict Cole* (2015); *Playing the Duke's Mistress* (2016); *The Scandalous Suffragette* (2019); and *The Master's New Governess* (2020). Besides the genre conventions that link Harlequin Historical romances more generally,[5] all four of these novels share the following characteristics: strong female characters, who challenge patriarchal ideologies; dual point-of-view narrations that switch between the female and male protagonists, which may be interpreted as an ongoing negotiation between intimate partners, as privileged within an Intimate Civility framework; and female protagonists, who are beings of desire. At this high level of description, there seems little difference between the feminist politics of the four novels, which may be no surprise given the feminist commitment expressed by Reid Boyd in Part One of this essay. If, however, we focus our analysis on the entanglement between desire and consensuality, then it becomes apparent that the two post-#MeToo novels are more overt in their representation of an embodied intersubjective negotiation initiated by female desire. For the remainder of this essay, we analyze the first-kiss scenes to show the distinction between the way female desire is represented in the pre- and post-#MeToo novels. First-kiss scenes may be seen as an initial site for consensuality, a moment in which the beloveds touch skin and are touched by each other.

Enticing Benedict Cole, set in Victorian England, features the relationship between Lady "Cameo" Catherine Mary St. Clair, an upper-class woman, and Benedict Cole, a Pre-Raphaelite painter. Yearning to be a serious artist, Cameo writes to Benedict asking for painting lessons, and when he denies her request, she disguises herself as an artist's model in order to learn from him by watching him work. The novel challenges patriarchal and class ideologies that deny women access to the art world as artists, and the relationship between Cameo and Benedict becomes one of mutual physical desire and artistic respect, as Cameo learns to become an artist in her own right.

The first kiss between Benedict and Cameo occurs the very first time Cameo models for him. When Benedict moves Cameo's namesake necklace from the fabric of her dress to her skin, their mutual desire becomes palpable:

> His lips came down at the exact moment she raised hers to his. They moved together as one, his strong arms lifting her from the chaise longue as she stood on tiptoe to reach him while a greater force thrust them together. Nothing stopped her seeking the hardness of his lips in that moment, causing an explosion within her that dived to the depths of her stomach, and flamed up again as a deep sigh opened her mouth. She let his cool tongue probe, meeting his hunger with hers, longing to taste him. She flung her hands around his neck as he wrenched her body even closer in his fierce embrace [53].

The sensorium expressed in this passage shows a tandem intersubjectivity in which both Benedict and Cameo reach for each other at the same time: his lips coming down and hers raising up; moving together as one; his arms lifting and her toes stretching. Cameo matches Benedict's desire with her own, and in the final sentence, she becomes an active subject flinging her arms around his neck, an act that occurs in each of the four novels as an expression and expansion of their relationality.

Also set in Victorian England, *Playing the Duke's Mistress* focuses upon the relationship between the actress Miss Calista Fairmont and Darius Carlyle, the Duke of Albury. Darius initially believes all actresses want to marry into the aristocracy, but Calista defies his expectations, and the more time he spends with her, the more he is drawn to her. Their first kiss occurs when Darius is taking Calista home from the theater after one of her performances. Calista presses him to tell her why he is being so kind to her when previously he has made it very apparent that he does not like actresses. Darius responds, "Haven't you worked it out by now, Miss Fairmont?":

> He pulled her into his arms. The blade of his lips parted hers, opening them to his searching tongue. Beneath her petticoats her legs threatened to send her slipping from the seat. The taste of him, like port wine, made her heady, and she opened her mouth wider, tasting him, wanting more. Her arms went to his neck as he pressed her to him, his hands on the curve of her waist. In that moment, the hardness of his body, the search of his lips, became all she knew. Around them the carriage and the London streets outside vanished [86].

As in *Enticing Benedict Cole*, in this scene, the male lover initiates the act through the first part of the paragraph. He pulls her into his arms, and his lips part hers with his tongue. She responds to his touch with her whole body, again meeting his desire with hers, her legs weak, her head spinning, her mouth opening wider. Her arms go to his neck sooner in this paragraph, and, again, simultaneously their bodies move together.

Redgold's first post-#MeToo novel *The Scandalous Suffragette* is arguably the most political, setting the romance between chocolate heiress and suffragette Violet Coombes and Adam Beaufort, Esquire, against a backdrop of British women's struggle for the vote. Unlike the first two novels, in which a difference in class also informs the politics of the romance, in *The Scandalous Suffragette* both Violet and Adam may be seen as belonging to upper-class society. The class distinction between them is that Violet comes from new money gained from her father's chocolate empire, while Adam is from old money, which his now-deceased father gambled away. When Violet causes a scandal through her suffragette activities, Adam proposes a marriage of convenience that will provide her with the freedom to continue her activism and will allow him to pay off the debts his father incurred.

Unlike the pre-#MeToo novels, in which the male beloved initiates the first kiss, in *The Scandalous Suffragette*, Violet is positioned as the active desiring subject from whom touch originates. Their first kiss occurs during the conversation in which Adam proposes a marriage of convenience to Violet. When she questions Adam about a husband's rights, Adam becomes outraged by the suggestion that he "would take [his] rights by force" (71). Worried she has offended Adam by suggesting that he might not behave in a gentlemanly fashion once they are married, Violet tries to remedy the situation by initiating their first kiss:

> Violet sought Adam's mouth with hers.
> He pulled back, but only for a moment.
> His mouth was hard as she pressed against it with her lips. There was a slight tingling sensation. Again he moved to pull away. In reply she pressed more intently, running the tip of her tongue between the firm edges of his lips, as though seeking access. As if she had spoken a secret password between them, his mouth opened over hers.
> Violet gasped. Under the sudden searching pressure of his mouth, her lips parted. Now there was more than tingling. She fell back against the cushions as he explored her mouth with his tongue. Her eyes fanned closed as her hands reached for more of him, her body pressed into the cushions. Still seeking her with the heat of his mouth, Adam wrapped his arms around her, as her lips yielded to him [72].

I quote this passage at more length than the previous novels because the kiss continues for much longer than the previous first kisses. Indeed, this kiss lingers and builds for another three paragraphs before Violet and Adam disentangle and discuss the logistics of the marriage and determine that they do not find themselves "repugnant to each other" (75). Violet approaches the kiss rationally, as a practical aspect of their marriage of convenience, but her body responds to Adam's skin touch almost instantly with a tingling sensation. Given the previous conversation about Adam being a gentleman, his movement to pull away may be read as a gesture of civility and surprise, rather than as an action that implies he does not give his consent to be kissed. Indeed, after the kiss ends, Adam says, "'You've surprised me upon every occasion we have met, Miss Coombes, But this, may I say, is the most pleasant surprise so far'" (74). Additionally, Violet's kiss and her wish not to offend him represent both empathy and respect, key aspects of Intimate Civility, which argues that "respect arises from empathy through attuned listening" (Reid Boyd et al.). Regardless of initial intent and thought, they soon open to each other physically as they become intimately entangled.

If *The Scandalous Suffragette* is the most sensual, then Redgold's final novel is the most restrained, dealing instead with the emotional and physical trauma suffered by a woman who has been sexually assaulted by her employer. In *The Master's New Governess*, Maud Wilmot is a governess, who runs away from her previous employment in order to escape from her abuser, Lord Melville. Ashamed and afraid, Maud poses as her sister Martha, also a governess, so she may work for widower Sir Dominic Jago, owner of the West Cornish Railway Line. Although Dominic expresses a wish never to marry again and Maud believes her passion "had been taken away" (187), their desire for each other grows as they spend companionable time together.

Their first kiss occurs after Maud agrees to dine alone with Dominic, each of them noting to themselves their growing attraction to the other. After dinner, Dominic gifts Maud a butterfly hair ornament, and she gives him permission to place it in her hair:

> A tiny shiver ran through her as it went in. He halted, momentarily, then pushed it a little further. Then he took his hand away....
> ....
> She caught his reflected gaze as it rested upon the comb in her hair, then travelled down, over her face, to rest on her lips.
> She saw her own lips open, like a flower to the sun.
> He didn't move.
> They were close, closer than they had been the night before in the woods, when she had realised the full force of her feelings for him.
> She'd stopped then, stood apart from him.
> But tonight, she would not.
> Maud turned and lifted her mouth to his.
> She felt his body pause, jerk, as he went to pull away.
> But their lips had already touched.
> Now she turned her body completely, lifting her arms to twine around his neck.

With a groan he pulled her to him, his mouth hard on hers.

She opened her lips, throwing back her head to drink him in. The taste of him, the brandy on his tongue and hers, the heat of his body beneath the white shirt, pressed against her satin dress.

He reached for her hair, curling strands of it around his fingers as he continued to search her mouth with his, in a wild, passionate discovery. She searched, too, for the truth of him, in that kiss, in that connection, that had flared between them for so long now [184–185].

This first kiss builds across the length of two pages and occurs late in the novel due to the caution and hesitation of the beloveds, aware of the power inequality between them and wary due to their painful pasts. Touch, however, erases fear, and Maud's shiver is like Violet's tingling sensation, skin responding to the other. The sensuality of Dominic sliding the comb into Maud's hair reads almost euphemistically like sexual intercourse, but importantly, Dominic waits for Maud to approach him. And she does. Reaching for him, opening to him, this kiss exposes not only a truth of Dominic but a core element of their knowing each other.

These four novels depict ongoing ethical relationships between intimate partners, who are beings of desire together. Defying personal prejudices and political ideologies, the four main couples in these novels feel together and demonstrate how intimate partnerships can be ethically navigated. Each of these novels challenges patriarchal ideologies, and the post-#MeToo novels, in particular, represent women who initiate physical intimacy by reaching for the first kiss. In our current world where touch is often forbidden and indeed life-threatening, these novels provide a place where we remember that ideologies change and we imagine a hopeful future where touch can be a way of feeling together without fear.

Notes

1. "Reid Boyd, like so many other feminists before her, makes clear that romantic-love mythology provides bedrock for the development of feminism. Faced with that fantastical adversary, men's advocates can argue they have excellent data demonstrating a growing narcissism among women and a neglect of men, facts that should lead right-thinking people away from the grip of feminism." (Dec 1 2019, https://gynocentrism.com/category/feminism-2/).

2. The word ruined was a damaging sexual slur against women in the 19th century, as used in *The Master's New Governess*. However, as with many words, subversion offers ways to reduce its sting, such as in Thomas Hardy's 1866 satirical poem "The Ruined Maid":

"Why Delia, my dear, this does everything crown,
Whoever supposed I should meet you in town,
And whence such fair garments, such prosperity?"
"Oh, didn't you know I'd been ruined?" said she?

Similarly, actress Nell Gwynne's quoted witty rejoinder, "Pray good people, be civil, I am the Protestant whore!" to the crowd that pelted her carriage with stones and rotten fruit and vegetables, thinking her to be Charles II's Catholic mistress (it's not her sexuality that justifies such uncivil treatment) made me first think about intimate civility.

3. The work of such writers, some of whom were nuns, resists definition. Their spiritual writing was sometimes in a sensual style, using the language of courtesy, chivalry, and romance to evoke the divine. Writers include Hildegarde of Bingen (1098–1179), Mechthild of Maldeburg (1210–1285), Hadewijch of Brabant (13th century), Julian of Norwich (1342–1416), Jane Leade (1624–1704), and Marguerite de Porete, who was burned at the stake for her writing in the 14th century. Marguerite was a Beguine, a lay order of nuns. Kristeva notes that the Beguines practiced a form of art installation they called secret gardens that she describes as "sensual, manual, cosmic, biblical and evangelical bricolage" (97).

4. We refer here to open humanism rather than closed humanism. Open humanism is concerned with human and personal values, and an authentic human existence.

5. See Harlequin Historical guidelines: https://harlequin.submittable.com/submit/28678/harlequin-historical-approx-75-000-words.

Works Cited

Ainsworth, M.D.S. "Attachments and Other Affectional Bonds Across the Life Cycle." *Attachment Across the Life Cycle*, edited by M. Parkes, J. Stevenson-Hinde, and P. Marris. Routledge, 1991, pp. 33–51.
Anzieu, Didier. *Les Enveloppes Psychiques*. Dunod, 1987.
Beard, Mary. *Women and Power: A Manifesto*. Profile Trade, 2017.
Belldene, Amber. "The Secret Sermon in Every Romance Novel." 2014. http://wonkomance.com/2014/10/09/the-secret-sermon-in-every-romance-novel.
Bowlby, J. "The Nature of the Child's Tie to His Mother." *International Journal of Psychoanalysis*, vol. 39, 1958, pp. 350–371.
Cixous, Hélène. "The Laugh of the Medusa." *New French Feminisms: An Anthology*. Edited by Elaine Marks and Isabelle de Courtivron. Harvester, 1980, pp. 245–264.
_____. *La Venue à L'écriture*. Union générale d'éditions, 1977.
Cixous, Hélène, and Mireille Calle-Gruber. *Rootprints: Memory and Life Writing*. Allen and Unwin, 1997.
Irigaray, Luce. *The Ethics of Sexual Difference*. Trans Carolyn Bourke. Cornell University Press, 1990.
Kristeva, Julia. *Teresa, My Love: An Imagined Life of the Saint of Avila*. Trans. Lorna Scott Fox. Columbia University Press, 2015.
Lorde, Audre. "The Master's Tools Will Never Dismantle the Master's House." *Sister Outsider: Essays and Speeches*. Crossing Press, 2007, pp. 110–114.
Meltzer, Donald. *Explorations in Autism: A Psychoanalytic Study*. Clunie, 1975.
Newman, Barbara. *From Virile Woman to Woman-Christ*. University of Pennsylvania Press, 1995.
Redgold, Eliza. *Enticing Benedict Cole*. Harlequin, 2015.
_____. *The Master's New Governess*. Harlequin, 2020.
_____. *Playing the Duke's Mistress*. Harlequin, 2016.
_____. *The Scandalous Suffragette*. Harlequin, 2019.
Reid Boyd, Elizabeth. 'Romancing Feminism: From Women's Studies to Women's Fiction." *Australasian Journal of Popular Culture*, vol. 3, no. 3, September 2014, pp. 263–272.
_____. "To the Mattresses: A Defence of Romance Fiction." *The Conversation*. 14 February 2017. https://theconversation.com/to-the-mattresses-a-defence-of-romance-fiction-72587.
Reid Boyd, Elizabeth, Madalena Grobbelaar, Eyal Gringart, Alise Bender, and Rose Williams. "Introducing 'Intimate Civility': Towards a New Concept for 21st-Century Relationships." *M/C Journal: A Journal of Media and Culture*, vol. 22, no. 1, 2019. http://journal.media-culture.org.au/index.php/mcjournal/article/view/1491. Accessed 21 July 2020.
Rose, Jacqueline. "Woman and Power: A Manifesto by Mary Beard Review—The Poison of

Patriarchy." *The Guardian* 22 November 2017. https://www.theguardian.com/books/2017/nov/22/women-and-power-a-manifesto-by-mary-beard-review.
_____. *Women in Dark Times*. Bloomsbury, 2014.
"The Scandalous Suffragette." *Smart Bitches, Trashy Books*. 1 April 2019. Review. https://smartbitchestrashybooks.com/reviews/the-scandalous-suffragette-by-eliza-redgold/.
Segal, Naomi. *Consensuality: Didier Anzieu, Gender and the Sense of Touch*. Rodopi, 2009.
Wright, Peter. *Feminism and the Creation of a Female Aristocracy*. Academic Century Press, 2018.

I Thought You'd Never Ask

Consent in Contemporary Romance

Courtney Watson

On May 19, 2020, British romance author K.J. Charles posted the following tweet about the subject of consent in contemporary romance novels: "I've just received an email complaining that there's too much consent in my sex scenes, and tbh I'm really struggling with why the hell you'd write that down and send it to someone" (@kj_charles et al.). The author and former editor's incredulity at the reader's objection to the amount of consent in her novels was clear throughout her eight-tweet viral thread, and the response from the online community of romance writers and readers in support of Charles's rebuttal was swift. The thread spread like wildfire as the initial tweet alone received nearly a thousand shares, over 10,000 likes, and hundreds of comments from readers eager to engage in discourse about the value and necessity of consent in romance novels.

Charles's thread was met with almost universal support by readers and fans who shared their own thoughts, which focused not only on the dearth of conversation about consent in romance literature, but also attitudes in the society it reflects. Editor Atlin Merrick weighed in on the real-world implications of the value of consent being modeled in literature by saying, "All of this times infinity but also? ALSO? It doesn't hurt that it models things we need in the real world, a world that is wretched and grim specifically because of lack of consent" (@kj_charles et al.). Merrick was not the only commenter to observe the lack of conversation about consent in the wake of multiple cultural movements that purported to demand it.

Fellow romance author Dana Staves also expressed frustration about the fundamental misunderstanding of the value of consent in literature, particularly romance novels but certainly not limited to that genre: "Wow. Just…. But I'm saving this thread because a discussion of what consent provides in romance is so important. It's not a box to check—absolutely. It's essential" (@kj_charles et al.). Later in the thread, Charles herself echoed this sentiment by discussing the ways in which consent can be used as an element of craft, particularly in the area of characterization: "Consent in a sex scene is not just a tick box (or if it is the author is doing it wrong). It's a tool for using a sex scene to develop the relationship in whatever way, and to inform the reader about character," (@kj_charles et al.) an idea that is expanded upon in greater depth in a subsequent blog post on her website titled, "Yes or No: Consent in Sex Scenes" (Charles).

While in hindsight the viral response to this thread may seem inevitable, especially given the fervor of comments from readers and fellow authors, the intensity and urgency of the discussion about the issue of consent in fiction is surprisingly not fully mirrored by scholarship. To clarify, while there is some extant scholarship about consent in romance fiction (general fiction as well, though that is beyond the purview of this discussion), it is limited in proportion to the comparative depth and scope of non-academic discourse on the subject. This suggests there is a great and urgent need for additional academic inquiry in this area, which offers opportunities for compelling interdisciplinary research, as well as a tempting frontier for emerging scholars. As perhaps the most dynamic and culturally responsive genre in literature, romance—and its many subgenres—is at the forefront of the first historical movement focused on the idea of consent and all of its nuances. As a genre largely driven by women—from the creators to the consumers—the implications and opportunities for the genre and everything it touches are vast. As such, we find ourselves in a dynamic historical moment with the potential to create meaningful cultural change by fostering further engagement in the discussion about consent.

While there is limited academic scholarship dedicated to contemporary romance and its many subgenres (particularly considering the size and popularity of the genre), there is an even more notable lack of critical discussion in the area of consent in contemporary romance. This, despite the presence of a lot of thoughtful conversation in this area beyond academia. An overview of both critical feminist theory and recent discourse—scholarly and otherwise—on the issue of consent in contemporary romance offers some insight when examined in the much broader context of cultural conversations via social media that have gained momentum during the #TimesUp and #MeToo movements. An evaluation of the evolution of consent in romance novels also sheds light on how contemporary audience expectations for consent can, and maybe should, be represented in literature. A thorough review of the extant landscape of discourse about romance in academic scholarship also reveals myriad opportunities for further engagement.

Consent, Media, and the Law

The romance reading community is not the only one to show concern about representations of consent in popular culture; there is an ever-growing body of legal scholarship dedicated to the study of consent as it is portrayed in mainstream media. Though this scholarship is primarily focused on television shows and movies, many of the themes explored by these legal scholars are also discussed at length by the romance community. In her 2018 article "Romance or Sexual Assault?" Courtney Anne Groszhans advances her argument in favor of "Yes Means Yes" consent legislation by pointing out that consent in sexual situations in television shows and movies is often vague or even nonexistent. (Groszhans 2018)

Citing Aya Gruber's *Consent Confusion*, Groszhans posits that consent is especially slippery in American culture because it is rarely modeled in a clear, outright way in the media: "The idea of consent is confusing because it is confusing legally, psychologically, and socially. The 'Yes Means Yes' legislation is a hard concept to grasp because Americans rarely see it on the movie screen" (Groszhans 224). To clarify, the legislation cited by Groszhans proposes affirmative consent, defined as "affirmative, conscious, and voluntary agreement to engage in sexual activity.... Lack of protest or resistance does not mean consent, nor does silence mean consent. Affirmative consent must be ongoing throughout a sexual activity and can be revoked at any time" (Groszhans 225). Groszhans goes on to argue that not only should the practice of affirmative consent be adopted in American education and culture, but it is essential for affirmative consent to be modeled in entertainment as well.

As it is described by Groszhans, the goal of affirmative consent is to eliminate ambiguity, something that has long been a topic of discussion among romance authors and readers. In her tweet thread, Charles cautioned against consent being treated as an "administrative preliminary," which is perhaps also a goal of the "Yes Means Yes" legislation, if not the only priority, as suggested by the inclusion of "ongoing consent throughout a sexual activity" (Groszhans 225). Another priority within the romance writing community's discussion of consent in romance novels, and, presumably, in the society they're meant to reflect, is types of consent, which is a concept that should absolutely be reflected in the real world conversation about consent.

Charles offers great clarity in her thread about different kinds of consent, and the ways in which the approach to consent is an essential part of character development. She says, "The way consent is portrayed in sex scenes is a huge part of characterization. E.g., the consent in *Band Sinister* is super verbalized because the experienced MC is not just 'getting consent,' he wants his inexperienced lover to explicitly voice his desires in order to understand them and become more comfortable" (Charles). This argument exposes yet another dimension in the conversation about consent, which is the idea that consent can be dynamic and nuanced; Charles even suggests that consent can be nonverbal, sharing a scenario from one of her novels: "Other MCs might prefer not to talk during sex at all. Maybe consent is conveyed in body language and eye contact. Maybe characters are operating with care. Maybe they aren't and it's not sought. Each of those choices tells you about the characters and their position right then" (Charles). While this nuanced take may not echo a legal desire for concrete, affirmative consent, it does offer insight into attitudes about consent both within the romance community and beyond.

One of the key sources of tension that arises when discussing consent, both in romance novels and in real life, is the idea that consent is a mood killer. While Charles—and many other authors cited in this essay—firmly advocate for the appeal of consent, there is still the perception of a lingering stigma that has been investigated by authors in multiple fields. The authors of one psychology study, "Is Consent Sexy? Comparing Evaluations of Written Erotica Based on Verbal Sexual Consent," used assertions that consent "ruins the mood" (Piemonte et al. 1) and performed research that suggests otherwise.

In their study, Piemonte et al. asked survey participants to read passages of erotic fiction that showed both consent and lack of consent. When surveyed, they determined that "U.S. adults judged the stories similarly and, if anything, considered the excerpts with verbal consent sexier ... indicating that public concerns about consent ruining sexual dynamics are potentially unwarranted" (Piemonte et al. 1). Interestingly, in their recommendations for future action the authors suggest media practices that echo the advice of bell hooks (2014), saying, "We discuss the potential utility of sexual media in normalizing sexual consent as an erotic aspect of sexual scripts" (Piemonte et al). The consensus seems to be that the best way forward, both in romance literature and in society, is to standardize consent to the greatest possible degree.

Throughout her article, Groszhans also emphasizes the necessity of affirmative consent being not only performed and demonstrated in popular culture, but also normalized, an idea that is nothing new to the romance community. Citing legal feminist scholar Catherine MacKinnon, Groszhans advocates for affirmative consent in television and movies as a way to combat societal bias and reluctance to engage, rather than reinforce it: "When so much of public consciousness is formed by the media, not seeing sexual abuse represented in public as it actually happens makes it seem to each sexually abused person as if they are the only one to whom it has ever happened" (Groszhans 226). The movement to normalize affirmative consent in popular culture, MacKinnon argues, would have a powerful impact on normalizing consent throughout society.

Feminism and Popular Culture

The idea that popular media is a tool of great value for advancing the agendas of social movements is nothing new. In her 2014 update to her 2000 book *Feminism is for Everybody: Passionate Politics*, bell hooks discusses the pervasive nature of mass media, and she argues that it is an ideal purveyor of feminist principles: "There should be billboards; ads in magazines; ads on buses, subways, trains; television commercials spreading the word, letting the world know more about feminism" (hooks 4). She goes on to discuss the inherent disconnect between feminist theory and its construction and dissemination by scholars and the way that it is understood beyond the ivory tower:

> Everywhere I go I proudly tell folks who want to know who I am and what I do that I am a writer, a feminist theorist, a cultural critic. I tell them I write about movies and popular culture, analyzing the message in the medium. Most people find this exciting and want to know more. Everyone goes to movies, watches television, glances through magazines, and everyone has thoughts about the messages they receive, about the images they look at. It is easy for the diverse public I encounter to understand what I do as a cultural critic, to understand my passion for writing. But feminist theory—that's the place where the questions stop (hooks viii).

Throughout the book, hooks addresses misunderstandings that she frequently hears about feminism and what it stands for, and she considers a multitude of strategies for bringing feminism to the mainstream.

hooks also calls for feminist thinking to be more widely disseminated: "In those circles, the production of revolutionary feminist theory progressed, but more often than not, that theory was not made available to the public. It became and remains a privileged discourse available to those among us who are highly literate, well-educated, and usually materially privileged" (hooks ix). This seems to be the crux of the issue limiting the scholarly conversation about consent in romance fiction. There is an abundance of rich conversation being had, which hooks would surely find heartening, but the overlap between the romance literary community and the feminist scholarly community remains somewhat marginal, at least publicly.

The Evolution of Consent

MacKinnon's theory applies to the romance genre, and it connects to research described by Laura M. Moore in her 2019 article "Sexual Agency, Safe Sex, and Consent Negotiations in Erotic Romance Novels."

Moore applies sexual script theory, which "asserts [that] sexual values and norms are learned through culturally available messaging. A primary site for that messaging is through erotic romance novels written by, and generally for, women" (Moore 92). Like many other scholars working in the field of romance studies, Moore notes the dearth of research on representations of consent within the genre: "Despite its mass popularity ... the social sciences have rarely examined this genre for key themes and messaging" (Moore 92). In her research study for this article, Moore applied qualitative analysis to 68 scenes in 20 romance novels in order to examine the role of consent in contemporary romance novels. Unlike the distinct lack of representations of affirmative consent observed by MacKinnon and Groszhan in movies and television, Moore found "successful consent negotiations" (Moore 92) in the majority of sexual encounters depicted in the literature she examined.

Like Charles, Moore also examined the idea of nonverbal consent, a relatively new concept, though it is not difficult to find examples within the genre wherein consent is implied. Moore attributes the dramatic increase in instances of consent being given prior to sexual encounters to changing attitudes and greater empowerment of women of the past several decades: "One of the major shifts in romance novel writing from the 1970s to today has been the increased focus on writing explicitly present and character-driven consent. The 'no means yes' and rape tropes found in romance novels of four decades ago has been thoroughly challenged by feminists, romance authors, and the general public" (Moore 93). Throughout this study, which examined 20 best-selling erotic contemporary romance novels, Moore noted a preponderance of examples of sex initiated by women, and the majority of sex scenes also featured affirmative consent between participating characters. It can be speculated, then, that one positive effect of the #TimesUp and #MeToo movements will be even greater attention paid to demonstrating ongoing affirmative consent when writing sexual encounters in romance novels.

Moore's study reinforces the idea that the romance genre is leading the charge to normalize consent in popular culture, an effort that will hopefully lead to additional scholarship in this area using a variety of critical lenses. However, her analysis reveals some limitations in women's sexual agency in the novels she included in her study: "This preliminary analysis revealed scripts addressing safe sex practices in this genre have not advanced substantially over the last decade and female characters are still portrayed as passive actors relative to negotiations for their own sexual health" (Moore 94). Overall, however, Moore identified the romance genre as being a fundamental actor in the broader cultural conversation about consent, providing essential standards for how consent should be modeled in popular entertainment: "However, the movement toward eliminating rape tropes in the genre has been successful and romance novelists are increasingly cited as some of the most skilled producers of explicit and sexy negotiation scripts in a cultural context where few such examples exist. The positive shifts in consent scripts over time could serve as a model for similar shifts in safe sex scripts in this genre" (Moore 94). As asserted by MacKinnon, this type of representation and modeling of consent, if replicated in television, movies, and other forms of popular entertainment, could provide a turning point in the national conversation about consent.

Greater scholarly investment in the issue of consent in romance literature is needed in order to advance, and, to some, legitimize, the value of the romance genre in the fight to expand representations of consent in popular culture. Moore expounds on this point by saying, "Many U.S. media and education outlets have failed to model updated cultural scripts that could improve the sexual health of its population. While the romance genre continues to be relatively ignored by scholars, its outreach is expanding. It is important for social scientists to focus on the genre's messaging and potential for initiating change" (Moore 94). While the limited amount of scholarship in this area is noteworthy, the interest expressed by scholars in the legal field and the social sciences suggests that this is a fruitful, and necessary, area to encourage cross-disciplinary efforts in order to incite meaningful change.

Romance Scholarship

While the lack of critical research on consent in romance literature is the primary concern of this writer, it is important to note that there is limited critical scholarship on popular romance in general. There are many theories about why this is the case, all well-synopsized by Jessica Van Slooten in her outstanding 2018 review, "Popular Romance, American Identity, and Feminist Criticism." Van Slooten offers an overview of the landscape by saying, "Popular romance fiction—from slim Harlequin category novels to longer stand-alone works—continues to be wildly popular and frequently maligned" (Van Slooten 1). She goes on to talk about how the strength of the romance market also makes the publication of marginally profitable genres possible. "The irony is that the commercial success of popular romance fiction likely subsidizes other publishing, including the celebrated literary fiction that graces most of the pages of the NYTBR. Popular romance fiction is a $1.08 billion industry, with women making up 84% of the readership" (Van Slooten 1). Van Slooten discusses cultural biases that have historically worked against the romance genre, as well as common stereotypes that long stigmatized the genre as being unworthy of either critical attention or academic scholarship.

These biases were first explored by scholar Pamela Regis in her groundbreaking 2003 text *A Natural History of the Romance Novel*, which provides a much-needed historical perspective on the genre as well as a critical framework for examining works within it. The book's introduction offers valuable, if dated, insight about the divide between romance literature and the ivory tower: "The romance novel has the strange distinction of being the most popular but least respected of literary genres. While it remains consistently dominant in bookstores and on best-seller lists, it is also widely dismissed by the critical community. Scholars have alleged that romance novels have helped create subservient readers, who are largely women, by confining heroines to stories that ignore issues other than love and marriage" (Regis, back cover). Examined in this context, it is interesting to consider the scholarly work that has taken place in the intervening years, and the directions in which it continues to grow.

Van Slooten offers further insight into the discord between romance fiction and academia by suggesting that romance novels were easy targets for early feminist critiques: "Consider second-wave feminist critiques of male domination within heterosexual relationships and intercourse alongside the fulfilling fantasy of 'happily ever after.' Consider, too, problematic tropes of trembling virgins and rapey rogues whose narrative destiny is to fall into something like marital bliss" (Van Slooten 1). There is no doubt that these tropes are part of romance fiction's beginnings, but, as Moore's research asserts, the genre has changed greatly over the past few decades. Charles reinforces this idea by affirming that consent is integral to the creative process of characterization, which is why romance protagonists written today have significantly more agency than their predecessors, no matter the trope (Charles).

While the field of academic scholarship in romance studies remains small and largely interdisciplinary, it is a fixture in popular culture studies and gaining steam with emerging literary scholars as well. "Fortunately, times are changing. Third-wave feminism embraces sex positivity, and many contemporary romance novels feature couples—of all genders and sexualities—who are well-versed in consent and power, explicitly and implicitly navigating these issues as they fall into orgasmic bliss" (Van Slooten 2). Van Slooten credits third-wave feminism for cultivating an academic climate that is well-prepared for robust engagement in romantic scholarship: "Feminist cultural studies provides tools for unpacking the complexity of popular romance fiction, paving a way for more nuanced readings and feminist stances" (Van Slooten 2). While conditions are ripe for romance studies to become a more popular and more widely-recognized field of academic study, the response has been somewhat limited so far; however, multiple sources have long insisted that the scholarly romance community is on the cusp of significant expansion. Issues like consent in contemporary romance offer exactly this opportunity for deeper and more meaningful critical engagement.

Contemporary Romance Scholarship

Among scholars, Van Slooten offers the clearest evaluation of the contemporary landscape of romance scholarship and conversation in her description of the myriad places it takes root: "A growing number of these [romance] readers are also scholars who have worked over the past 40+ years to develop a rich, diverse, interdisciplinary scholarly community. Popular romance scholars find community in numerous places, including the venerable Romance Writers of America (RWA) association" (Van Slooten). The epicenter of romance scholarship is the International Association for the Study of Popular Romance (IASPR), which has published its online peer-reviewed *Journal of Popular Romance Studies* since 2010. Interestingly, both the IASPR and the journal were created by scholars Eric Selinger and Sarah Lyons to support the enthusiastic following on their blog *Teach Me Tonight*, a forum dedicated to the discussion of romance novels.

Romance studies also features under the larger umbrella of studies in popular culture: "(PCA) features a vibrant popular romance division, and scholars gather at the PCA's annual conference to engage in community connections and share research. Popular romance blogs like *Teach Me Tonight* and…. *Smart Bitches, Trashy Books* offer more informal gathering places for scholarly inquiry to flourish" (Van Slooten 2). Van Slooten's discussion of these settings of inquiry as "informal" provides an important key, perhaps the linchpin, to understanding the hybrid nature of romance scholarship and offers insight into the dearth of published, peer-reviewed scholarship on the issue of consent in contemporary romance novels. As suggested by the viral popularity of Charles's tweet thread, this conversation is extant and thriving within the romance community—but only if you know where to look.

Indeed, it is within this informal community—an aggregate of romance writers, scholars from myriad fields, and readers of the most popular genre in the world—that the most robust discussion about urgent topics like consent in romance novels is taking place. Within this heady mix of scholarship and fandom lies a wealth of discussion on topics ranging from tropes and diversity to classic analysis and the mysteries of love itself. Catherine Roach, author of the superlative *Happily Ever After: The Romance*

Story in Popular Culture, does an excellent job of exploring the tensions within the aca-fandom (academics who are also fans of the genre), a category of scholar-reader that Roach both identifies as and discusses at length (Roach 34).

Building on Regis's research as well as her own metamorphosis from academic to romance author, Roach crafts a compelling theory about romance scholarship that distills down to the suggestion that the origin story of many, if not most, romance scholars is markedly different from those studying in other literary fields (Roach 30–35). In her review of *Happily Ever After*, Van Slooten discusses how "Roach's structural approach to her own book bridges the divide between scholarly and popular writing… [Roach] explicitly situates herself as 'a multi-positioned aca-fan-author' … reflected, for instance, in Roach's approachable voice, lack of jargon, and infusion of romance imagery and language" (Van Slooten 2). While this hybrid approach to the romance genre is ascribed only to Roach, in this instance, it can perhaps be widely applied to many working within the genre. Much of the writing being done across multiple platforms, particularly online, does not fit traditional definitions of scholarship so much as informed public discourse, but maybe it should.

Roach's monograph/memoir is a treasure trove of both the history of scholarship within the romance genre and also a thoughtful source of perspective about the many communities invested in discourse about the romance genre. The romance genre simply belongs to more people than any other genre of literature, particularly among those that receive critical attention. It bridges academic disciplines, and there is a wealth of fertile ground for scholarly exploration to build upon the existing discourse. Of particular interest for this research, of course, is the iceberg of conversation that has taken place about—or adjacent to—the discussion of consent in romance novels, how it has evolved, and the work ahead. It is also important to note that Roach and Hannah McCann explore this need further in their chapter on sex and sexuality in romance fiction in the recently-published book *The Routledge Research Companion to Popular Romance Fiction*, saying "More work remains to be done in continued discussions about the meaning of consent, seduction, and BDSM and the relationship between fictional depiction and real-life experience around issues of assault, traumatic reenactment, healing, agency, and desire" (422). Additional scholarship on consent in romance fiction would certainly aid in this effort.

Roach addresses the subject of consent directly in one chapter of her book, and she does so in a very interesting way. In "Notes from the Imagination," a hybrid critical/creative nonfiction interlude, Roach features her academic self in conversation with her romance novelist alter ego,

Catherine LaRoche, author of regency romance novels *Knight of Love* and *Master of Love*. This creative exercise, though entertaining, offers valuable insight into the inherent conflicts between the romance novel industry and feminist academic discourse.

One notable passage draws correlations between the romance genre's preference for the ever-commanding alpha male and the very real specter of rape culture in our society. "Roach: 'But I'm worried about the extent to which the seduction by this dominant and powerful alpha male can sound like a rape. Consent is so central to good sex, and can go so wrong. Do you know the figures on college campuses about the prevalence of unwanted or coerced sexual contact...'" (66). LaRoche counters this claim by asserting that, "In romances—straight or gay—the hero is typically some version of the quintessential male but with the assurance that he is a figure of honor who will do no harm" (66). LaRoche then goes on to suggest that the alpha hero archetype in romance novels is actually a deeply feminist figure: "So, yes, the heterosexual romance with the alpha hero upholds the patriarchal ideal of masculinity but with the feminist twist that this hero's power is never used against the heroine. In fact, his power is never misused at all, for any unjust purpose of exploitation" (Roach 66). This is a thought-provoking idea, one that is both obvious and yet also radically subversive.

The idea is met with incredulity by Roach: "But how realistic is that? That this tycoon-billionaire-duke-sheik-alpha male is, underneath it all, a feminist boy scout?" (66). Roach then argues about the need for realism to ground these stories, suggesting that more realistic depictions of romantic love might better serve the genre and its audience. LaRoche counters with the idea that not only is the fantasy of romance the point, it is also essential for addressing critical issues in our society: "People talk about romance as an escapist fantasy genre that women read in order to get away from the drudgery.... But I think the role of fantasy is much more profound. It's where we work out deep conundrums of the culture, like the problem of female desire in a patriarchal world" (67). Romance novels themselves may well be the key to a greater cultural conversation about consent, one that would be well-supported by further scholarly examination and engagement in the topic.

At the end of the chapter, Roach asserts that there is a brighter, more connected future for discourse about the romance genre. She also suggests that fully exploring the possibilities may require a new kind of scholarly inquiry, one that might represent a significant departure from traditional approaches:

> So let me end with a quick and sober summary.
> There are clearly transgressive and progressive possibilities offered by romance fiction, as well as constraints and complicated questions posed by the genre. There is as well the strange and seductive pleasure of this question: How

to understand the creative and fruitful possibilities of ludic research, of play and performance, of a wholehearted engagement of the self—Roach and LaRoche coming together—pointing toward another model of the academic life? And what new possibilities of academic writ—[76–77]

In a telling moment, Roach is cut off mid-sentence by LaRoche exclaiming her joy at the happily-ever-after ending she sees on the horizon for academic scholarship and the romance genre. Roach ends the chapter by acknowledging the possibilities that lie ahead, as well as all the work that needs to be done in order for major issues in the genre and our society—like consent—to have the full engagement of academic scholarship.

Roach is not the only author to suggest that discourse about romance novels, by necessity, often departs from traditional academic scholarship. In their 2009 book *Beyond Heaving Bosoms*, authors Sarah Wendell and Candy Tan offer an incisive look at the landscape of the romance genre, its detractors, and the inherent value that greater discourse and academic scholarship holds. As the proprietors of the popular romance blog *Smart Bitches, Trashy Books*, Wendell and Tan are well positioned to offer insight into the challenges the genre has faced to gain legitimacy within the cultural conversation.

Wendell and Tan cite no less than bestselling romance author Nora Roberts when discussing the uphill battle the genre has faced to be taken seriously: "As Nora Roberts says, 'Romance is the hat trick of easy targets: emotions, relationships, and sex.' Add to that hat trick the instant handicap of being a genre written mostly by women, mostly for women, and the stereotypical images that surround both the readers and the writers, and it's a one-stop express to Highly Denigrated Genre land" (Wendell and Tan 126). However, like Van Slooten and Roach, Wendell and Tan see the genre as chronically overlooked by scholars, particularly considering the high stakes of culturally relevant topics examined in romance writing: "Because romance deals with one of the most elemental blocks of human relationships.... The genre is huge, creative, evolving, and a multivenue crossroads of just about every other type of fiction. And it has been ignored for far too long" (9).

Like their counterparts in academia, Wendell and Tan feel the romance genre is deserving of far more scholarly attention than it receives, though they also argue that the tide may finally be turning: "From Pamela Regis's *A Natural History of the Romance Novel* to the Professors Brilliant at *Teach Me Tonight*, a blog devoted to scholarly examination of the genre, there are some big, big brains examining the power of the romance, and the power hidden within it. The political, social, and yes, feminist implications of the genre are examined with full brain powers on" (132). Beyond making this observation, Wendell and Tan also advocate for more scholarly engagement in the cultural discourse about the romance genre.

Wendell and Tan also engage with the subject of consent in romance novels, though somewhat obliquely. The authors argue that the genre has largely evolved past the violent rape fantasies frequently seen in romance fiction through the 1980s, and that today's romances are characterized by their greater commitment to consensual sex: "But despite the number of rape and conquer scenes that littered Old Skool romance like discarded petticoats on the floor of the nearest pirate ship, current romance creates not so much a conquering through sex as it does a cohesion, with both sides equal players in the sexual, emotional, and physical boom-shaka-laka" (156). Though rape in romance novels has not yet been completely relegated to the past, it has been marginalized throughout much of the genre.

In addition to evolving approaches to consent, Wendell and Tan credit the romance genre for its contributions to the sexual education of many of its readers. The authors also discuss how romance novels represent many readers' "first introduction to sex. Long before they had any actual sex, they read about it in various configurations and in various historical time periods" (Wendell and Tan 157). They cite scholar Laura Vivanco's analysis that romance novels' greatest contribution may in fact be the role they play in readers' education about their own sexual autonomy and agency, saying that her analysis "that romance novels are one of the few genres that focus not only on women's sexuality ... and sexual enjoyment, reveals romance as a source of both the sexual teaching and the sexual healing ... and, more important, are responsible for shaping attitudes towards sexuality" (Wendell and Tan 156). In addition to exploring the fundamental educational contributions the romance genre has made to its readers, the authors also imagine an expansive role to be played by an emerging generation of romance scholars, one that does not seem out of reach.

Conclusion

As the flurry of the responses to Charles' tweet thread shows, the discourse about consent is alive and well in the wake of the #TimesUp and #MeToo movements. It also reveals opportunities for greater engagement in this area of research by the academic community in the still-emerging field of romance scholarship, a field that is disproportionately smaller than the vast and diverse nature of romance readership might suggest. The readership's desire to discuss consent in romance novels and amplify its presence in the broader cultural conversation suggests an urgent and immediate need for thoughtful and immersive critical engagement in order to support rapidly changing cultural demands for comprehensive consent within literature and, more importantly, in the values of the society it reflects.

WORKS CITED

Charles, KJ. "Yes or No: Consent in Sex Scenes." *KJ Charles*. 20 May 2020. https://kjcharleswriter.com/2020/05/20/yes-and-no-consent-in-sex-scenes/.
Charles, KJ (@kj_charles), et al. "I've just received an email complaining that there's too much consent in my sex scenes, and tbh I'm really struggling with why the hell you'd write that down and send it to someone." Twitter. 19 May 2020. https://twitter.com/kj_charles/status/1262618284928774146.w
Groszhans, Courtney Anne. "Romance or Sexual Assault? Ambiguity of Sexual Consent in the Media and How Yes Means Yes Legislation Can Help." *Hastings Women's Law Journal*, vol. 29, no. 2, 2018, pp. 224–240.
hooks, bell. *Feminism is for Everybody: Passionate Politics*. 2nd ed., Routledge, 2014.
Kamblé, Jayashree, Eric Murphy Selinger, and Hsu-Ming Teo, editors. *The Routledge Research Companion to Popular Romance Fiction*. Routledge, 2020.
Moore, Laura M. "Sexual Agency, Safe Sex, and Consent Negotiations in Erotic Romance Novels." *European Journal of Social Sciences*, vol. 2, no.2, 2019, pp. 92–96.
Piemonte, Jennifer L., Staci Gusakova, Marissa Nichols, and Terry Conley. "Is Consent Sexy? Comparing Evaluations of Written Erotica Based on Verbal Sexual Consent." *Psychology & Sexuality*, 2020. pp. 1–10.
Regis, Pamela. *A Natural History of the Romance Novel*. U of Pennsylvania P, 2003.
Roach, Catherine. *Happily Ever After: The Romance Story in Popular Culture*. Indiana UP, 2018.
Van Slooten, Jessica. "Popular Romance, American Identity, and Feminist Criticism." *Resources for Gender and Women's Studies: A Feminist Review*, vol. 39, no. 1, 2018, pp. 1–6.
Wendell, Sarah and Candy Tan. *Beyond Heaving Bosoms: The Smart Bitches' Guide to Romance Novels*. Touchstone, 2009.

PART THREE

History and Historicity

"Say, could that lass be I?"

Outlander, *Transmedial Time-Travel, and Women's Historical Fantasy*

Ashley Elizabeth Christensen

A dedicated adaptation of a series of novels, Starz's *Outlander* opens most episodes with an otherworldly title sequence consisting of abstract shots from the series and the breathtaking Scottish Countryside, juxtaposed against an ancient feminine ceremony meant to call forth the magic of standing stones, set amidst a haunting ballad about the disappearance of a lass; it's an eerily cognizant representation of what *Outlander* as a franchise stands for: women, historical fantasy, and a deep mistrust of the (masculine) historical record. Based on a traditional Scottish folk tune, "Skye Boat Song," in 1829, Robert Louis Stevenson revised the lyrics and integrated the original's structure into a poem, "Sing Me a Song of a Lad That Is Gone." The poem serves as a testament to Bonnie Prince Charlie's daring escape from the English to the Isle of Skye after the massacre at Culloden, disguised as a young serving maid to mistress Flora MacDonald (Donelan 49).

Playing with gender fluidity already present in the original, *Outlander* series composer Bear McCreary adapted the poem, recording a new version with vocalist (and wife) Raya Yarbrough; only in this version, our subject is no longer a "lad" but a "lass" seeking her way home. While this "lass" ostensibly refers to series' protagonist Claire Fraser, a 20th-century nurse who inadvertently travels to 18th-century Scotland on the eve of the 1745 Jacobite Uprising, and whose disappearance precipitates the overarching conflict of the series, the title sequence also refers to "the inexplicable 'disappearance' of women—their names, subjectivities, desire—from culture and patrilineal genealogies" (Donelan 31). The title song serves as a succinct exemplification of the franchise's thematic priorities that extend beyond the romantic hijinks of two relatable leads, specifically a rediscovery of feminine domestic contributions within the historical record and intensive literary identification.

Diana Gabaldon, author of the original series of novels on which the television show is based, extends current debates about history's biased narratology and its deconstruction by utilizing the compelling foundation of women's historical fiction—which has the ability to apply retroactive critique against historical marginalization—and intensifies it by literally transposing a (loosely) contemporary female character into a historical context. Beyond jumpstarting a captivating tale of adventure and danger, Claire's transposition as a modern woman into a pre-feminist context, struggling not only to survive in a brutally patriarchal world but also to carve out agency for herself, provides multiple points for readers to semiotically engage with and connect their own journey through different patriarchal contexts to Claire's, resulting in a process of intensive reader/viewer identification that subjectively positions them within the narrative as a fellow "lass" who is dedicated to a decidedly feminine vision of historical narratology—a potent strategy that is in part responsible for the undeniable success of the *Outlander* franchise across demographic boundaries, such as gender, race, and sexual orientation.[1]

Anthony Guy Patricia's chapter, "Gabaldon and the Practice of Gay Male Homoerotic Reading" is a compelling example of the above as he charts his own critical and personal reactions to Gabaldon's narratives as a homosexual man who, through Claire's heterosexual subject position, is invited to objectify and emotionally desire Jamie, which he recognizes as intense literary identification. Utilizing the work of Laura Green, Patricia defines the concept of literary identification and its priority within the narratives of *Outlander* as an

> "elaboration of bonds between and among readers, characters, and authors," of which one factor is a "reader's recognition of aspects of her or himself in a fictional character." [Literary identification] signals an "occurrence emerging from the encounter of the psyche of a reader and the rhetorical construction of a narrative by its author." This, in turn, makes it relatively easy for her readers to suspend their disbelief willingly. Indeed, readers may well be inclined to think that, if it was an actuality, traveling through time would likely feel for them exactly as it did for Claire. Hence, because the character of Claire is a fictional representation of a human being who encounters the extraordinary in a wholly believable way, Gabaldon's readers, regardless of their gender or orientation, can empathize with her to the point that they do not question the sheer impossibilities inherent in her initial story [109].

The concept of *Outlander* is strongly based in the series' propensity to foster connections between readers/viewers and the narrative, especially for women, due to the narrative's privileging of the female perspective and revaluing of the domestic feminine—a realm where many a historical woman has been banished with the insinuation that such contributions are ultimately superfluous to the construction of the historical record. *Outlander*, and other similar narratives, in many respects, posit a contradictory position to this perspective by using a strong and competent heroine who is able to survive using the limited tools at her disposal and her own (modern) skills. The manner in which Gabaldon positions Claire's use of these tools in turn suggests that readers/viewers too could apply their own different skill sets and use them just as effectively though perhaps in a different fashion than healer Claire (Ty 58). In Gabaldon's version of feminine historiography, feminine earthy desires and potential are elevated as even spiritual in nature, as Jamie observes to Claire after ruminating on his own mortality, "A woman is ... infinite possibility" (*Echo in the Bone* 513). Beyond a romantic sentiment whispered to his wife in bed, Jamie's observation is a coded message about the implications of recognizing oft-ignored female contributions to society, culture, and the historical record, and the series' propensity to prioritize such.

The above is an example of *Outlander's* historiography, as the series is quick to complicate and deconstruct the myth of an objective masculine historical record. After she returns to the 20th century, Claire argues that historians' "greatest crime is that they presume to know what happened, how things [come] about, when they only have what the past chose to leave behind—for the most part, they think what they were meant to think, and it's a rare one that sees what really happened, behind the smokescreen of artifacts and paper" (*Dragonfly in Amber* 907). Moreover, she calls the dashing Bonnie Prince "a fool, and a drunkard, and a weak, silly man" and his compatriots "all fools ... who drank too much together, and filled themselves with Charlie's foolish dreams. Talk is cheap" (*DA* 906). By acknowledging the failures of historians and the historical record, the narrative both recognizes and validates the reader/viewers' frustration at the invisibility of women and other marginalized populations within the historical record. Additionally, the series proposes an alternative feminine history through the use of meta-historiography to engage with the reader/viewer's own socio-cultural position within contemporary patriarchal contexts, which serves as an integral component of the series' successful strategy of literary identification. Such identification is an essential piece of the puzzle which explains the series' popularity and fandom. Whereas white, heterosexual men are spoiled for choice in their identification with popular fictional narratives and the characters which populate them, women are given decidedly fewer options and less flexibility. In a cultural environment where femme consumers often have to place themselves into a fraught subject position in order to enjoy masculine pop culture narratives, *Outlander*, for many, represents a breath of fresh air.

Publishing the first volume in 1991, Diana Gabaldon's *Outlander* series began modestly enough with an original slate of ten novels, the ninth of which was released in November 2021. In the intervening years, *Outlander* has exploded from one series of novels to several other genres, from a spin-off series focused on a major queer character to the aforementioned and ongoing television series (2014–). Its popularity has grown to such proportions that the economic and political imperatives that lie behind *Outlander*'s narrative have effected real-world consequences, most notably with the "Outlander Effect" in the tourism industry, wherein sites mentioned or used in filming have seen an astounding 67 percent increase in visitors and revenue, 70 percent of which are women (Mailman). Indeed, even beyond tourism, and even despite the critical derision often assigned to texts within the women's romance/historical fiction genre, the series was creating political waves before even airing its first episode.

British fans of the series were perplexed when, in August 2014, *Outlander* premiered in the United States but did not in the United Kingdom, despite the production being shot on location and being a co-production between both British and American companies. It was not until the infamous Sony Email Hack three months after the show's premiere that fans were given answers why—David Cameron's government had halted distribution negotiations for the series in fear that such a pro–Scottish narrative would skew the results for the Scottish Independence Referendum that was scheduled for September 2014 (Shacklock 317).

Outlander is rarely sympathetic to the English Imperialist plight; the subjugation and attempted eradication of the Highland clans and culture dominates the narrative, and the rape of uber-masculine hero Jamie Fraser at the hands of English dragoon Jack Randall reflects this targeted violence and the repeated attempts to justify the treatment of native Scots through political theater and manipulation, such as the Act of Union and England's refusal to allow Scotland to engage in another referendum after being forced out of the European Union despite the overwhelming majority of the Scottish population voting to remain. Yet, after contributing over 40 million pounds and 2000 jobs to Britain's economy in its first season alone, *Outlander* is not even broadcast in one of its countries of origin and where a majority of the narrative is set. While there have been halfhearted attempts to rectify this, such as broadcasting the first season almost three years after it had already aired and after the series had moved onto multiple subsequent seasons, most fans utilize international streaming services and other legally hazy methods to access the series. Such an intense reaction and its real-world consequences seems startlingly at odds with a fictional property that has had the moniker "mommy/mummy porn" applied to it with a fair amount of critical and social derision.

As both a series of novels and a television show, *Outlander* has enjoyed immense success, though neither is without the controversies and paradoxes commonly associated with romance narratives, such as being insistently heteronormative (John Grey notwithstanding) and encouraging of nuclear familial units. Yet, the narratives are ineffably pro-birth control, and much of Claire's medical knowledge is deployed to that end, both in attempting to help women reproduce certain modern birth control methods with varying degrees of success and educating others about such methods' efficacy in allowing women agency in their reproductive roles[2] and health. The limitations of Claire's expertise in preventing pregnancy without 20th-century medical technology are often rectified by knowledge imparted to her by other historical women. When Jamie raises an objection to their daughter employing such techniques, Claire is quick to point out, "remember, Jamie—Bree comes from a time where women can decide whether or when to have babies, with a fair amount of certainty. She'd feel such a thing was her right" (*The Fiery Cross* 182).

However, whereas the television show's treatment of birth control, including terminating unwanted pregnancies, is reasonably progressive, *Outlander* posits a decidedly more ambivalent position on abortion in the novels. When Claire and Jamie's daughter, Bree, is raped soon after her own impromptu marriage and finds herself pregnant and with a missing/kidnapped husband, Claire communicates to Bree that abortion is an option if undertaken early enough—even over Jamie's vehement patriarchal objections. Claire once again re-educates him, arguing "I know what it is to bear a child. I know what it is to have your body and your mind and your soul taken from you and changed without your will. I know what it is to be ripped out of the place you thought was yours, to have choice taken from you…. And it isn't something anyone should do without being willing" (*Drums of Autumn* 828). Yet for all her defense of Bree's right to choose, only a couple pages later, Claire also reveals

> I had never done an abortion though I had had some experience as a resident, in the post-care of miscarriage. On the rare occasion a patient had asked it of me, I had referred them to a colleague. I had no absolute objections; I had seen too many women killed in body or spirit by untimely children. If it was killing—and it was—then I thought it not murder, but a justifiable homicide, undertaken in desperate self-defense [*DoA* 831].

Ultimately, Bree decides not to terminate her pregnancy, in the novels ostensibly because the child may also be her husband's, though in the television series Bree articulates it is primarily for herself. This ambivalence continues in the same novel as Bree's unplanned pregnancy, where Gabaldon also features a botched abortion which claims the life of the woman involved and places the life of the slave she forced to perform the procedure at risk, further clouding a pro-abortion message. Yet Gabaldon's contradictory stance on the appearance of birth control and abortion in her narratives is one example of a common paradox found in romantic fiction: progress mixed with orthodoxy. In *Outlander*, and other romantic narratives, it is this marriage of opposites that holds much responsibility for the breakdown in critical conversations between (academic) feminists and the popular lay-reader/viewer.

Another example of this paradox at work can be seen in the prevalence of sexual assault within romantic narratives, including moments of "dubious" consent. In Gabaldon's novels, and the television series based upon them, sexual assault and hazy consent are common. For example, in the third novel, while separated from Claire, Jamie has a disturbing sexual encounter with Lady Geneva Dunsany, wherein she withdraws her consent after first penetration and Jamie continues having intercourse with her. Astutely, the creators rectified this problematic moment by establishing explicit consent within the show's adaptation of the same scene, a decision fans of the books roundly applauded. However, unlike many other dominant popular cultural narratives, the effects of trauma and recovery are always a priority in *Outlander*, and it is not only women who are victimized.

Even less common is the rape of a hegemonic masculine hero early in the series, though satisfyingly, his rapist (and all others throughout the series) is brutally punished. Black Jack Randall is first nearly trampled to death by a herd of wild highland cows before then dying in the battle of Culloden, presumably by Jamie's hand. The man responsible for the sexual assault of young Mary Hawkins is brutally cut down by Jamie as he springs Claire and Mary from their prison (notably in the show, it is Mary herself who strikes down her attacker). Stephen Bonnet, Bree's attacker, is captured due to her actions, tried as a pirate, and left to drown with the tide before Bree calmly executes him herself. The roving band of degenerates who abduct and assault Claire in the sixth novel and fifth season of the show are brutalized by Jamie and his settlers when they catch up. Even the lone survivor of the massacre gets his due when in the novels he is later smothered to death by Mrs. Bug, an elderly housekeeper; or in the television series where he escapes being smothered only to be poisoned with essence of hemlock by Marsali, Claire's medical apprentice and daughter-in-law, after Marsali asserts that unlike Claire, she is not bound by the Hippocratic oath.

The television series has drawn much attention for its presentation of sexual violence, and the thoughtful representation of such serious subject matter is a difficult balance to strike, as creators must convey both the horror of the action taking place while avoiding any prurient overtones or triggering the audience. These concerns are then further exacerbated by the condensation of the original narrative for adaptation to screen. As Kathryn

VanArendonk wryly notes, "because the series is more narratively compact than the books, it also feels like characters are experiencing or being threatened by sexual assault all the time" ("*Outlander* Drew a Line…"). The prevalence of sexual assault in the original series also poses philosophical questions about the ethics of adaptation; if there is an assault in the source material that fundamentally affects a character and the plot, are adaptors duty bound to include it in the television narrative? Regardless, in comparison to other shows like it, such as HBO's *Game of Thrones*, *Outlander* proves that filmmakers can portray sexual assault without being exploitative. The assaults are never sexualized, and the creators draw a clear demarcation between rape and consensual sex that prioritizes female pleasure.

When Bree is attacked by Stephen Bonnet, the camera does not follow to witness her brutalization, but instead focuses on the complicity of those present who can hear Bree's screams, as the men in the room

> carry on as if nothing untoward is happening…. However, the looks on the barmaids' faces tell a much different story. The creeping horror as they realize what is going on is only matched by the resignation that this is way the world is for women and they are powerless to stop it. In the current #MeToo era, this feminine sorrow is all too familiar [Fikse].

It's difficult to argue against those who feel that the novels and show rely overmuch on narratives of sexual assault. This debate will only be exacerbated by the recent season five finale, which saw the story of Claire's assault accelerated in the narrative.[3] But once again, the showrunners present a complex and nuanced depiction of sexual trauma, foregrounding Claire's emotional experience and attempts to cope, as she dissociates and regresses inside herself to an idyllic 1960s where her family from both the future and past come together to celebrate an all-American Thanksgiving.

As is par for the course in *Outlander*, Claire's rapists meet horrifically bloody demises shortly after her assault in a manner that is both disturbing and gratifying to the viewer by placing them in a position of narrative complicity in the rapists' punishment and the avenging of Claire's victimization. The above suggests that romantic genres, hybridic like women's historical fiction or otherwise, are engaging in equally philosophically complicated conversations as their masculine counterparts, though the conventions may differ greatly. However, it is difficult to engage in such when critical conversations surrounding femme-focused properties like *Outlander* are steeped in tones of borderline sanctimonious feminist horror which ignores reader/viewer-made semiotic meaning, instead positing the consumers of such content as ostensible traitors to feminism at worst, and mindless dupes at best. Simply put, sexual assault is a common element in American romances (and culture) and merely asserting that such depictions all fall into the "rape as a plot device" argument ignores the manner in which these texts handle the personal experience of being attacked, recovering from trauma, how readers may relate or connect to these narratives, and what they say about the greater conversation surrounding sexual assault in the United States and Great Britain. I would also strongly caution any critic, especially feminists, against speaking for or making generalizations about survivors of sexual assault and how they may or may not feel about pop culture portrayals of sexual violence. To effectively discuss *Outlander* as a pop culture entity, we must acknowledge the above paradoxes and controversies[4] commonly found within texts in the romance genre in order to engage with why such fiction continues to be so alluring and how fan engagement can engender real-world economic development, as the "Outlander Effect" clearly shows no signs of abating.

The *Outlander* series is a women's historical romance with metahistorical elements as emphasized by its time-travelling narrative, as "we ultimately encounter Claire as a character who facilitates the reader's re-conception of time and history by destabilizing the absoluteness with which both are associated" (Potter 283). Due to this meta-historicity, the franchise presents a paradoxical version of feminism characterized by clear overtones of feminism or feminist thought in conjunction with traditional narrative tropes of the romance. In many ways, it is a marriage between complicity and critique. But moreover, due to the series being based upon intensive reader identification, the narrative complexities of Claire's differing feminist contexts offer an alternative history for contemporary (women) readers who fail to recognize themselves in the so-called historical record by emphasizing how feminine strength and resistance is an integral part of humanity's history, even if it was not recorded in "official" (i.e., male/masculine) histories.[5] The reorganization and prioritization of the feminine perspective in the *Outlander* series, and other popular non-academic narratives like it, allows readers/viewers the opportunity to conceive history, and women's contributions to historical progress, in a new light that is distinguished by equal consideration of the domestic sphere as an integral component in the formation of culture and history.

Even as the scope of the series began to expand to include other narrative perspectives, Claire's personal narrative remains the only instance of first-person, experiential narration, while all others are subjected to third-person narrative styles. This form encourages an intense personal connection between the reader/viewer and the character of Claire, allowing her competency within patriarchal contexts to serve as retroactive historical absolution. This element of the text is evidenced by the fact that it is primarily women (70 percent) who engage in *Outlander* tourism in Scotland, despite the gender of viewership being close to an even split between male/female, motivated to visit the series' historical sites because they feel as connected to them as the fictional women in the novels and show, despite those women's real-life counterparts not being present in the historical record. This reader/viewer engagement could be read as an extension of Janice Radway's arguments about the subversive act of reading the romance itself—the phenomenon of women engaging in *Outlander* tourism is an amplification of Radway's arguments about the romance's place in allowing women to make time for themselves and find emotional nurturance within such texts, but dialed up to eleven because no longer are these readers limited by their own physical environment or the subsequent endings of such narratives.

The original series and the television adaptation of *Outlander* are hybrids of several genres, a common feature of contemporary romantic narratives given that the genre of romance is often derided critically, within both popular culture and the academy, yet even then such texts still face an uphill critical battle. While the first novel of the series was marketed as a romance, it was a "designation ... to which [Gabaldon] agreed to only at the urging of her agent.... But Gabaldon ... exacted a promise from the publisher: If the book became 'visible' (e.g., made its way to the *New York Times* best-sellers list), then they would re-situate it as 'general fiction'" (Petersen). Even as *Outlander's* identity as a romance is in flux, readers often interpret it as such and Gabaldon is able to leverage the market even despite her protests that she's not completely a part of it. Perhaps some could find such equivocating problematic considering the success of *Outlander*, but with such ambivalent, but often contemptuously negative reception largely propagated by a primarily male critic base, it's not difficult to understand why an author would be wary of such a designation used by both anti-feminists and feminists alike to mock such content and narratives in the name of ostensibly protecting an infantile (femme/woman) reader who is apparently unable to engage in critical thinking, reading, or meaning-making on their own.

For example, Victoria Kennedy has focused on taking feminized cultural content like *Outlander* and the novels of Philippa Gregory to task for their apparent failures to speak to a clear academic feminist identity. Acknowledging "threads" of feminist rhetoric in Gabaldon's series, she argues that positing the novels as a feminist historiography would not be "critical enough" (118), nor take into account the aspects of the texts she personally finds disturbing—such as Claire's decision to return to Jamie through the stones after a separation of twenty years, which Kennedy interprets as a choice to return to a nostalgic pre-feminist context despite Claire carefully weighing options, extensively preparing, and exercising her agency to choose which historical context she exists in and where she derives the most fulfillment. Regardless of whether a critic personally agrees with Claire/Gabaldon's decision, the emphasis from the outset is on the fact that it is her decision in a world where such decisions are often not in the hands of the women whom they affect. It is also a critical mistake to conflate discussions of symbolic agency and sexual agency within the romance or its derivatives. Kennedy problematically connects Claire's decision to return through the stones directly to various moments in the texts where "dubious" consent (another common trope in the romance genre) is present during sexual situations, despite there not being an instance of Claire and Jamie engaging in sexual acts without clear consent even after the infamous spanking scene, arguing "how is the contemporary woman reader to understand these scenes of 'dubious' consent? Do the novels force the woman into a masochistic subject position wherein her access to pleasure from the narrative can only come from a belief in her own subordination?" (124).

While Kennedy makes salient points about specific moments in the text, like use of "dubious consent" tropes during sexual interactions outside of the series' main couples, her arguments can be somewhat limited in their discussion of the hybridic and complicated nature of the contemporary romance genre; but more problematic is her conception of the typical romance reader as a mindless dupe, powerless to enact active reading strategies, make semiotic meaning, or tell fact from fiction. In some ways, it is Kennedy who forcibly places the *Outlander* reader in the position of "negotiated reading" she so fearfully cautions other critics about. Any feminist critic worth their salt would have a simple time paging through the latest romantic bestseller, pointing out all the ways in which the narrative fails to adhere to a rigid set of academic feminist expectations, but such examinations are ultimately reductive and fail to posit engaged critical consideration of the cultural and popular feminist power of the genre and can position consumers of such narratives as mere victims who have been duped into their own subjugation, passively ingesting a rigid conception of singular semiotic meaning, which has apparently been dictated by the critic, not the reader who has purposely sought out such narratives for consumption.

With such reactions, as well as the ire generated by sexist denunciations of feminized genres, it's not difficult to understand why author Diana Gabaldon might be reluctant to have her work clearly codified as romance. But as Tania Modleski attests in her foundational work *Loving with a Vengeance*, "even the contemporary mass-produced narratives for women contain elements of protest and resistance underneath highly 'orthodox' plots. This is not to say that the tensions, anxieties, and anger which pervade these works are solved in ways which would please modern feminists: far from it" (25).

Yet, for all her moments of "dubious" consent in the novels, Gabaldon often subverts and plays with traditional romance conventions. When Claire and Jamie are forced to wed both for Claire's protection and expedient political circumstances, it is Jamie who is a virgin and Claire who has been sexually active, not only with her previous husband but with others before her first marriage as well. In fact, when Claire and Jamie first meet it is through her own nurse's training that Claire is able to save his life (as opposed to the hero saving her), and at the end of the first novel in the series, after offering himself up as a sacrifice to secure Claire's release by proving his commitment and allowing his captor to take a mallet to his hand, Jamie is again rescued by his wife after she kills a wolf with her bare hands during her own escape—not the other way around. But most importantly, Claire and Jamie often take turns saving each other from the various dangers they encounter and are equally responsible for their own successes as well.

However, the greatest digression from traditional romance narrative in the *Outlander* series is the brutal assault of its masculine hegemonic hero, Jamie Fraser, by Captain Black Jack Randall. In horror, Claire considers "one never stops to think what underlies romance. Tragedy and terror, transmuted by time. Add a little art in the telling ... to make the blood run fast and maidens sigh. My blood was running fast, all right, and never a maiden sighed like Jamie, cradling his mangled hand" (*Outlander* 534). Despite strong assertions that Claire's decision to return to a nostalgic pre-feminist context is problematic, Claire is *not* an 18th-century woman, a fact she struggles to barely conceal (often getting her in trouble), and a conceit that Gabaldon uses to mount several poignant critiques about the evolution of gender roles and feminist thinking over time. When abducted by a roving band of criminals and murderers, Claire is informed by another (male) time-traveler who happens to be travelling with them that "you [Claire] don't act afraid of men. Most of the women from now do. You oughta act more afraid" (*A Breath of Snow and Ashes* 344). Nor is Claire unaware of her own subject position in the past; though she is "for the most part, able to ignore the fact that [she] was legally [Jamie's] property. That didn't alter that it was a fact—and he knew it" (*ABoSAA* 601).

And while the series spends copious amounts of time exploring Claire and Jamie's relationship, Claire's professional identity is just as important to her personal fulfillment as her identity as a wife and mother, regardless of what historical period she finds herself in. When her daughter asks about her calling as a healer, Claire replies, "Jamie's a part of me. So are you.... But neither of you is all of me. I am ... what I am. Doctor, nurse, healer, witch—whatever folk call it, the name doesn't matter. I was born to be that; I will be that 'til I die. If I should lose you—or Jamie—I wouldn't be quite a

90   Part Three: History and Historicity

whole person any longer, but I would still have that left" (*TFC* 684). Claire's words come to pass on multiple occasions, from her twenty-year separation from Jamie, his (mistaken) death by drowning, to Bree deciding to return to the 20th century with her own family. In Gabaldon's narrative and many other romances, women really can seemingly have it all—a fulfilling career, a grand romance, motherhood, and the ability to possibly save lives. They have their cake and eat it too.

While it would be easy for academic feminists to refer to the aforementioned controversies of the franchise as a fly in this supposed ointment, to do so in order to write off the franchise is to continue to reduce readers and viewers of *Outlander* to an inferior subject position—an act already being perpetrated by patriarchal cultural stratification and traditions that disempower the femme/woman fan as passive and easily manipulated. Yet conversely, as robust fan engagement with the series suggests, readers and viewers are connecting with the franchise and identifying with its characters in compelling ways. And despite Gabaldon's seeming ambivalence about the classification of her series and its adaptation as a romance, she is unwavering in her support of fans' connection and identification to her narratives as being subversively powerful, and an element of her fiction she is willing to explicitly defend.

When Starz's Chief Executive Officer Jeffrey Hirsh mockingly insinuated that only women are fans of *Outlander* before dismissing their interest as being resultant of Sam Hueghan's (Jamie Fraser) shirtless physique,[6] Gabaldon was quick to correct him and his sexist notions of female fanbases, responding by emphasizing that while women do watch *Outlander*, they are joined by men in that enjoyment: "What they mostly say they like is the intelligence of the story and the complexity and strength of the relationship between Jamie and Claire. They also love the visual beauty of the show and the emotional depth of the acting…. If [Hirsh is] looking for a place to lean in, though, I think maybe 'intelligence' might be a good place to start" (Roots). While shockingly tone-deaf, considering Starz has the highest female 18+ audience composition in all of premium cable (Roots), Hirsh's comments are unsurprising in a narrative television landscape where award-winning dramas gleefully drape the female form (and do violence unto it) in scenes like one would hang a photograph on a blank wall. Any television series that privileges the female gaze is bound to discomfit the patriarchal powers that be.

The female gaze is an integral component of Gabaldon's series, and readers are often treated to detailed descriptions of Jamie's physique, as well as Claire's (and others') admiration for his physical prowess even as he enters his late fifties. However, the female gaze encourages and appreciates not only Jamie's physical vulnerability but his emotional vulnerability as well. On their homestead on Fraser's ridge, Claire observes she hasn't "seen him with his shirt off for a long time and paused to enjoy the sight. Beyond the simple pleasure of seeing his body flex and move, whipcord muscles moving easily" (*Written in My Own Heart's Blood* 811).

Fortunately, through the process of adaptation, the female gaze has remained a priority for Starz's *Outlander*. The television series' uncommon privileging of the female perspective, especially in the genre of prestige television where the male gaze is obsessively normalized, has garnered praise for being one of the few shows on air which presents the female gaze as the new normal.[7] While the sexual objectification of women through the male gaze strips them of their humanity, corresponding objectification in the (heterosexual) female gaze allows the male subject to maintain his humanity while being looked at as "Claire watches Jamie, and the audience watches Claire watch Jamie" (Lopez 47). From Jamie's equally dramatic wedding reveal midway through the first season, in full Highland regalia no less, to his care and consideration of Claire's emotional needs, Jamie is a character fashioned to appeal to femme/women audiences, a novel experience in a media landscape dominated by the male perspective and gaze.

As Araceli R. Lopez asserts, "the Jamie-centric gaze of the television show also emphasizes that by coming from a space of non-privilege, women writers and specifically female directors present sexual objectification while still maintaining the objectified subject's humanity.... When Jamie wants it, he enjoys being gazed at. Arguably framed in a heterosexual female gaze, the show reiterates that men too are beautiful creatures to be looked at. And that is okay" (52–53). By extension, this femme/female perspective also allows for the reconceptualization of masculine gender roles that acknowledges their futility in expressing the emotional complexity and depth of the masculine experience.

In many ways, Jamie does encapsulate the typical romantic hero, from his good looks, prowess as a warrior, and spectacular lovemaking skills, to his birthright as Laird of Lallybroch. But in many ways, he also complicates those expectations or outright fails them—"These include Claire's dual love for him as well as for the (more feminine) Frank, Jamie's failure to raise his biological children, his close friendship with Lord John Grey,[8] a homosexual man who expresses a deep and abiding love for Jamie, and, finally and more controversially, Jamie's victimization at the hands of Black Jack Randall" (Phillips 55). But the above "failures" do not undermine Jamie's status as a hero within the narrative, nor does the fact that Claire saves Jamie just as, or more, often than he saves her. This is most evident in the first novel, and during the first season of the series, when Jamie is raped by Jack Randall. The rape of a hegemonic masculine character is rare, and of a romantic lead rarer still, but where *Outlander* excels is in tackling the emotional aftermath of such an assault. Even after he's been rescued by Claire, both from Randall and from his own suicidal ideations after the attack, Jamie's recovery takes time, and it is not a smooth journey. Even after decades, vestiges of the assault are still present in his psyche as he continues to cope, with Claire's support.

Jamie's assault at the hands of Black Jack Randall and its aftermath is one example of how *Outlander*, and other romance narratives, have evolved to include serious social issues, "such as spousal or child abuse, alcoholism, racism, and mental and physical illness. While this aspect might not seem to be appealing on the surface, it speaks to the needs of many readers as it allows them not only to confront real-life problems through fiction, but also to envision healthy, hopeful, and successful solutions to them" (Ramsdell qtd. in Frankel). These elements can be seen in several *Outlander* storylines.

One notable example is the efforts of Stephen Bonnet to assert a legal and physical claim to Bree's son Jeremiah, a possible product of his rape of her, in a ploy to claim young Jeremiah's inheritance of the wealthy plantation of River Run. Unfortunately, rapists attempting to claim paternal rights over the resultant children of their assaults is very much a reality in the United States, and oftentimes, even when wrongdoing has been recognized by the court (a rarity itself), the rapists succeed on the basis of their biological relationship.

Even with elements of science fiction, high fantasy, and romance, storylines such as the above demonstrate the effectiveness of the central conceit of the series, both novels and television—the transposition of a highly relatable/identifiable contemporary woman into a past historical context. As journalist Sonia Saraiya astutely observes, "It's wish-fulfillment fantasy from the point of view of a woman—but undercut with the cold horror of taking the conceit seriously. The bygone era of tartan dress and skirling bagpipes look and sound lovely—but what if someone from the modern era was actually transported to that time period? How would she survive?" (qtd. in Frankel). Herein lies the appeal of the series, as reader/viewer engagement is rooted in this literary identification and so experiences this reality though their identification with the contemporary Claire, and later Bree and Roger, who also hail from the 20th century.

When Claire witnesses a group of druid women perform a ritual to "call forth" the power of the stones early in the first novel, she observes that "they should have been *ridiculous*, and perhaps they were. A collection of women in bedsheets, many of them stout and far from agile, parading in circles at the top of a hill. But the hair prickled on the back of my neck at the sound of their call" (*Outlander* 33, emphasis mine). Initial reactions to *Outlander* may mimic Claire's early skepticism and near dismissal of these women as "ridiculous," but their feminine call is responsible for Claire's own time-traveling journey. Though it's her historian husband Frank who first brings her to the standing stones, she returns on her own, seeking out a flower she saw growing at the base of the stones and drawn to the place where she saw the women performing their sacred ceremony. The reader/viewer is placed in a similar narrative position, whereby they too are given the option to ignore the women's call, or step forward. While it is important to engage in a dialogue about the feminist/anti-feminist elements within the expansive series and its many properties, to center the conversation on a reductive feminist pass or fail is to approach the narrative (and others like it) with a limited scope that lacks the necessary nuance to engage with the complexity of the romance and hybrid romance narratives, as well as the highly personal connections made by those who consume them.

Gabaldon snappily conceptualizes and recognizes the feminist nature of her novels as being as equally complex as those who read them, stating, "[*Outlander*] is about a woman, who is quite confident in who she is as a woman, and that's one definition of feminist—you take yourself at your own worth, and you demand that others take you at your own estimation" (Petersen). While such a vague definition of feminism may rankle with academic feminists, its focus on personal meaning, identity, and reader engagement is on brand for both the series and the romance genre in general.

Popular women's fiction, like the romance and the historical novel, have often been characterized by their supposed feminist failures, yet the engagement of women and femme consumers with these genres strongly argues that despite these so-called critical feminist failures, fans of these narratives read moments of resistance and subversion within them, or that at the very least, feminist critics need to engage with these genres in a nuanced fashion that posits the consumers of such narratives as active participants capable of creating meaning out of popular feminized genres.

Approaching such texts with a sense of feminist critical superiority and judgment can result in a restrictive conversation that leaves both the critic and the reader/viewer dissatisfied and frustrated that neither is being heard. As Kathryn VanArendonk articulates, "this is a different argument from one that posits *Outlander* is feminist—that idea is fascinating, but it puts a value on the series as espousing and performing a particular political position.... Whether or not it is feminist, Outlander is unusually, stubbornly female, in a genre that so often is not" ("Why *Outlander*'s Birth Scene is so Unusual"). For the television series, and the novels that it is based on, this stubbornly female focus, emphasized by Claire's first-person narrative priority and the female gaze, is what draws fans in, again and again. Gabaldon's compelling use of techniques that encourage literary reader identification, which have been effectively translated to its onscreen counterpart, ensures a connection between reader/viewer and text—a connection that can be so powerful that fans can give life to this identification and emotional bond by travelling to Scotland itself to walk a mile in Claire Fraser's shoes, should they be so inclined.

Notes

1. Yvonne Leach's "*Outlander* from Book to Screen: Power in Gender and Orientation" presents a fascinating examination of how literary identification has affected the adaptation of the novel series, due to showrunner Ronald Moore relating more to Jamie, whereas Gabaldon clearly identifies with Claire. A poignant example of this difference, Leach points out, is the mishandling of the "spanking" scene from the books, which the television show places in a first season episode that is narrated by Jamie, regardless of the fact that Jamie is not given his own perspective or narrative voice until the third book of the series, so marking a departure by the show's creators.

2. Critics have noted the growing presence of birth control and other protective measures in romantic fiction but have limited their scope to texts that take place during modern/contemporary contexts and male-centric condom use, specifically (duPlessis 83). It's unclear how prevalent discussions of birth control are in women's romantic historical fiction, simply because it has yet to be included in the critical conversation, so *Outlander*'s discussions of reproductive agency could be representative of the genre or be considered an outlier. Regardless, both *Outlander* properties center such discussions from a female point-of-view, often emphasizing the imbalanced procreative and child-caring burdens which fall upon women in a patriarchal society.

3. Each novel is adapted into one season of the television series. Claire's assault is in the sixth book, but fifth season of the show.

4. Another controversy with *Outlander* relates to its treatment (or lack thereof) of race. Gabaldon's depictions of racial difference, slavery, or racially motivated violence leaves much to be desired, though it is debatable which narrative entity (novels vs. show) fails the most in this respect. On the one hand, while the novels engage more with race, they often do so in a stereotypical and oftentimes privileged manner; on the other hand, the show attempts to rectify moments of racial insensitivity, but does so by refusing to engage with race as often or deeply as the novels (Prescott). However, it must be noted that viewers and readers of color still engage with *Outlander* in subversive and powerful ways that draw attention to the racial failures of both the novels and the show while still deriving enjoyment from its narrative. This is exemplified in *Blacklanderz*, a community site dedicated to viewers of color who engage with *Outlander* on multiple levels through blog posts they call Convos.

5. Fernando Pagnoni Berns and Leonardo Lando argue "following this idea, *Outlander* can be read as a warning about the frailty of social contexts, which are just circumstantial and with proclivity to potential stagnation and even regression to previous historical stages. Second, the progressive theory allows just one temporality, just one and only one history, both privileged by universalism, while other potential histories and bifurcations are left just as footnotes. Claire's journey puts into crisis both, the model of history as continuous national improvement and the existence of just one universal temporality" (105).

6. "Outlander—you can say that it's great because women like it because she's a surgeon who goes back in time, but there's also another side of that, which is there's some eye candy for that audience and people like when [Heughan] has his shirt off. You have to be really thoughtful about when you're looking at a piece of content and whether it's really going to be female or not. And it's not easy" (Qtd in Roots).

7. The female gaze as an aesthetic norm for the TV series takes some time to fall into place—there are several instances in the first season where the male gaze is apparent, such

as Jack Randall's attempted rape of Claire (S1E08). While the episode was primarily directed by a woman, due to scheduling conflicts she was unable to shoot the final scenes so another (male) director was brought in—which is clearly evident in the titillating manner in which the scene is shot, but also in its focus on Caitriona Balfe's exposed and bouncing breasts (Leach).

    8. The fascinating relationship between Jamie and John Grey deserves more consideration than I am able to give here, but the friendship, including John's romantic feelings for him, never render Jamie less of a "man" and as a character, John Grey was so popular with readers that Gabaldon has dedicated an entire spin-off series to his exploits with rumors of a possible Starz adaptation circulating as of Summer 2021.

Works Cited

Donelan, Carol. "'Sing Me a Song of a Lass That Is Gone': Myth and Meaning in the Starz Original Series Outlander." *Quarterly Review of Film and Video*, vol. 35, no. 1, 2018, pp. 31–53.
duPlessis, Nicole M. "Men, Women and Birth Control in the Early Outlander Books." In Frankel, *Outlander's Sassenachs*, McFarland, 2016, pp. 82–96.
Fikse, Alyssa. "What Outlander Gets Right About Female Sexuality and Sexual Assault." *SYFY Wire*, 19 February 2019, www.syfy.com/syfywire/what-outlander-gets-right-about-female-sexuality-and-sexual-assault.
Frankel, Valerie, ed. *Adoring Outlander: Essays on Fandom, Genre, and the Female Audience*. McFarland, 2016.
_____. *Outlander's Sassenachs: Essays on Gender, Race, Orientation and the Other in the Novels and Television Series*. McFarland 2016.
_____. *Scots, Sassenach, and Spankings: Feminist and Gender Roles in Outlander*. Amazon Publishing, 2015.
Gabaldon, Diana. *A Breath of Snow and Ashes*. Random House, 2005.
_____. *Dragonfly in Amber*. Random House, 1992.
_____. *Drums of Autumn*. Random House, 1997.
_____. *An Echo in the Bone*. Random House, 2009.
_____. *The Fiery Cross*. Random House, 2001.
_____. *Outlander*. Random House, 1991.
_____. *Voyager*. Random House, 1994
_____. *Written in My Own Heart's Blood*. Random House, 2014.
Kennedy, Victoria. "The Way We Were: Nostalgia, Romance and Anti-Feminism." In Frankel, *Outlander's Sassenachs*, McFarland, 2016, pp. 117–129.
Leach, Yvonne D. "Outlander from Book to Screen: Power in Gender and Orientation." In Frankel, *Outlander's Sassenachs*, McFarland, 2016, pp. 130–151.
Lopez, Araceli R. "Gazing at Jamie Fraser." In Frankel, *Outlander's Sassenachs*, McFarland, 2016, pp.44–53.
Mailman, Erika. "The Outlander Effect: The Popular Book and TV Series is Increasing Travel to These Scottish Sites." *The Washington Post*, 14 February 2020, www.washingtonpost.com/lifestyle/travel/the-outlander-effect-the-popular-book-and-tv-series-is-increasing-travel-to-these-scottish-sites/2020/02/13/900a2dfc-4c26-11ea-b721-9f4cdc90bc1c_story.html.
McAlister, Jodi. "Traveling Through Time and Genre: Are the Outlander Books Romance Novels?" In Frankel, *Adoring*, McFarland, 2016, pp. 94–106.
Murphy, Shaunna. "How 'Outlander' Turned 'Mommy Porn' Legit." *Revelist*, 12 July 2016, www.revelist.com/tv/outlander-mommy-porn/3366/as-the-fifty-shades-movies-and-other-femaleskewing-hollywood-projects-were-greenlit-the-often-grossly-sexist-mommy-porn-chatter-became-unavoidable/2.
"Outlander Tourism Effect a 'Double Edged Sword.'" *BBC News*, 15 February 2020, https://www.bbc.com/news/uk-scotland-highlands-islands-51488784.

Pagnoni Berns, Fernando Gabriel, and Leonardo G.A. Lando. "Reviewing Linear Time: History Repeating All Over Again (Now Against You)." In Frankel, *Outlander's Sassenachs*, McFarland, 2016, pp. 105–116.
Patricia, Anthony Guy. "Gabaldon and the Practice of Gay Male Homoerotic Reading." In Frankel, *Adoring*, McFarland, 2016, pp. 106–122.
Petersen, Anne Helen. "'Outlander' is the Feminist Answer to 'Game of Thrones' and Men Should Be Watching." *BuzzFeed*, 4 August 2014, www.buzzfeed.com/annehelenpetersen/watch-outlander.
Phillips, Jennifer. "Confrontational Content, Gendered Gazes and the Ethics of Adaptation in Outlander and Game of Thrones." In Frankel, *Adoring*, McFarland, 2016, pp. 162–181.
_____. "Jamie's 'Others': Complicating Masculinity and Heroism Through His Foils." In Frankel, *Outlander's Sassenachs*, McFarland, 2016, pp. 54–67.
Potter, Mary-Anne. "'Everything and Nothing': Liminality in Diana Gabaldon's Outlander." *Interdisciplinary Studies*, vol. 21, no. 3, 2019, pp. 282–296.
Prescott, Amanda-Rae. "Outlander: We Need to Talk About Jocasta Owning Slaves." *Den of Geek*, 16 April 2020, https://www.denofgeek.com/tv/outlander-jocasta-slavery/.
Roots, Kimberly. "Outlander Author Diana Gabaldon Counters Starz Exec's Take on Show's Lusty Female Audience." *TV Line*, 29 July 2019, www.tvline.com/2019/07/29/outlander-diana-gabaldon-response-starz-jeffrey-hirsch-premium-female-audience/.
Shacklock, Zoe. "On (Not) Watching Outlander in the United Kingdom." *Visual Culture in Britain*, vol. 17, no. 3, 2016, pp. 311–328.
Ty, Eleanor. "Melodrama, Gender and Nostalgia: The Appeal of Outlander." In Frankel, *Adoring*, McFarland, 2016, pp. 58–67.
VanArendonk, Kathryn. "Outlander Drew a Line Between Rape and Sex. Does It Need so Much Rape, Though?" *Vulture*, 23 December 2018, www.vulture.com/2018/12/outlander-season-4-sex-rape-wilmington.html.
_____. "Why Outlander's Birth Scene Was so Unusual." *Vulture*, 11 September 2017, www.vulture.com/2017/09/outlanders-birth-scene-why-it-was-so-unusual.html.

"Place the glass before you, and draw in chalk your own picture"
The Recasting of Jane Eyre

LUCY SHEERMAN

Jane Eyre *as Romance*

The publication of Jane Eyre, in 1847, under a male pseudonym, ensured a stormy reception for the novel and its author. The mystery over the identity of its authorship was compounded by a sense of outrage and shock about its characters and plot, a coarseness that many reviewers believed was particularly inexcusable if its author was a woman. Few reviewers attacked with such force as Elizabeth Rigby, writing anonymously in the *Quarterly Review*, who condemned the "repulsive vulgarity" of the book and its author (175). She notes that the book is "remarkable" for "combining such genuine power with such horrid taste" (163), making her attack all the more deeply personal when she concludes her essay by stating that "the impression she leaves on our mind is that of a decidedly vulgar-minded woman—one whom we should not care for as an acquaintance, whom we should not seek as a friend, whom we should not desire for a relation, and whom we should scrupulously avoid for a governess" (174). In her article "The Victorians Regarded Charlotte Brontë as Coarse and Immoral—and Deplored Jane Eyre" Lucasta Miller notes the way that this review frames the author of *Jane Eyre* as an agent of "political liberalism and personal libertinism" and also reveals the queasy disdain with which literary London greeted the outmoded Byronic protagonists the Brontës brought to life in their work (Miller).

Rigby's review vacillates between fascination with the book's "novelty and originality" (163) and vexation with its "sheer rudeness and vulgarity" (163). Objecting as much to the author as to its narrator, the review reveals Rigby torn between outrage at the novel's most scintillating scenes (in particular, Rochester's proposal to Jane) and the urge to offer its isolated protagonist practical advice on her predicament. Charlotte Brontë found Rigby's review lastingly upsetting, even going so far as to write a scathing riposte in her rejected "Preface" to *Shirley*, entitled, "A Word to the 'Quarterly.'" Rigby's review offers a critical reading of *Jane Eyre* which still resonates. The compelling, even overwhelming, presence of Jane and Rochester which so disgusted Rigby continues to concern contemporary critics. The multifaceted and enthralling narrator and the complex, flawed hero she falls in love with also remain influential on contemporary romance. Certainly, Rigby aligns Jane Eyre squarely with her author, as so many readers have continued to do: "The inconsistencies of Jane's character lie mainly not in her own imperfections, though of course she has her share, but in the author's" (167).

The fascination with the book's authorship, their gender, class and political and moral compass all bubble away throughout this review as though these are intrinsic to a reading of the book, and an understanding of the author will give a clue to its meaning and moral. What complicates this interpretation of the novel is the romance of its author's backstory, which captivated readers as soon as the author was revealed to be not male, but female, and not a woman who "for some sufficient reason … forfeited the society of her own sex" (176) (by implication, as Miller points out, a fallen woman), but the daughter of a parson.

In *The Brontë Myth*, which charts the growth of Brontë mythology, Miller demonstrates how Charlotte Brontë was herself complicit in the blurring of identities between her own autobiography and that of her protagonist. The author of *Jane Eyre* had "transformed personal experience, through art, into something universal with which every reader could identify" (13). Her male pseudonym was, initially, a veil between her highly personal work and the public; however, she began to use the circumstances of her life and background in order to excuse the faults of her sisters' work when she wrote a posthumous "Biographical Notice of Ellis and Acton Bell."

Elizabeth Gaskell was only continuing this strategy when she used the family's life stories to distract attention from the more shocking aspects of their books in *The Life of Charlotte Brontë* (1857). Its publication ensured that Charlotte Brontë's life and work have remained contested sites of meaning and misreading. The iconic status of *Jane Eyre* as an apparently autobiographical text is blurred with the real biography of its author. Gaskell was still smarting on her friend's behalf ten years after the review was published. In her *Life* she returns to the notorious review, describing its "cowardly insolence" (359), downplaying Charlotte's response to "the stabbing cruelty of the judgement" (360) on a writer who has led "a wild and struggling and isolated life" (360) and thus projecting the suggestion of coarseness and impropriety back onto Rigby.

The conflation of biographical and literary approaches to rereading and rewriting the Brontës continues even now. The experience of reading most fanfiction or Brontë-inspired work frequently tends to perpetuate a conflation of *Jane Eyre* with *Wuthering Heights* and the intensity of the Brontës' personal lives with the brooding moors that surround the parsonage. Reviewers and critics frequently turn to the dramatic circumstances of the writing and publication of the Brontës' books in any discussion of their writing.

Rigby vividly summons the figure of Jane Eyre and her author in order to face judgment:

> [she] is one of those ladies who put us in the unpleasant predicament of undervaluing their very virtues for dislike of the person in whom they are represented. [...] One feels provoked as Jane Eyre stands before us—for in the wonderful reality of her thoughts and descriptions, she seems accountable for all done in her name—with principles you must approve in the main, and yet with language and manners that offend you in every particular [167].

Jane Eyre the narrator, summoned here by Rigby, dominates the reader now just as she did in 1847. Her dominating voice continues to reverberate in contemporary romance novels and to shape the writing of romance and the conflicts to which its narrator gives voice. Rigby's fierce reaction to what George Lewes described in his review of *Jane Eyre* as the book's "strange power of subjective representation" (437) throws into relief the way in which the book's influence on romance novels continues to be examined and revised by both writers and critics.

For Rigby, this impossible-to-like heroine, taking control of her own story and its irredeemable hero, should have "no chance, in the purer taste of the present day; but the popularity of *Jane Eyre* is a proof how deeply the love for illegitimate romance is implanted in our nature" (166). In her article about the reception of *Jane Eyre* during the Victorian period, Miller states that Rigby's attitude of contempt is not surprising. The idea of a romance between Jane, a plain and friendless governess, and of Rochester, older and her employer, superior in wealth, power and influence, was considered provincial and naïve by reviewers such as Rigby and "the new, progressive Victorian establishment, who had moved their focus from Romantic individualism to social amelioration" (Miller). Significantly, Miller points out the effect of Brontë's act of feminism in making her main protagonist and narrator an apparently powerless figure. "Her assertiveness," she argues, "is indeed feminist, relocating the Byronic ego in the figure of the poor, plain governess. But her erotic masochism reflects the Fifty Shades of Grey view of gender relations" (Miller).

In her *New York Times* review of *Fifty Shades of Grey*, "She's Fit to Be Tied," Maureen Dowd also makes this link: "James writes like a Brontë devoid of talent" (Dowd), her statement echoing Rigby's scornful repulsions of Brontë's literary ambitions and her novel's status as "illegitimate romance" (Rigby). Dowd condemns the book for its adherence to old-fashioned romance tropes, arguing that "James cleaves to hoary conventions out of Harlequin: powerful and wealthy heroes with a sense of entitlement who need to be rescued; smart and strong-willed heroines who tame their men" (Dowd).

In her essay "Sorry, but *Jane Eyre* Isn't the Romance You Want It to Be," Erin Blakemore argues that what seemed most shocking and revolutionary to its Victorian readers was Jane Eyre's passionate self-love and sense of self-worth: "In the 1840s, Jane's love for herself was so subversive it bordered on revolution. In 2019, her love of Rochester is so shocking it borders on treason. In any era, its relationship to the love it explores is uneasy, volatile. Nearly two centuries after it was published, *Jane Eyre* confounds every expectation" (Blakemore). However, Mrs. Fairfax's comment to Jane on her betrothal to Rochester that "[g]entlemen in his station are not accustomed to marry their governesses" (265) might equally summarize Rigby's sense of disdain for this improbable and unequal match. It is this inequity which still continues to trouble and perplex critics and to problematize the book's influence on contemporary romance novels.

Even though she acknowledges the powerful hold that *Jane Eyre* has for many readers, Jean Wyatt finds the relationship between Jane and Rochester emblematic of a dysfunctional power balance within the idea of romantic love. She equates romantic love with passivity, expressive merely of the "desire for desire" (202) in her essay "A Patriarch of One's Own." She concludes that "[t]he apparently revolutionary nature of Jane's egalitarian marriage allows an old fantasy to get by the ideological censors of her readers, so that we all, feminists and Harlequin romance readers alike, can enjoy the unending story of having one's patriarch all to oneself forever" (214).

Germaine Greer gave the keynote speech to the 2016 Brontë Society Conference which marked the bicentenary of the birth of Charlotte Brontë. In her lecture, subsequently published as a paper in the journal *Brontë Studies*, she makes similar assessments to Rigby about the legitimacy of writing romance, when she states that "though it is invariably described as a classic *Jane Eyre* is one of the most romantic novels ever written" (5). Greer wonders why it is "*Jane Eyre* with all its improbabilities and imperfections that is the most influential of the Brontë sisters' novels" (4). Indeed, she asks "whether this phenomenon might not have its sinister aspect. What if *Jane Eyre* is the archetypal Mills & Boon romance?" (4).

Of course, if *Jane Eyre* is the archetypal Mills & Boon romance, then, Greer surmises, "*Fifty Shades of Grey* has its roots deep in the humus of *Jane Eyre*" (4). She, like Rigby, summons the author into view, seeing "Charlotte Brontë as standing at the head of a main stream in low-brow female literature" (4). For Greer a romance is certainly, by definition, the obverse of literary quality, of a "classic": *Jane Eyre* "presents neither a broad canvas nor an unforgiving miniature. It taps a broad vein of unvoiced female fantasy that continues to be reworked to this day" (5).

Like Rigby, Greer equates the novel's pretentions to literary quality with concerns about class; here, once again romance is linked to "low-brow" literature and the "main stream" of popular work such as *Fifty Shades of Grey*. Greer implicitly positions herself as a discerning reader on the higher ground of literary quality, from which she can observe Brontë at the "head of a main stream" of "female fantasy" and discern the contradictory mutability of her narrative vein, one which appears to offer feminist empowerment but also manifestly succumbs to the patriarchal world *Jane Eyre* inhabits, even as she, and Bertha, her alter ego, rage against it (Greer). Class and status is, of course, at the heart of Jane Eyre's story, as well as her author's. Jane's progression from slavery and oppression to freedom and self-mastery is predicated upon kinship with the recently freed slaves with whom she aligns herself repeatedly throughout the novel. However, as numerous critics have shown, this narrative serves only to free Jane and the voices of the enslaved peoples to whose voices she lays claim to remain silenced, particularly in the symbolic figure of Bertha Mason, who never utters a word. In the next section I want to look in more detail at the influence of *Jane Eyre* on contemporary romance and to consider, in particular, the way in which its singular narrative voice and the travails of its narrator serve to eclipse other stories and voices.

The Price of Freedom in Jane Eyre

Cora Kaplan, opening her book *Victoriana* with a chapter on *Jane Eyre*, describes this work as a "mnemic" text, one which has an influence on culture so ubiquitous that it becomes impossible and futile to try to map it (15). In her book she traces the conflation of biographical and literary approaches to rereading and rewriting Victorian narratives, with a chapter that focuses on *Jane Eyre*. In particular she examines neo-Victorian writers and critics who have restored the affective subject firmly to the center of their responses to the Brontës and other works of the Victorian period. It is a strategy which she argues evades the poststructuralist threat of the disappearance of the author and reintroduces the idea of firsthand narrative or biography as a medium which might convey or hold absolute historical truth, "a 'real' history, certifying the materiality, depth, and moral authority of authors" (40). Her chapter on *Jane Eyre* explores its long history as a mnemic symbol for critics, for whom it offers the possibility of "exploring the highly charged emotions that, over time, have frequently accompanied critical responses to Charlotte Brontë's most enduring novel" (16).

As we have seen, *Jane Eyre* is a book that endlessly puzzles and provokes its readers with characters and situations that remain vividly engaging. It is also a book which navigates trauma, with a focus on the feelings and emotions of the individual, and in so doing it shares some of the central tenets of contemporary romance.

The dominance of Jane's voice and perspective forces the reader's attention onto her narration and permits the obliteration of the stories of other figures on whom she stakes her claims for freedom. The figure of slavery, which is summoned at various points throughout the novel as a metaphor for the cruelty and oppression Jane experiences, is the price paid for Jane's freedom and reabsorption into the world of the novel in which she is an outsider for so long. Gayatri Chakravorty Spivak identifies the "territorial and subject-constituting project" of imperialism which is enacted in *Jane Eyre* in her essay, "Three Women's Texts and a Critique of Imperialism." She points out that "the female individualist, not-quite/not-male, articulates herself in shifting relationship to what is at stake, the 'native female'; as such (within discourse, as a signifier) is excluded from any share in this emerging norm" (149).

Jenny Sharpe explores the problematics of autobiography and the status of the self in relation to Spivak's analysis of *Jane Eyre* in *Allegories of Empire*. She notes that the contradictory paradigm of *Jane Eyre* in relation to colonialism lies in the fact that it is the work of a woman "writing her life" as well as a narrative which claims to constitute "the record of her struggle to articulate the social injustices all women suffer" (31). Jane's self-expression and freedom is thus achieved by suppressing the resistance and rebellion with which she has hitherto aligned herself:

> There is no character of a West Indian slave to be found in *Jane Eyre*; she remains inaccessible except through Jane's own acts of rebellion. Yet, the figure of slavery, coupled with the shadowy existence of Rochester's West Indian wife, points to the presence of a racial memory. A faint imprint of the "black slave" can be discerned in the narrative demand on Jane to dissociate herself from the anger that is so crucial in establishing her childhood resistance (39).

Sharpe's analysis of *Jane Eyre* reconsiders the reading of Rochester's first wife as Jane's symbolic other, "the monstrous embodiment of unchecked female rebelliousness and sexuality" (45). There are, of course, clear parallels between Bertha and Jane before the process of socialization which permits Jane's reentry into the domestic and patriarchal sphere. It is evident in Jane's rage at the beginning of the novel at the rigid patriarchal structures enforced at Gateshead including her punishment by the figurative head of the household, John Reed, who calls her a "bad animal" (9), her imprisonment in the red room, where she is compared to a "mad cat" (12) and her banishment from the family to the top floor where she is deemed "not worthy of notice" (27). Bertha, however, continues to be associated with emotional excess and the animal rage experienced by the child Jane. "Intemperate and unchaste" (306), she may be demonic "the foul German spectre—the Vampyre" (284)—or inhuman, as when Jane witnesses how "it grovelled, seemingly, on all fours; it snatched and growled like some strange wild animal" (293). Bertha is both the literal obstacle to Jane's marriage to Rochester and a symbol of the fraught domestic sphere into which a happy ending must draw her.

Part of the power of *Jane Eyre* lies in these contradictions and in this essential instability which demands a constant re-mapping of its status and function as romance in order to accommodate the narrator on terms which permit her autonomy and freedom. In order to do so, her rage, fear and visceral response to lack of freedom must become, and remain, exorcised in the figure of Bertha, who in turn comes to represent the figure of the rebel slave with whom Jane, the narrator, had previously allied herself. Sharpe reads this conflict into the female-authored *Bildungsroman*, noting that the contradictions exist within the form itself:

> *Jane Eyre* charts the success of its heroine in resolving the conflict between self-determination and socialization that structures the *Bildungsroman*. As a female *Bildungsroman*, however, it also stages the impossibility of such a resolution because the socialization of women means submitting to a male head of household (42).

Further, Sharpe argues that in presenting the novel as an autobiography, Brontë compounds the blurring of identity between narrator and author and the slippage of agency. The publication of the book under a pen name "demotes the author to the lesser role of editor so that a fictional character can speak as a woman," once again suggesting a globalizing female voice arrived at through the "displacement of the woman writer *of* the text" (37).

As Kaplan points out, one of the effects of this intense focus on the competing critiques of feminist and postcolonial readings of agency in Jane Eyre is to further compound its influence:

> It tends to reify *Jane Eyre*'s position as an ur-text—not just as an origin for modern fiction and modern subjectivity, or of progressive and aspiring feminism, but a uniquely powerful articulation of the project of empire (28–29).

In spite of a huge shift in the way in which it is analyzed and discussed with the introduction of class, race and colonial critiques, *Jane Eyre* has continued to be regarded as a romance; in fact, following Kaplan, in many ways it is a mnemic romance, so far-reaching that it is hard to imagine contemporary romance without its influence—the complex hero-villain, the gothic house, the false hero, the interrupted wedding, the fierce love rival, the friendless central protagonist, the fiery narrator navigating a hostile universe, and of course the search for and belief in the healing power of love in spite of apparently impossible obstacles. It is therefore possible to read contemporary romance novels arguing with and responding to its influence without directly referencing the novel at all. Certainly, it is a text that continues to provoke intense affective reactions amongst readers and critics—of both attraction and repulsion.

Critics of the contemporary romance novel frequently cite the continued influence of *Jane Eyre* on romance novels. Tania Modleski's *Loving with a Vengeance*, one of the first to study women readers and their relationship to mass-market romance fiction, notes that the literary lineage of "Harlequins can be traced back through the work of Charlotte Brontë and Jane Austen" (15). Pamela Regis, author of *A Natural History of the Romance Novel*, another foundational text of romance novel criticism, dedicates a whole chapter, entitled "Freedom and Rochester," to *Jane Eyre*. She describes the way that "Jane's story compels" (85). In fact, Regis uses the plot line of *Jane Eyre* to explore her hugely influential breakdown of the romance novel into eight essential elements.

Regis defines one of these "essential narrative elements" (27) as the barrier: "a series of scenes often scattered throughout the novel establishes for the reader the reasons that this heroine and hero cannot marry. The romance novel's conflict often consists entirely of this barrier between the heroine and hero" (32). When considering the essential role of a boundary which must be overcome in romance plots, Regis describes the way in which Jane overcomes the barriers of inequality in status, age and gender with Rochester as both emblematic and an inevitable use of the romance plot:

> In the final courtship, however, when Jane leaves Marsh End to travel first to Thornfield and then to Ferndean to find Rochester, it is she who courts Rochester. This final courtship cements Jane's freedom. As an examination of the barriers and points of ritual death in the novel will show, freedom, for Jane, is independence—emotional, financial, and physical. In the course of the novel, she becomes self-possessed. She controls her emotions. She gains and then acts from a base of financial independence. She governs her movements—where she will live and how. She is, in short, free, and Brontë finds the romance novel form a natural medium for this theme of freedom (87).

For Regis, the degree to which Rochester and Jane can authentically meet as equals by the end of the novel is in no small part due to Jane's independence and defiance of authority: "In *Jane Eyre* Brontë draws a character who pursues affective individualism in almost everything she does" (91).

Regis's account of *Jane Eyre* focuses on the achievement of freedom in the novel and Jane's negotiation of this—in her dealings with Rochester, her Aunt Reed and her cousin, St. John Rivers. She traces the way in which slavery as a metaphor permeates the book and its account of Jane's struggle for autonomy. In her essay "Jane Eyre and the Secrets of Furious Lovemaking," Sandra Gilbert describes the different female role models that Jane encounters and must reject in order to acquire her freedom. "To Jane, who vehemently declares that 'I am a free human being with an independent will' [282], all these modes of sexual slavery represent a degradation far more radical than the self-abnegation of the consumptive and the self-repression of the governess" (359). Bertha Mason, her furious alter ego, represents the possibility of a narrative in which Jane does not choose the happy ever after of "practicing unearthly renunciation or gaining earthly reward" (360). Instead, we see Bertha filled with rage and sexual desire, which render her "both masculinized and, as it were, animalized" (360). "Unlike any of the Englishwomen we encounter in *Jane Eyre*, however, Bertha is the product of a symbolic as well as literal tropic in which desire flourishes" (360). Made symbolically "other" than Jane in the narrative, it is therefore possible to sacrifice Bertha, and thus Jane's overpowering and rebellious feelings of rage and desire, to achieve a happy ending.

The compelling force of the plot and of its narrator thus permits Brontë, and indeed her reader, to experience Bertha's "rage and sexual desire" without aligning themselves with its inevitable and insuperable narrative consequences. The uncomfortable anger and desires of the heroine are projected elsewhere. Such a reading takes us back to the power and force of Jane's narrative, its affective individuality. Swept along by the intensity of her story, the reader is not given permission to stop and question or contest the inexorable arc of this gothic love story in which, as Gilbert argues, "CINDERELLA MEETS BLUEBEARD" (357). Because of its structural constraints, it appears that the romance form as constructed here limits the capacity to reconcile outside experiences and points of view with that of Jane. In fact, both Bertha, who so frequently symbolizes the hidden history of literal slavery, and St. John Rivers, who represents the shift in colonial focus from the West Indies to East India represent counterpoints to Jane's narrative. Its oppositional framing seems to obscure them, pushing them to the peripheries both of the story's focus and of the domestic sphere, a site previously occupied by the young Jane.

Control Over Narrative and the Affective Voice in Jane Eyre

Critical analyses of the suppressed stories and subjectivities of *Jane Eyre* have permitted an exploration of the narratives of colonialism and racism which lie beneath this novel. Kaplan's analysis of critical responses to *Jane Eyre* demonstrates the strong feelings the work evokes, the extent to which Jane's powerful and intimate storytelling style compels people to listen but also blocks out alternative voices and narratives.

As discussed above, Spivak has demonstrated how Jane's expression of desire for freedom from a hostile system does not represent or include Bertha or colonial women oppressed by racism (245). In fact, Spivak argues that "Bertha's function in Jane Eyre is to render indeterminate the boundary between human and animal and thereby to weaken her entitlement under the spirit if not the letter of the Law" (249). In *Allegories of Empire*, Jenny Sharpe makes an explicit connection between the "mesmerising focus" (29) of Jane Eyre's narration and the exclusion of other versions of the past. The power of Jane's autobiographical narrative, which, as Regis says, "compels" the reader, has the effect of obscuring the narratives of the slaves with whom Jane allies herself but who are not, like Jane, granted a voice or freedom within the novel.

In focusing on the influence of *Jane Eyre* I want to begin to consider the ways in which the romance genre has inherited and addressed these constraints to the representation of point of view and suppressed histories and the extent to which the plot structures and narrative style of the romance novel might be complicit in such exclusions.

It is precisely in this "mesmerizing focus" which has always so enthralled and fascinated readers that many critics have discovered silences and erasures which threaten to overwhelm the reader and obliterate other points of view and perspectives and undermine the radical potential of this romance story and the contemporary novels and fanfiction it continues to influence. In this section I will therefore explore how this dominant authorial voice is countered and encountered—how this complex intertwining of the narrator and author has influenced contemporary readings, and how authors have shaped their work in response to this sense of erasure and disappearance.

In her essay "Reading Jane Eyre While Black: The Privilege of Escapism is Not Allowed for Me," Tyrese L. Coleman describes her experience as a young reader, exploring classics from *Sweet Valley High* to *Jane Eyre* where "the protagonists looked nothing like me," when she decided to make the "conscious decision to envision every character in every book I read as black, regardless of how the author portrayed them" (Coleman). However, when it came to reading *Jane Eyre* she found this to be impossible, because she found that:

> Bertha Mason's madness is predicated on the fact that she is not white. My mental switch—which I think is actually a universal part of the reading experience for everyone, regardless of race—means that I must confront this racist stereotype. Even if I wanted to, I would be barred from ever seeing any part of myself in Jane—because to be Jane would mean to be in direct opposition to myself. (Coleman)

The author Alyssa Cole describes a similar experience to that of Coleman in an interview about her writing with Rachelle Hampton, "One Romance Novelist's Fight for Diverse Love Stories." As a child "she would buy tabloid romances at supermarkets and use Wite-Out to alter the descriptions of *ivory* or *pale* skin, changing them to brown. 'My career on some level is making sure people don't have to do that'" (Hampton). Cole's historical novels set in the 19th century do not flinch from the history of slavery and racism that this context inevitably includes: "When Cole and writers like her include racism in their romances, it is not to make white readers uncomfortable or to ruin the escapism associated with a genre that, by definition, must end happily. Leaving the realities of life as a Black woman on the cutting room floor isn't escapism to those who experience them—it is erasure" (Hampton).

Jean Rhys addressed the suppressions and silences of *Jane Eyre*, rewriting the story from Bertha Mason's point of view in *The Wide Sargasso Sea* (1966). It is a creative work which precedes the critical analysis by postcolonial scholars of Brontë's novel. Cora Kaplan points out, when she discusses *The Wide Sargasso Sea* in *Victoriana*, that "banishing the Victorian happy ending is one effective narrative strategy for dispersing the long shadow that the imperial imagination cast on colonizers and colonized" (154). Recent rewritings of *Jane Eyre* have reconfigured its account of desire even while they remain in thrall to the compulsion to repeat its narratives of trauma and conflict.

In taking account of the influence of *Jane Eyre* on romance fiction it is worth noting there is a consistent overlap with the conventions of the Gothic—in fact they arguably go hand in hand. Victoria Holt, Mary Stewart, and Daphne Du Maurier all explicitly nod to the influence of this novel in their books while their first-person narrators remain firmly in control of the telling of the story and, therefore, of an account of their romance. Even more than Jane Eyre, these narrators are explicitly unreliable, the lapses and ellipses of the story told in *Jane Eyre* have become an integral part of the character and narrative itself.

Holt's hugely successful Gothic romances were quite explicitly conducted and commissioned as a response to *Jane Eyre*. Amanda Jones points out in her essay "Madness, Monks and Mutiny: Neo-Victorianism in the Work of Victoria Holt" that Holt's first novel, *Mistress of Mellyn* (1960), was written in response to her agent's suggestion that she write a new version of *Jane Eyre* (3). Jones argues that in this book Holt was "talking back to Jane Eyre and Victorian society, *Mistress of Mellyn* takes the theme of madness from Brontë's novel and rewrites it as a reaction to the limited opportunities open to women" (4). Jones explicitly makes clear that Holt's novels all referenced *Jane Eyre* and the Brontë oeuvre extensively. She cites the critics Diana Wallace, who described Holt's collective novels as "a rewriting of *Jane Eyre*," and Joanna Russ, who described Holt's first-person female narrators as "latter-day Jane Eyre[s]" (3–4).

Unlike Jane Eyre, who claims to speak for all women, in these works the heroines are frequently complicit with the ousting, silencing and disappearance of their predecessor. Symbols of femininity are frequently repressed or expunged in these books, which also portray their female narrators in situations in which they are threatened with powerlessness, silence, and marginalization. Like Jane they are described as being friendless and without family and, specifically, without strong maternal influence. The dominant female narrator of *Jane Eyre* has been encroached upon by the dynamics of both the plot conventions of gothic romance and its overbearing heroes and the mansion, haunted by the events of the past.

It is also worth noting that, as Kaplan observed of *The Wide Sargasso Sea*, many of the novels which explicitly echo *Jane Eyre*, such as Du Maurier's *Rebecca* and Taylor's *Palladian*, have been severed from the possibility of a happy ending and thus from the status of romance. The Byronic ego that Charlotte Brontë seized for her plain and poor governess heroine has been displaced, and only the erotic masochism remains.

Writing Bertha, Bertha Writing

When contemporary romance novels summon the ghosts of Jane Eyre and Bertha Mason it is frequently because they are codifying themes of problematic desire and anger. Often, they are also harnessing Jane's fiery self-belief and independence. References to Jane Eyre that appear in romance novels frequently form a shorthand, codified allusion to a shared reading history: the bookish girl who reads her way out of trouble, the self-discovery of a heroine who finds her voice and independence, the discovery of a reciprocated and fulfilling love with another person, gothic secrets and a happy ending, in that order.

While the dominant narrative voice of *Jane Eyre* can seem to obliterate alternative or contradictory viewpoints, many neo-Victorian critics and authors view the return of such subjectivity as fundamental to the introduction of narratives and voices excluded by, or diverging from, the Victorian worlds they echo. Sara Collins has talked about the influence of *Jane Eyre* on her bestselling gothic novel *The Confessions of Frannie Langton* (2019), a book which tells the story of a girl who learns to read on a plantation in Jamaica and then travels to London where she becomes a servant in a grand house in London and falls in love with her employer, Mrs. Benham. While it is not explicitly a romance novel, the developing love affair and rapport between Frannie and Mrs. Benham is at its heart. The novel, like *Jane Eyre*, uses the first person narrator, one which is frequently unreliable and explicitly partial in the life story it recounts. Frannie may omit details intentionally, or she may be unable to relate them because of trauma, madness, and amnesia. The story thus merges the lost or silenced narrative of Bertha with the female *Bildungsroman* of Jane. Its presentation as a confession means that the other voices and narratives of those who shape her story are not given expression until the final confessions, testimony, and correspondence that feature at the end of the novel.

Interviewed about the inspiration behind the book by the *For Colored Girls Bookclub*, Collins makes a direct link between the desire to create a narrative about a slave which also included a love story:

> I was really fed up of looking to history and to fiction for black characters, especially in the 18th and 19th century, and finding only victims. I wanted a black protagonist in a novel set in the early 19th century to have a love story and a gothic adventure. Then occurred to me that in fact the two go together. That the thing to do with slavery is to find the different stories, to find the love stories and to find the adventures [Collins, *For Colored Girls Bookclub*].

The story is told from the point of view of its protagonist Frannie Langton; like *Jane Eyre*, it uses an intimate confessional mode which drives the story forward. Frannie's narrative hinges on a powerful individual subjectivity, but it is that of a black woman, a former slave from Jamaica, which is also the birthplace of Bertha Mason Like Jane, Frannie's bleak childhood and the books she illicitly reads are integral to her story. In *The Confessions of Frannie Langton*, a passionate love affair develops between Frannie and Mrs. Benham. However, Frannie's past involvement in the terrible racial experiments conducted by her master, in collusion with Mr. Benham, continue to haunt her. The subtexts and narratives which were suppressed in *Jane Eyre* are revisited and explored in this neo-Victorian revisioning of the experience of a black woman's history in Victorian Britain and in one of its colonies. Benham's wife, like Bertha and Frannie herself, is not free. She is silenced and controlled by her marriage and addicted to opium as a means to escape from it.

Collins' novel closely follows the first person narrative and revelatory style of *Jane Eyre*. This structure, as well as its homage to the gothic horrors and hauntings of *Jane Eyre*, Toni Morrison's *Beloved*, and Rhys's *The Wide Sargasso Sea* makes a resolution of the novel in a happy ending unbelievable. All of Frannie's narrative seems to lead the reader inexorably to the impossibility of a woman of her race and traumatic history securing lasting happiness in the society she describes.

In her interview, Collins makes the connection between *Jane Eyre* and *The Confessions of Frannie Langton* explicit:

> I as a bookworm inherited a lot of my ideas about love and romance from those classic gothic romances. I grew up reading *Jane Eyre* and *Wuthering Heights*. Although I wouldn't class it as a gothic romance, my other sensibility towards romance was shaped by *Pride and Prejudice*. So you have Mr. Rochester, you have Mr. Darcy, you have Heathcliff. All of these gothic heroes. All of them have this one unifying feature in common: that the object of attraction is a white woman, usually one who starts out as quite helpless, with a few exceptions. [...] But in my opinion there had not been a novel featuring a black protagonist where love was, at least for the protagonist, the main, redemptive thing, even if it is a disordered, dysfunctional romance [Collins, *For Colored Girls Bookclub*].

In *The Confessions of Frannie Langton*, Collins creates a narrative that brings its protagonist, Frannie, vividly to life, empowered, literate and, eventually, freed from slavery. It also allows her to come down from her attic room in the servants' quarters and to find friendship and love with her employer. Paradoxically, in a novel about a search, which parallels Jane's, for freedom, independence, acceptance, and love, it closes with its protagonist imprisoned and facing execution. Jane's double, Bertha, is once again summoned in the final scene when she faces a morning "pink as flames" (371) and imagines being reunited with her lover. This is another example of a romance inspired by *Jane Eyre* which cannot sustain the weight or promise of a Victorian happy ending. Nevertheless, Frannie's confessions track a romance for its protagonist and, at the novel's close, envision a reunion with her beloved: "the mind is a different place, and there, soon, we will have days together" (371).

In *Jane Eyre*, Charlotte Brontë created a heroine like herself: passionate, angry, and, as Gaskell reports in her *Life of Charlotte Brontë*, "plain, small, and unattractive, in defiance of the accepted canon" (308). Like Jane, Frannie Langton is summoned out of absence as well as the desire for a heroine who resonates with both Collins' literary influences and the reality of her experience as a black reader of "classic" novels. Collins presents a heroine who, just as Jane Eyre does, finds herself through books and goes on to discover the powerful possibility of writing her own. While Brontë wanted a heroine able to achieve autonomy and love in an environment that suppressed for women with no connections, money, or beauty, writers such as Collins seek to find the same for characters who are oppressed and silenced by Victorian narratives of race and colonialism.

The desire for love is central to these novels. Kate Mitchell and Nicola Parsons, in their introduction to *Reading Historical Fiction: The Revenant and Remembered Past*, have described the necessity that the reader of work which revisits the past should be open to "a poetics that is also an ethical figuring; a poetics of the other" (12). In the rewritings of *Jane Eyre*, and most especially in the romance novels it has so influenced, it is possible to see a reconfiguring of what Lewes called Jane's "strange power of subjective representation" (437) so that other voices are encountered and heard. Historical romance novels are particularly sensitive to the politics of narrative voice, point of view and affective individualism, and this is evidenced in a shift in the narrative structures and techniques, a departure from first to second or third-person narrative, and the introduction of point of view for both romantic protagonists. This is evident in restorative historical works in which characters such as Grace Poole or Bertha Mason, who were previously denied agency because of class or race, are given voice.

In her essay "Mining the Neo-Victorian Vein: Prospecting for Gold, Buried Treasure and Uncertain Metal," Marie-Luise Kohlke questions why some romances are considered "admissible as neo-Victorian 'literature,' whereas mass market historical fictions about the same period are dismissed," (29) although she argues that "few critics would want to extend the term 'neo-Victorian' to include all romance novels set in the nineteenth century à la Harlequin historical fiction and bodice rippers" (29). She notes Cora Kaplan's assertion in *Victoriana* that historical fiction set in the Victorian period is "a genre that has become so capacious and lucrative that it contains several mini-genres including [...] mass-market romance" (88). It is precisely here—in the romance novels that continue to respond to the influence of *Jane Eyre*—that it is possible to see a reassessment of, and a bearing witness to, different subjectivities and experiences. Jane Eyre's voice remains as powerful as ever, but its strength has summoned other compelling voices that present different versions of the past and of the romance novel and of the possibility of a happy ending.

"Am I a monster?" The Black Heroine's Quest for a Happy Ending

In her essay, "'Am I a Monster?' *Jane Eyre* Among the Shadows of the Freaks," Chih-Ping Chen relates Charlotte Brontë's depiction of otherness to the history of Victorian freak shows. In these shows she notes that viewers found an affirmation of Britain's "normality" and "superiority" when they saw that "indigenous people—American Indians, Hottentots, 'Kaffirs,' and unknown racial types—became booked in the same venues as the physiologically monstrous bodies" (370). Chen connects Rochester's exhibition of Bertha to the disbanded wedding party with these freak shows, describing him as a colonial collector and exhibitor. The third floor of Thornfield Hall, in which Bertha is hidden away, also holds a collection of outdated furniture, discarded by the Rochester family, and suggests a colonial museum—giving the mansion, in Jane's words, "the aspect of a home of the past—a shrine of memory" (377). The house itself is the material expression of the family's colonial past. Chen traces the way in which Jane's fear of being outside this system and the mansion itself is manifested in the alien figure of Bertha:

> Bertha's image of monstrosity locates Jane's anxiety about her social status and self-image. Such anxiety is made explicit in her cry—"Am I a monster?" (293)— when she senses Mrs. Fairfax's seeming disapproval of her marrying Rochester and becoming the mistress of Thornfield Hall. Bertha's anomalous figure thus becomes a signifier of the tensions between the derogatory gaze of the society that continuously alienates Jane and Jane's struggles towards assertion and acceptance [380].

Edward Said observed in *The World, the Text, and the Critic* that Brontë's exorcism of the West Indian Bertha is "a way of telling us that denizens of the outlying Empire are useful as a source of wealth or as a moral ordeal for English men and women to experience, but never are they people to be accepted into the heart of metropolitan society" (273). The neo-Victorian novels under discussion can be read as a reconstruction of metropolitan society, as figured in and by Brontë's novel and its quest for a happy ending, which exhibits a different account of colonial history and point of view.

In this final section I want to examine two contemporary neo-Victorian novels and mass-market romances, which, like *The Confessions of Frannie Langton*, focus directly on the experience of slavery and reexamine the way in which it is represented and voiced. Beverly Jenkins' novel *Forbidden* (2016) and Alyssa Cole's *An Extraordinary Union* (2017) both figure characters who have been enslaved, and both are also romances. Jenkins and Cole have spoken about the significance of giving voice to enslaved people and of their own meticulous use of primary sources and research in order to find a way of doing so. Collins, Jenkins, and Cole's novels include author notes at their close citing the historical sources and figures which inspired these stories and characters. All three authors have talked about the extent to which their reading became an inspiration for their rereading and rewriting of romance. In her author's note to *An Extraordinary Union*, Cole states that she wanted to "extend" the tropes of American Civil War narratives which were based on the "omission of a whole swath of people, generally of a darker hue" (257). In all three works the "mesmerizing focus" of Charlotte Brontë's writing is reread and resisted. Bertha, described by Gilbert and Gubar in *The Madwoman in the Attic* as Jane's "truest and darkest double," is also recast (360). These works evidence the way that in contemporary rereadings and rewritings of *Jane Eyre*, increasingly, Bertha is not read as a metaphorically black character. The distinction between white Creole and slave has been elided and Bertha is frequently read as black.

The prologue of Jenkins' novel *Forbidden* is set in 1865 at the close of the American Civil War, while its main action takes place five years later. Cole's *An Extraordinary Union* is set in 1861 and 1862, at its beginning. Both are neo-Victorian novels which address the history and impact of slavery on their central characters. In these novels slavery has shifted to being a literal rather than a figurative subject. The novels follow the perspectives of their central protagonists, using third person narration, which permits a shift away from the dualities of Brontë's first person narrative technique and the oppositional strategies and metaphors which follow. Both Cole and Jenkins are explicitly writing romance, and a happy ending is thus integral to the plots and narrative arcs of the books. The search for, and commitment to, love and a happy ever after for their protagonists is at the heart of these works.

Forbidden traces the story of Eddy Carmichael and Rhine Fontaine. The prologue opens with Rhine at the plantation in which he grew up, viewing the ruins of the mansion at the end of the war which has been razed to the ground by a fire set by his great aunt, which killed her and his father, the owner of the plantation and 300 slaves. The scene is haunted by the memories of the slaves who lived there and the atrocities they experienced. At the outset of the novel he is passing as a white man, a decision made possible because of his mixed-race parentage, the child of one of the plantation's slaves and the plantation's owner.

Eddy is, like Jane Eyre, described as self-reliant and independent. She is in the course of making her way to San Francisco to set up her own restaurant when she is robbed and left to die in the desert. Rhine finds her and feels an instant attraction which he attempts to develop, although Eddy believes an equal relationship to be impossible because of his race. Eddy is freeborn and has also been told that she is descended from an African queen, just as Rhine was. Like Rochester, Rhine is established and wealthy with powerful political allies and business connections and enormous influence in Virginia City. At the beginning of the novel he is also engaged to the daughter of an influential white family from the town and owns extensive property. Like Rochester, he also holds a secret that could bring him shame and disgrace amongst these white townsfolk. The novel sees Rhine take the decision to stop passing as white in order to be with

Eddy and end his engagement to Natalie Greer, and it culminates in Rhine's public announcement of his racial background. It takes place at a political gathering of his associates, hosted in his saloon, and results in rejection by the white townsfolk. The novel builds slowly up to this declaration scene as Rhine discovers that he wants to cast off his fake identity and thus makes plans to break with his counterfeit past. It is a scene which mirror's Rochester's panic when he believes his brother-in-law is about to denounce him and reveal his married state to the house party he is hosting. Rhine's rejection of the racist society and values in which he had become complicit also allows him to make a relationship with Eddy possible and to be formally embraced into the black community of the town.

An Extraordinary Union is a gothic romance set during the civil war. The heroine, Ellen Burns, also referred to as Elle, is a spy for the Loyal League. She is working undercover in Richmond as a mute slave in the mansion of Caffery, a confederate senator. Her eidetic memory means she can recall huge amounts of information without needing to transcribe it; she can therefore gather intelligence for the Unionists.

Ellen has a number of characteristics shared with both Jane and Bertha. Like Jane and Eddy she is physically tiny; her nickname at the Caffery mansion is Li'l Bit: "You a li'l bit too small and a li'l bit too dark, but you still pretty all the same" (11). Her disguise as a mute slave echoes Bertha's silence in *Jane Eyre*—Bertha never speaks a word either through direct or reported speech in the novel. Ellen is abused by her mistress, Susie Caffery, the senator's daughter, in scenes reminiscent of the cruelty focused towards Jane. Jane's anger at her invisibility and lack of status as a woman without power is frequently linked to images of slavery. This is compounded in a scene in which Blanche deplores "the anathematized race" of governesses (177). This is once again made literal in the case of Ellen when she is abused and criticized in attacks that are directly linked to her race. Ellen cannot respond when Mrs. Caffrey says of her: "a regular darkie isn't very smart, what do you expect from a simple one." Ellen's fierce desire to speak back is countered with a fear of being the center of attention:

> Elle wanted to scream, to shout the words of Scott, or Keats, or Donne. But that would be foolish [...] in the end they'd still think her a slave, just one who could perform a special trick. She'd be a source of amusement for their guests, like a beast that could dance on its hind legs. Even people who considered themselves her friends had treated her as such, and Elle never wanted to be anyone's parlor act again.

While for Jane books offer a means of escape, for Ellen they figure, initially, as a prison. As a child she was recruited by abolitionists to tour the country reciting tracts of literature in order to evidence that "negritude did not have to equal idiocy" (19), an ordeal that "had made her feel like something unnatural" (35). The display of her talent for strangers echoes Rochester's exhibition of Bertha, compounding the sense that she is treated, as Bertha was, as a freak show display: "Elle still felt a strange sort of shame and anger when she thought of how she'd been treated. She'd been the Venus Hottentot of the abolitionist crowd, with the exception that it was her cerebral lobes that had been of interest to the gawkers" (35).

It is not just Ellen who compares herself to a circus act or describes herself as unnatural. Bertha was described in *Jane Eyre* as "some strange wild animal, but it was covered in clothing" (293). In *An Extraordinary Union*, Susie echoes this description when she points at Ellen and states that the function of fine clothing is "to separate people like us from them [...] Animals" (129). Ellen is trapped in the regurgitation of canonical works; the anglo-centric texts and narratives she was required to learn limit and control her. When Susie describes her as "ugly" (95) Ellen's knowledge of literature affirms it, with its definition of an idealized beauty that is other than her own: "she could catalogue in her mind all the things people considered beautiful, straight from hundreds of source works. Skin pale like cream, light eyes in shades of blue and violet. Lips that seduced with their pink sweetness. Hair that flowed like silk [. .] all the supporting text of years of devoted reading and remembering pushed up behind Susie's careless insults, giving it power" (95–96). It is a scene which echoes Cole's description of using Wite-Out as a child to alter the descriptions of romance novel heroines.

The oppressive nature of these texts shifts when Ellen is required to learn the ancient Chinese work of military strategy, Sun Tzu's *The Art of War*, to become a member of the Loyal League. It is a connection that is made explicit when the hero, Malcolm McCall, mistakes her quotation from Tzu as Shakespeare. Ellen retorts, "Not all that sounds profound is from the Western canon" (142). As in *Forbidden*, the main barrier to a developing romance between Ellen and McCall is their inability to conceive of a relationship between a white man and a black woman. They do not have any other narratives they can refer to, to make the idea real or concrete. While Ellen was previously unable to imagine a story for herself and McCall because there were no stories or texts to which she could refer to ground the idea in possibility, their move away from the dominance of these narratives, as well as their use of quotes from literature which reflect their developing relationship throughout their courtship, means that their rereadings can become a become a source of freedom rather than constraint. While *Jane Eyre* is not directly cited, its influence runs through the novel, and, tellingly, Ellen Burns' name mirrors that of Jane's best friend, Helen Burns, with its suggestion of elemental fire, as well as hurt and destruction. The Caffery mansion can be read as Thornfield Hall, the gothic mansion with secret and forbidden rooms, a place that displays and perpetuates colonial power and abuse.

Not all of the characteristics associated with Bertha are mapped onto Ellen. Susie Caffrey is the superficial mouthpiece of racist patriarchy throughout Cole's novel, just as Rhine's fiancée, Natalie Greer, was in *Forbidden*. Bertha's "intemperate and unchaste" characteristics are transferred onto them in both novels (306). As well as being representatives of hostile and denigrating attitudes towards slavery and race, they are also the agents of anger, rage, and revenge, particularly when the hero rejects a union with them. Nevertheless, it is Ellen who burns down the Caffery mansion in order to free both McCall and herself from captivity, and it was Rhine's enslaved aunt who burned down his father's mansion.

In the reframing of the neo-Victorian narrative of race and romance which takes place in these novels there is a departure from the globalized account of female experience evidenced in the narrative of *Jane Eyre*. There is also a reframing of the exhibition of otherness and the construction of a literary metropolis in which the voices of black slaves are centered. For the contemporary reader and writer, though, the blurring of the narratives of Jane, Bertha and Charlotte Brontë herself persists, in part due to the dualistic structure and tensions of the genre's tropes and their oppositional framing. The reader must continue to read between what is said and not said, even as these novels revisit suppressed voices and repressed histories. Both *Forbidden* and *An Extraordinary Union* explore the roles and voices available to their protagonists, reflecting the history of the historical figures they summon as well as that of their authors. Anchored in past events and mirroring real characters, the voices of author, narrator and protagonist inevitably overlap with the real experiences of the author. As in Jane Eyre, reader, author and protagonist intertwine, creating a disequilibrium between narratives about and of the past so that history is both inhabited and burned away.

Works Cited

Blakemore, Erin. "Sorry, but Jane Eyre Isn't the Perfect Romance You Want It to Be." *JSTOR Daily*, 27 February 2019, https://daily.jstor.org/sorry-but-jane-eyre-isnt-the-perfect-romance-you-want-it-to-be/.
Brontë, Charlotte. "Biographical Notice of Ellis and Acton Bell." *Wuthering Heights, Agnes Grey, and Selected Poems*, London: Smith, Elder & Co, 1850.
_____. *Jane Eyre*, edited by Margaret Smith, Oxford University Press, 2008.
Chen, Chih-Ping. "'Am I a Monster?' 'Jane Eyre' Among the Shadows of Freaks." *Studies in the Novel*, vol. 34, no. 4, 2002, pp. 367–384. JSTOR, www.jstor.org/stable/29533530. Accessed 10 June 2021.
Cole, Alyssa. *An Extraordinary Union*, Kensington Books, 2017.
Coleman, Tyrese L. "Reading Jane Eyre While Black: The Privilege of Escapism Is Not Allowed for Me." *Literary Hub*, 28 August 2017, https://lithub.com/reading-jane-eyre-while-black/.
Collins, Sara. *The Confessions of Frannie Langton*, Penguin, 2019.

_____. "For Colored Girls Book Club + Sara Collins." *For Colored Girls Book Club*, https://www.forcoloredgirlsbookclub.com/interviews/interview-with-sara-collins. Accessed 11 October 2020.
Dowd, Maureen. "She's Fit to Be Tied." *New York Times*, 1 April 2012, Section SR, p.1. https://www.nytimes.com/2012/04/01/opinion/sunday/dowd-shes-fit-to-be-tied.html.
Gaskell, Elizabeth. *The Life of Charlotte Brontë*, edited by Angus Easson, Oxford University Press, 2009.
Gilbert, Sandra M., and Susan Gubar. *The Madwoman in the Attic: The Woman Writer and the Nineteenth-Century Imagination*, Yale University Press, 2020.
Greer, Germaine. "How the Child Bride Vanquished the Savage Father: Jane Eyre and Wish Fulfilment." *Brontë Studies*, vol. 43, no. 1, January 2018, pp.4–13.
Hampton, Rachelle. "One Romance Novelist's Fight for Diverse Love Stories." *Slate*, 25 September 2020, https://slate.com/culture/2020/09/alyssa-cole-romance-novels-racism-diversity.html.
Jenkins, Beverly. *Forbidden*, HarperCollins, 2016.
Jones, Amanda. "Madness, Monks and Mutiny: Neo-Victorianism in the Work of Victoria Holt." *Neo-Victorian Studies*, vol. 12, no. 1, 2019, pp. 1–27, http://www.neovictorianstudies.com/past_issues/12-1-2019/NVS-12-1-1-A-Jones.pdf.
Kaplan, Cora. *Victoriana: Histories, Fictions, Criticism*, Columbia UP, 2007.
Kendrick, Sharon. *The Forbidden Innocent*, Harlequin Mills & Boon, 2011.
Kohlke, Marie-Luise. "Mining the Neo-Victorian Vein: Prospecting for Gold, Buried Treasure and Uncertain Metal." *Neo-Victorian Literature and Culture: Immersions and Revisitations*. Routledge, 2014.
Lewes, George Henry. "Review of Jane Eyre." *Fraser's Magazine*, December 1847, pp. 690–694.
McLellan, Erin. *Stocking Stuffers*, Erin McLellan, 2019.
_____. "The Victorians Regarded Charlotte Brontë as Coarse and Immoral—and Deplored Jane Eyre." *Independent*, 10 March 2016, https://www.independent.co.uk/arts-entertainment/books/features/victorians-regarded-charlotte-Brontë-coarse-and-immoral-and-deplored-jane-eyre-a6923616.html.
Mitchell, Kate, and Nicola Parsons. *Reading Historical Fiction: The Revenant and Remembered Past*, Palgrave Macmillan, 2013.
Modleski, Tania. *Loving with a Vengeance: Mass-Produced Fantasies for Women*, Archon, 1982.
Regis, Pamela. *A Natural History of the Romance Novel*, University of Pennsylvania Press, 2003.
Rigby, Elizabeth. "Vanity Fair and Jane Eyre." *Quarterly Review*, Dec. 1848, pp. 153–185.
Roach, Catherine M. *Happily Ever After: The Romance Story in Popular Culture*, Indiana University Press, 2016.
Said, Edward. *The World, the Text, and the Critic*, Harvard UP, 1983.
Sharpe, Jenny. *Allegories of Empire: The Figure of Woman in the Colonial Text*, University of Minnesota Press, 1997.
Spivak, Gayatri Chakravarty. "Three Women's Texts and a Critique of Imperialism." *Critical Inquiry*, vol. 12, no. 1, Autumn 1985, pp. 243–261.
Stein, Charlotte. *Sweet Agony*, HarperCollins, 2015.
Victoria (Eve's Alexandria). "Review of Sweet Agony," *Goodreads*, 4 August 2020, https://www.goodreads.com/en/book/show/24381552-sweet-agony.
Vivanco, Laura. *For Love and Money: The Literary Art of the Harlequin Mills & Boon Romance*, edited by John Lennard, Humanities-Ebooks, LLP, 2011.
Wendell, Sarah. "Origin of the Romance." *Smart Bitches, Trashy Books*, 3 October 2005, https://smartbitchestrashybooks.com/2005/10/origin_of_the_romance/
Wendell, Sarah, and Candy Tan. *Beyond Heaving Bosoms: The Smart Bitches' Guide to Romance Novels*, Simon & Schuster, 2009.
Wyatt, Jean. "A Patriarch of One's Own: Jane Eyre and Romantic Love." *Tulsa Studies in Women's Literature*, vol. 4, no. 2, 1985, pp. 199–216. JSTOR, www.jstor.org/stable/463696. Accessed 7 Oct. 2020.

Part Four
Representation Matters

"The Realness" in Jasmine Guillory's Sista Lit Rom Com Novels

CAMILLE S. ALEXANDER

Romance novels can be critiqued for sometimes lacking racial representation, appearing to be populated solely by white characters. Belinda Edmondson contends that the romance novel was "an essentially white form, based on European chivalric tradition" that even today justifies emphasizing white characters by concluding that "black people weren't … romantic subject[s]" (191). This presents an issue for non-white romance novel enthusiasts, who may feel alienated by the characters depicted on some romance novel covers. Romance novels featuring skinny, white, female protagonists with long, flowing hair and princes with bodybuilding physiques may be as popular as they once were, but the genre has evolved, creating a space for non-white characters and socio-cultural experiences reflecting racial differences.

African American romance writer Jasmine Guillory's novels depict relatable African American female characters, often in plausible situations. Her novels combine the rom com with sista lit, providing an amusing take on black romantic relationships in the 21st century, but also incorporating a level of reality called "the realness," which some romance novels may lack. Guillory's novels can be described as sista lit rom com, as she incorporates elements of both genres in her fictional representations of romantic relationships, centering on African American female characters.

The rom com is "a light, comic movie or other work whose plot focuses on the development of a romantic relationship"[1] or "a humorous film, novel or play about a love story that ends happily."[2] Rom coms are feel-good texts, arriving at protagonists' happily-ever-after through a series of amusing events. These texts, peopled with "fallible, funny heroines" and a "breezy style," focus on "the romantic escapades of contemporary young women" like "the novels' intended readers" (Mabry 193). However, rom coms typically lack an element of reality, which is an important component of sista lit.

Sista lit speaks "to the modern condition of being female, independent, single, and black" (Guerrero 89). Sista lit omits heaving bosoms with pink nipples and ripped bodices, indicative of some romance novels, and instead depicts the realness of black life by incorporating the layered experiences of being black in predominantly white societies, such as in the U.S. The denizens of *RuPaul's Drag Race* (2009–) define the realness as "the truest version of something or someone"—an element of a person or event that cannot be imitated (Borge par. 21). The realness is an important element of black life and plays a crucial role in sista lit, moving the genre towards an authenticity often lacking in rom coms. In sista lit, the realness is key to presenting black women and their experiences in a manner that is as close to reality as possible with few forays into the absurd.

The sista lit rom com is a welcome contribution to the romance novel genre, deviating slightly from typical sista lit and particularly from authors like Terry McMillan or Pearl Cleage. While McMillan's and Cleage's novels incorporate romantic relationships and humor, these events are minimal, and the protagonists are typically successful, professional black women centered on career, family, and friends. Sista lit prioritizes friendships, much like those portrayed on the television series *Girlfriends* (2000–2008) and in McMillan's novel *Waiting to Exhale* (1992), emphasizing the tight-knit bonds black women share. The typical rom com novel, such as Zoe May's *Perfect Match* (2018) or Camilla Isley's *I Have Never* (2017), depicts romantic relationships comically, including the requisite amount of drama to propel the narrative. Rom coms sometimes reduce falling in love to a series of comedic events, often presenting female protagonists as inept singletons fixated on finding Mr. Right. A Cinderella-type courtship seems highly relevant in the typical rom com, while other aspects of daily life are often minimized or neglected.

Conventional rom com and sista lit novels make some missteps, highlighting one component of women's lives or resting on opposite sides of the fiction spectrum—too absurd or too serious. These genres leave a gap in the romance novel genre that could successfully merge falling in love with daily life, incorporating the realness in the process. While romance novels often address "the romantic escapades of contemporary young women similar to the novels' intended readers," A. Rochelle Mabry notes that they reflect a limited perspective (193). These protagonists are exclusively white, as are their love interests, but an all-white cast can be unrealistic. Guillory shifts the rom com novel narrative, disrupting its often traditional themes in ways that seem almost mundane, by integrating characters of various races and ethnicities; avoiding stereotypical behaviors and situations; and presenting non-white characters as plausible, ordinary people, not addendums to comedic, white-centered narratives.

Guillory's storylines provide candid discussions on race atypical to many romance novels, which can sometimes avoid race. Romance novel plots are sometimes plagued with unrealistic locations, events, and characters that alienate readers by requiring them to suspend all disbelief. Guillory's novels are often set in plausible locations; include everyday events; and contain non-white protagonists while also adding the requisite amount of humor to classify them as romantic comedies. While contributing to the rom com, Guillory enriches sista lit without sacrificing plausible characters or content. Guillory's novels, while not creating an entirely new subgenre in the romance novel genre, do significantly refocus the genre. As such, Guillory accentuates the rom com by offering more convincing plots while staying true to "the realness" of sista lit.

Guillory appeals to rom com audiences by integrating romance with a relatable amount of humor while satisfying sista lit readers by featuring successful African American female protagonists navigating contemporary life and experiences. There are currently five novels in Guillory's unnamed series; the first four will be discussed here. The novels are sequential, including previously introduced characters. The first two novels engage in discussions of interracial relationships, whereas the third and fourth novels delve into black relationships with the fifth novel incorporating characters over the age of 50.

The Wedding Date (2018), Guillory's first novel, introduces Alexa Monroe, a beautiful, voluptuous, thirty-something, African American woman who is a successful former lawyer employed as the Berkeley mayor's chief of staff. Alexa is trapped in an elevator with Drew Nichols, a handsome, "tall white guy," and doctor (2). Incorporating the elevator scene satisfies a rom com element to the novel rather early in the plot. Drew, who is in town to act as a groomsman in his former girlfriend's wedding to his former best friend, finds Alexa attractive, intelligent, and fun. To lighten the pressure of attending the wedding, he asks her to "Be [his] date this weekend" (12). Drew begs Alexa to "[c]ome to the wedding … protect me from … disaster," and she agrees (12).

From the onset, Alexa views this relationship as temporary, confiding in her best friend, Maddie, that "this guy is out of [her] league" because "[h]e's hot … funny … flirty, and … a doctor" (29). Alexa believes that she is "your standard short black girl with big boobs and hips who can barely look him in the eye" (29). This discussion provides one of the many examples of the realness that Guillory incorporates into her novels. Alexa is

124   Part Four: Representation Matters

honest, albeit slightly self-judgmental, about her long-term chances with Drew. Not only are race and physical appearance barriers to their relationship's success, but Drew confesses that he is "not a girlfriend kind of guy" (9). If Alexa allows herself to momentarily believe their relationship has longevity, Drew's elevator confession eliminates that possibility. Yet, despite his doubts, Drew finds Alexa to be "cute … funny and smart" (26).

Alexa and Drew's relationship has the requisite amount of sex to promote the story's physical attraction element, making Drew wonder why they had not "been doing this since thirty seconds after that elevator got stuck" (82). Alexa, who is typically "worried about how [a lover] felt about her body" and is "self-conscious" after sex, is still "able to throw herself into the whole experience from the first kiss" (82 and 83). These feelings, which do not usually accompany casual sex, are telling, revealing that while Drew and Alexa view their relationship as short-term, it has the depth, longevity, and friendship to lead to a long-term, companionate relationship.

Their relationship has the realness; they enjoy sex and each other's company, but they also communicate and work towards becoming better acquainted. When Drew makes an uncomfortable confession to Alexa, she immediately thanks him "for being honest and not bullshitting" her, placing honesty at the forefront of their relationship (90). Alexa and Drew have great sexual chemistry, suggesting a strong physical connection to reinforce their burgeoning romance. The realness is demonstrated again when, throughout the relationship, they experience doubts, driving them apart despite their emotional and physical bond. Yet, when they both stop "bullshitting" and conclude that they are happier together, the relationship has enough foundation for longevity, which sista lit often includes but rom coms can disregard.

Guillory's second novel, *The Proposal* (2018), follows closely on the heels of *The Wedding Date*. This novel, which begins with a dose of absurdity progressing to the realness, centers on the relationship between Carlos Ibarra, a funny, handsome, Latinx, thirty-something, up-and-coming pediatrician, and Nikole Paterson, an attractive, career-minded, African American freelance writer with impressive credentials. Carlos and Nik meet at a Dodgers' game where Nik's part-time boyfriend, Fisher, stages an uncomfortable public proposal, placing their private lives on the Jumbotron during the seventh inning and misspelling her name "NICOLE" (2). The absurdity of this proposal highlights the novel's rom com theme. While men of color are rarely depicted as saviors, Guillory includes a scene in which Carlos essentially saves Nik by intervening when a reporter attempts to interview her on camera immediately following the proposal rejection. The inclusion of a Latino as the "knight in shining armor" in this scene is refreshing as men of color can sometimes be reduced to physical or sexual beings rather than developed as fully as white male characters.

Guillory implies that, in the court of public opinion, black and brown women are often subjected to excessive scrutiny and sometimes outright cruelty. When Fisher proposes at Dodger Stadium, Nik observes, as she leaves the stadium with Carlos and his sister Angela, that the "few [people] they did see gave her dirty looks" because "she was the bitch who broke the pretty blonde boy's heart, live on the JumboTron" (10). The nature of this public response is problematic on various levels. Nik, the black "girl," should be grateful because Fisher, the "pretty blonde boy," asked her to marry him. Nik is immediately cast in the "black bitch" role for saying no as if, because she is black and he is white, she is not allowed to refuse. Yet, Nik realizes early in their relationship that it is temporary and problematic, which the aftermath of the proposal reveals.

Immediately after Fisher's proposal, Nik feels like she is living a "nightmare," engaging in an internal monologue that they only dated "for five months" and the fact "[t]hat he loved her was news to her" because "he'd certainly never said *that* before" (3). Fisher, who is taken aback by Nik's hesitation, wonders why she has not "even put the ring on" and asks, "Are you saying no?" (3). As Fisher waits on bended knee for a response, Nik makes logical statements, such as "we've never discussed this"; "we aren't really in a place"; and "I wish you'd brought this up … before now" (3). In response, Fisher tells Nik, "We're great together! Live a little! Give us a shot!" (3). Fisher refuses to acknowledge that they are not in love. Before the public proposal, Nik had "actually started wondering … how much longer this Fisher thing would last," because he bored her and "she didn't really think he was … that interested in her, either" (19). Nik's inner musing raises warnings about Fisher and their relationship that she ignores, leading to the unwanted proposal.

At the end of the novel months after the thwarted proposal, Fisher reemerges in Nik's life, offering an unpleasant performance of the realness as he stalks her at home and attempts multiple times to embrace her. Fisher encourages Nik to date him again because their relationship was "[m]utually beneficial" (301). Fisher reminds Nik that people "who look like [her] don't usually get to go to the places" he took her (302). The racist connotations of Fisher's statement are clear, as is the superficiality of their former relationship. To add insult to injury, Fisher punctuates his toxically masculine, racist speech with a fouler action: he "smacked her butt" (302). Guillory writes a response to this violation that many women would enjoy; Nik punches his face, knocking him to the ground.

Guillory incorporates elements of contemporary life that many people find harmless, like using social media, and in *The Proposal*, social media is a tool and a weapon. When Nik reaches the safety of Carlos's car, she receives texts from Fisher, referring to her, his intended fiancée, as a "fucking bitch" (13). His harassing texts continue all evening. In one text, Fisher mentions that he "saw [her] potential when no one else did. [She] was lucky to be with" him (29). Two days later, Nik notices that her social media feeds, which are linked to her career and success as a writer, are filled with comments ranging "from insulting to abusive" because many men "seemed personally insulted that she, a black woman ... rejected a white man" (31–32). The implied threats in Fisher's text messages and her social media feeds, which reduce her to an addendum in a white male narrative, accentuate some pitfalls black women face with interracial dating or marriage. Guillory emphasizes the realness of racism as some of Nik's messages used her "least favorite insult for black people" (32). Yet, despite Nik's growing apprehension, she responds as many women of color would: she keeps "tweeting her way through it, because she used Twitter professionally" and her "'brand'" was a "sarcastic, witty, tough-skinned woman who nothing could bother" (32). Guillory demonstrates how black women internalize strength, independence, and self-reliance; feel "less satisfied, and more burdened than everyone else"; and believe "it is their responsibility to overcome life obstacles alone" (Harris-Perry 202). The realness here is that Nik assumes a tough exterior "when she felt overwhelmed and outnumbered" by the threatening and aggressive text messages and social media feeds (32). While the proposal should have been dismissed, the event becomes dangerous and emotionally damaging because Nik is a black woman.

Once Nik and Carlos begin a relationship, Guillory uses the realness to expose the fissures. Nik cannot commit to a long-term relationship. She believes that relationships are one-dimensional and that Carlos's love for her is problematic. She hesitates to get close to Carlos because in previous relationships, she learned that "[s]omething terrible always happens when a man says 'I love you'" (29). She admits to Carlos that "this isn't what I want" (261). Nik prefers their casual relationship and is "happy going along the way [they] had been going" (261). While some rom coms feature women seeking committed relationships and hesitant men, Guillory reverses this script with Nik and Carlos.

Nik's commitment phobia is more realistic today when women—particularly women of color—may not be as focused on marriage and children as they were in the past. Today, black women may place more emphasis on their careers, reflecting the reality of increased divorce rates, economic independence, personal goals, and fewer available eligible partners, with "seventy single black men" per "one hundred single black women" (Beamon 3). Therefore, Nik and Carlos's path to a permanent relationship is fraught with underlying issues based on more than just her commitment phobia. Nik acknowledges that in previous relationships she lost her identity and sight of her career goals in favor of pleasing a man. Concluding that she and Carlos can have a successful relationship involves relinquishing the hold prior experiences have on her while embracing the possibilities without losing her identity. In the end, Nik and Carlos find a balance to maintaining their relationship, careers, and extended families.

The Wedding Party (2019), the third novel in Guillory's series, reintroduces characters from the previous novels and incorporates Alexa and Drew's wedding. In this novel, Alexa's best friends, Maddie Forest and Theo Stephens, have an unlikely romance. Maddie is an attractive, African American, thirty-something, entrepreneur, and owner-operator of a celebrity styling business. She is the only child of a single mother, Vivian, with whom she shares a close relationship. Theo, Alexa's co-worker, is the handsome, African American, highly intellectual, communications director to the Berkeley mayor, and he has political ambitions. Theo, like Maddie, is the child of a single mother and has a younger, equally successful brother named Ben.

At first glance, Maddie and Theo seem like the ideal power couple—an ad for black excellence and love with one minor issue: they "don't even like each other" (62). Maddie thinks Theo is "boring, self-important, and pedantic" (1). When Theo sees Maddie, "the grin dropped from his face" (3). They become intimate unintentionally when Theo, responding to a dare, dances for Maddie. After kissing, they spend "half the night having fucking incredible sex" (29). The terms of their relationship follow Guillory's pattern of beginning with a short-term, friends-with-benefits arrangement. Maddie and Theo impose an additional term: their agreement ends "with [Alexa and Drew's] wedding" (75). Maddie believes this addendum is necessary to conceal their arrangement from Alexa, who they suspect will interfere and campaign for their relationship to evolve into a more permanent one.

Maddie and Theo's relationship should be straightforward—friends-with-benefits, no strings; however, like Guillory's other characters, Maddie and Theo begin to rely on each other, and their relationship unwittingly evolves. Yet, when Maddie is considered for a television stylist job, she shares her news with Theo, justifying this sign of intimacy by claiming that "for twenty years it had been Maddie and Alexa all the time … now it was Alexa and Drew" (95). Theo also becomes susceptible to the tug of intimacy and relationship permanence. After a trying day, Theo visits Maddie's apartment, where they spend time talking. When Theo states that he refuses "to let [her] keep being so nice to" him, she counters, stating that she thought he "deserved a little something" because he "had a bad day" (143). This "little something" is allowing Theo to drop in unexpectedly, spend the night when he is locked out of his apartment, and to feel comfortable in her space. Maddie also listens to Theo recount the day's events, which is not typical for the casual relationship that they believe they have.

The Wedding Party incorporates race, evoking the realness through authentic portrayals of black experiences, such as in their careers, and Theo's problematic day is directly related to his subjectivity as a professional, black man navigating spaces that are predominantly white-populated. Theo's position in the mayor's office often places him in trying situations requiring composure, and his first sleepover at Maddie's home is prompted by a Twitter battle with a journalist over the mayor's universal pre-K program. In the aftermath, Theo concludes that, "people like [him] can't get away with blowing their fuse at work," and they must "work twice as hard and be twice as good" (144). The untenability of Theo's predicament is disheartening yet common among ambitious people of color. In this statement, Theo articulates the "black tax," an axiom that "black people must work harder than their counterparts to achieve similar outcomes" (Mays par. 1).

Although she is a business owner, Maddie is acutely aware of the burden of being black in a professional setting—particularly for women trying to establish their careers. Maddie views hosting a styling show as a chance to help women who "didn't know all of the unwritten … rules that seem to come up everywhere" (92). These "unwritten rules" preclude women of color from jobs by deeming them "not a culture fit" (192). Guillory's use of the realness in these scenes reveals that, while some Americans may continue to delude themselves claiming that the U.S. has become a post-racial society, racism remains a critical social and economic issue, impacting people of color in tangible ways.

In keeping with the rom com formula, *The Wedding Party* includes the requisite number of absurd situations. In one of these scenes, Theo, who seems so formal, breaks into a well-choreographed dance in his living room for Maddie. Maddie contributes to the hilarity by entertaining Alexa in her den while Theo hides in her pantry naked and cold. Theo and Maddie also maintain an active sexting schedule in public to add excitement to their clandestine relationship and to the novel's hilarity. Despite the numerous amusing scenes throughout the novel, the best may be at the end, occurring on Alexa and Drew's wedding day. In keeping with the rom com formula, Maddie and Theo separate after a misunderstanding.

At a rally for the mayor's universal pre-K program, Theo receives a blow to the head; knocked unconscious, he requires emergency medical care. Maddie takes full responsibility for Theo's care, accompanies him to the hospital, remains with him all day, and takes him home to monitor him throughout the night. The next evening, Maddie returns to Theo's house after Ben gives her a much-needed break. She surprises Theo, who is telling Ben that he cannot be in love with Maddie because she is "still the same shallow person [he] thought she was" (278). This thoughtless comment comes after Ben observes that Theo is "obviously in love with her" and

Maddie "has sister-in-law material written all over her" (277). Theo disparages Maddie to Ben because he cannot admit to anyone—particularly to himself—that he is in love with her, and "he was resentful because he somehow didn't know how to function without her" (275). When Maddie overhears Theo's comments, she is unnerved but leaves the house calmly because "she didn't want Theo or his brother to see how upset she was" (280).

For three weeks, Maddie and Theo stubbornly refuse to reconcile, although each is miserable without the other. At the rehearsal dinner, Guillory reintroduces Carlos and Nik, who notice that Maddie is not accompanying Theo. Nik gives Theo some sound advice: "complications don't matter," reminding him that all relationships have difficulties to overcome (318). The next day, when Maddie and Theo go to Alexa's home to help her prepare for the wedding, Alexa convinces each of them to get more champagne from a closet where she locks them "in until [they] figure [their] shit out" (323). Alexa also takes the opportunity to yell through the door that "Everyone knew!" about their relationship (323). While locked in the closet, Maddie and Theo are forced to face each other. They finally admit their feelings—the hurt, loneliness, and misunderstandings leading to this moment. Being locked in the closet is amusing, but the outcome—two people who love each other finally admitting it—is the realness.

Guillory's fourth novel, *Royal Holiday* (2009), picks up where *The Wedding Party* ends—with Maddie off to England for a Christmas styling job with a special client—Meghan, the Duchess of Sussex. In this novel, set largely at Sandringham Estate, the Duke, Duchess, and Queen make appearances, which are delightful additions to this sista lit rom com. In this novel, Guillory addresses black couples over 50, who are often neglected in both rom coms and sista lit. Maddie's mother, Vivian Forest, an attractive, vibrant social worker, is previously introduced; this novel follows her relationship with a dashing, Afro-Brit Oxford grad, and the Queen's private secretary, Malcolm Hudson.

Initially, Vivian hesitates to accompany Maddie because of work and family obligations. Vivian was recently offered a promotion, effective upon her current supervisor's retirement. In addition, there is the issue of Vivian's sister Jo, whose "cancer had been in remission ... for six months" (12). Vivian feels guilty for leaving Jo and her social work job during the busy Christmas season. Yet she agrees because Maddie declares that she will "decide for both" of them and because "it warmed [Vivian's] heart to know her daughter still wanted her mom with her for Christmas" (4).

Upon arriving at Sandringham, Maddie is immediately swept up into a whirlwind of work-related activities, and Vivian is left on her own. On her first day at the Sussexes' residence where she and Maddie are staying,

Vivian decides to "go downstairs showered, with her hair in place, and with a bra on" because there may "be a prince in the kitchen" (12). This element of the realness is relatable, as many women are concerned with the impression their appearances have, while the humorous possibility of a "prince in the kitchen" maintains the rom com formula. While the Duke is not there, she does see Malcolm "standing by the back door" waiting to sample fresh scones (14). Finding him attractive, Vivian nicknames Malcolm "Hot Chocolate" and wonders if he will "leave" or come in (15). The Sussexes' cook, Julia, introduces Vivian to Malcolm, stating that Vivian "needs a tour of Sandringham Estate," and Malcolm agrees (18).

While Vivian and Malcolm are clearly attracted to each other, they both hesitate to become closer for various reasons, including their ages. Initially, Malcolm cannot imagine "what … prompted him to offer Vivian Forest a tour of Sandringham" other than there is "something about Vivian's smile [that] made him want to talk to her for longer than it took to eat his scones" (21). He is also mesmerized by "her bright smile, glowing skin, and curvy body" (22). Malcolm is at a loss, struggling to converse with Vivian. He wishes that "he knew more about trees" so "he'd be able to tell Vivian about" the trees around them (24). To avoid making "a fool out of himself by rambling about trees," he asks about her flight (24). Malcolm concedes that around Vivian he is a "fifty-two-year-old man … acting like a teenager with a crush" (28).

Vivian, "who … celebrated her fiftieth birthday almost five years ago," is delighted with Malcolm's company (13). After their tour of Sandringham, she realizes that she "hadn't lost track of time like that talking to a man in years"—a revelation freeing Vivian from misguided notions about romance over fifty (41). Vivian is somewhat jaded by other men, "who wanted women around to take care of them" (84). Vivian and Malcolm begin a decidedly traditional romance, exchanging letters delivered between Sandringham and Sycamore Cottage by estate employees, but this old-fashioned communication—particularly today—is not a negative reflection on their ages. Instead, Guillory develops their romance cautiously, as both are world-weary; as divorcees, they are deliberate, laying the foundation for a permanent relationship, which is the realness.

At the end of their first date, Malcolm is driving them back to Sandringham when he declares "I just have to do this," stops the car over between some trees, "pulled her to him, and kissed her" (104). Initially, Vivian "didn't kiss back," but she eventually "grinned, wrapped her arms around his neck, and leaned forward" to kiss him (105). Vivian's participation in the kiss proposes that middle-aged women can take control of their sexuality. This kiss initiates the physical side of their relationship, and, finding Malcolm's kiss "firm, powerful, and somehow also tender,"

Vivian realizes "she'd forgotten ... how great a really good kiss could be" (105). Afterwards, Vivian tries to convince herself that theirs "is just a little Christmas fling," but she knows this relationship means more (105).

Malcolm suggests that Vivian stay "a few extra days in London," but she hesitates, again reaffirming her notion that theirs is a "fling" despite all contrary indications (112 and 113). Yet she eventually agrees. When Vivian and Malcolm are finally alone together in London, they are shy and awkward around each other, which could be related to the gap between this and past relationships or the novelty of the situation. Vivian invites Malcolm up to her hotel room for a nightcap, remembering "that she'd packed everything this morning and ... left her suitcase ... in ... the sitting room" in anticipation of staying at Malcolm's home, per his invitation (175). Before she can fully explain why her suitcase is packed, "Malcolm was kissing her so hard she could barely breathe" (175).

This scene, initiating their sexual relationship, is interjected with the realness, as Vivian and Malcolm disrupt aging and intimacy tropes. Research on sexual activity among older adults "suffers from inadequate descriptions of the population" (Rheaume and Mitty 342). The paucity of research on middle-aged black women and intimacy indicates that ageist and racialized notions about this demographic persist. Guillory disrupts these notions about middle-aged black women—and particularly about middle-aged black couples—by including intimate scenes between Vivian and Malcolm.

Vivian and Malcolm's intimacy provides another example of the realness as, while there is initial caution, once they discover a mutual sexual attraction, they proceed with as much passion, intensity, and enthusiasm as younger characters would. On their first night together, Vivian pushes Malcolm "down onto the couch" in her hotel room, stating "tonight there's no way either one of us is leaving this ... room" (175). Before transferring to the bed, they spend time "kissing, touching, exploring each other's bodies," and Malcolm discovers "what made her gasp, what made her sigh, what made her giggle" (177). Vivian participates, running "her hands up and down" Malcolm's body and placing her "lips on him" (178). Guillory removes all rom com elements during sex by avoiding comedic comments about aging and by drawing attention to their physical attraction and passion. Their intimacy emphasizes the romantic sista lit aspect of the narrative and the erotic.

For black women, revealing the erotic can be problematic, which is influenced by sexualized and stereotypical perceptions, and because "women have been made to suffer and to feel both contemptible and suspect by virtue of its existence" (Lorde 88). Among the stereotypes black women endure is that of their "naturally animalistic, wanton and licentious ways" (Morgan 36). However, Audre Lorde's exploration of the erotic is all-encompassing. Lorde addresses the passion for everything women do rather than emphasizing only the sexual. Yet, the sexual is critical as "the desire for closeness and sexual contact can endure for a lifetime" (Rheaume and Mitty 342). Guillory's emphasis on intimacy and the erotic in Vivian and Malcolm's relationship is the realness, addressing the necessity for sexual intimacy among middle-aged, black adults and by portraying this as neither comedic nor unique.

There is another aspect to race that Guillory incorporates into *Royal Holiday* that reflects the sista lit genre. Vivian's inquiry about whether Malcolm is the Queen's first "Black private secretary" highlights racial issues that many black female and male readers may be familiar with (35). Malcolm is the Queen's first black private secretary in the novel, but her actual immediate staff is predominantly white. Placing Malcolm in a critical position in the royal household suggests a mythical post-racial attitude in the UK and monarchy that is inaccurate. Guillory imbues Malcolm with the realness as he admits to enduring "years of hard work," ignoring "tiny insults and jokes" and "naysayers," and keeping "a straight face and a low voice when he wanted to pound on a table and yell" while performing his work duties (35). Malcolm's success is noteworthy, but his path was difficult, signifying the realness behind many black professionals' success stories in western, white-majority nations. Media images denigrating black men and women drive these professional experiences. These images are "class specific," reflecting "unprecedented media reach, and transnational racial inequality" (Winfield 198). Skewed media depictions often cast middle-class, well-educated, successful black men like Malcolm "as effeminate sissies or nonthreatening 'sidekicks' to a white protagonist" (Winfield 199). Guillory strays from these depictions with Malcolm as she did with Theo in *The Wedding Party*. Malcolm is neither effeminate nor a white character's sidekick, and he is driven by personal success and the desire to set a positive example for his nephew Miles, thus emphasizing the importance of the black family in the process.

While media images of black men can be problematic, black women fare no better. Aida Harvey Winfield observes,

> middle-class Black women are depicted as "Black Ladies" whose potentially unrestrainable sexuality is safely confined to heterosexual marriage, "educated Black bitches" who are manipulative and controlling, or "modern-day Mammies," who uphold white-dominated structures, institutions, or bosses at the expense of their personal lives [198].

While some of Guillory's black female characters come dangerously close to these descriptions, such as Maddie, who is accused of being an "educated

Black bitch," Guillory works, as a black author, to deviate from stereotypical black characters. Vivian blends some elements of these tropes, but there is also an effort to depart from them. Throughout *The Wedding Party* and *Royal Holiday*, Vivian delineates from the "educated Black bitch" by using her education to resolve issues and provide support, not control or manipulate others. Vivian's "sexuality is" not "safely confined to heterosexual marriage"; she is divorced and her physical relationship with Malcolm is freeing, not restricting.

In professional and personal settings, black women are assumed "to conform to controlling images of the modern mammy" (Winfield 201). As Vivian is helpful and comforting as a social worker, there is an inclination to label her a mammy. Vivian's naturally caring nature and extensive social work career guide her attentive interactions with others and her responses to their concerns. The burden is often placed on black women to care for everyone except themselves, reinforcing the mammy image. While Vivian occasionally places others before herself, such as hesitating to leave Jo or her job over the holidays, labeling her a mammy is still inaccurate.

Mammies are characterized by obesity, leading to a label of asexuality; obsessive concern for whites; and self-imposed servility. Malcolm describes Vivian's body as "curvy," not large, and often comments on her attractiveness. Her sexuality is present in her physical relationship with Malcolm. Vivian supports her clients; however, she also wants "to serve as an example and mentor to the younger black women in [her] field" (97). Finally, Vivian is not servile. When she meets the Duchess, she is formal and respectful. In her interaction with the Queen, she "dropped into a quick curtsy," but she speaks to the monarch politely yet conversationally (72). While it may be easy to assume that Vivian is a mammy character because she is caring, she does not represent this caricature of black womanhood. In Vivian, Guillory employs the realness by creating a black female character who deviates from racialized and gendered stereotypes about age, romance, and black women.

One of the major complaints lodged against romance is its exclusivity—the genre seems to focus on a limited portion of the population as characters yet is expected to be marketable across race and ethnicity. Throughout her first four novels, Jasmine Guillory explores romantic relationships between characters who are black, Latino, and middle-aged adults. She includes interracial, black, and middle-aged couples without fetishizing or marginalizing them. Guillory, writing in the sista lit rom com genre, incorporates the realness in her novels; her characters, settings, and events are humorous and yet often authentic and relatable. Guillory crafts unique rom com narratives with relationships that are initially tenuous, reflecting how couples weigh their options before committing to a long-term companionate relationship. Unlike some previous iterations of the romance novel and the rom com, Guillory's novels appeal to wider audiences and are not geared largely towards white female readers. As a result, Guillory's sista lit rom com novels reflect a more inclusive romance novel with more realistic portrayals of diverse couples falling in love, providing an accurate articulation of the realness.

Notes

1. "Romantic Comedy," *Merriam-Webster*, last modified 2020, https://www.merriam-webster.com/dictionary/romantic%20comedy.
2. "Romantic Comedy," *Collins Dictionary*, last modified 2020, https://www.collinsdictionary.com/dictionary/english/romantic-comedy.

Works Cited

Beamon, Nika C. *I Didn't Work This Hard Just to Get Married: Successful Single Black Women Speak Out*. Lawrence Hill Books, 2009.
Borge, Jonathan. "Decoding 'RuPaul's Drag Race': 16 Terms You Need to Know." *Marie Claire*, 16 March 2015, https://www.marieclaire.com/culture/news/a13716/rupaul-drag-race-terms-to-know/. Accessed 6 April 2020.
Edmondson, Belinda. "The Black Romance." *Women's Studies Quarterly*, vol. 35, no. 1/2, Spring–Summer 2007, pp. 191–211.
Girlfriends. Created by Mara Brock Akil, performances by Tracee Ellis Ross, Golden Brooks, Persia White, and Jill Marie Jones, Grammnet Productions, 2000–2008.
Guerrero, Lisa A. "'Sistahs Are Doin' It for Themselves': Chick Lit in Black and White." *Chick Lit: The New Woman's Fiction*, edited by Suzanne Ferris and Mallory Young. Routledge, 2006, pp. 87–101.
Guillory, Jasmine. *The Proposal*. Jove, 2018.
_____. *Royal Holiday*. Berkeley, 2019.
_____. *The Wedding Date*. Jove, 2018.
_____. *The Wedding Party*. Jove, 2019.
Harris-Perry, Melissa V. *Sister Citizen: Shame, Stereotypes, and Black Women in America*. Yale UP, 2011.
Isley, Camilla. *I Have Never*. Pink Bloom P, 2017.
Lorde, Audre. "The Uses of the Erotic: The Erotic as Power." *Sister Outsider: Essays and Speeches*. Crossing Press, 1984, pp. 87–91.
Mabry, A Rochelle. "About a Girl: Female Subjectivity and Sexuality in Contemporary 'Chick' Culture." *Chick Lit: The New Woman's Fiction*, edited by Suzanne Ferris and Mallory Young. Routledge, 2006, pp. 191–206.
May, Zoe. *Perfect Match*. HQ, 2018.
Mays, Anthony D. "The New Black Tax and the Cost of Being a Minority in Tech." *Huffington Post*, 4 August 2017, https://www.huffpost.com/entry/the-new-black-tax-and-the-cost-of-being-a-minority_b_59853a4fe4b0bd82320297c5. Accessed May 31, 2020.
McMillan, Terry. *Waiting to Exhale*. Viking, 1992.
Morgan, Joan. "Why We Get Off: Moving Towards a Black Feminist Politics of Pleasure." *The Black Scholar*, vol. 45, no. 4, 2015, pp. 36–46.
Rheaume, Chris, and Ethel Mitty. "Sexuality and Intimacy in Older Adults." *Geriatric Nursing*, vol. 29, no. 5, 2008, pp. 342–349.
"Romantic Comedy," *Collins Dictionary*, last modified 2020, https://www.collinsdictionary.com/dictionary/english/romantic-comedy.

"Romantic Comedy," *Merriam-Webster*, last modified 2020, https://www.merriam-webster.com/dictionary/romantic%20comedy.

Winfield, Aida Harvey. "The Modern Mammy and the Angry Black Man: African American Professionals' Experiences with Gendered Racism in the Workplace." *Race, Gender & Class*, vol. 14, no. 1/2, 2007, pp. 196–212.

Eating Disorders and Romance

Ellen Carter

Eating disorders (EDs) and body image concerns are cultural and societal issues of growing contemporary significance. Research shows three-quarters of American women report that body image worries interfere with their happiness (Reba-Harrelson et al.), roughly twenty percent have an ED or disordered eating (Lester 18), and two-thirds of American women and three-quarters of men are classified as overweight or obese (Yang and Colditz). ED diagnoses are both prevalent and increasing (Galmiche et al.) with an estimated thirty million Americans suffering from an ED, five times as many as schizophrenia and double the Alzheimer's rate. Given this incidence, it is troubling that EDs are difficult to treat, with anorexia nervosa having one of the highest mortality rates among mental health diagnoses (Smink et al.).

Given these findings, it is encouraging that 21st-century romance fiction is increasingly including characters with EDs. However, despite this positive sign that romance fiction is diversifying to portray a broader panoply of the lived experience of its culturally and politically aware, engaged, and active audience, this depiction remains flawed. In this essay I compare real world data on EDs with fictional depictions and argue that these novels perpetuate inaccurate cultural norms about "good" EDs and patients, as well as portraying a rosier-than-reality impact on long-term mental and physical health. In other words, just as the romance genre idealizes intimate relationships, these novels idealize EDs.

Corpus and Methodology

I analyzed twenty-one contemporary romance novels or series published between 2001 and 2019, each of which has a main character with an ED. I identified ED romances through two Goodreads lists—"Eating disorders in romance novels" (Goodreads, "EDRN") and "M/M Romance with Body Image Disorder" (Goodreads, "MMRBID")—as well as additional online research. However, not only will I not have identified all ED romances, but I was unable to access all the novels I did find, so my corpus of twenty-one books is a convenience sample; the bias inherent in this sampling technique means my findings cannot be generalized.

One example of bias introduced by my sampling method is the corpus's breakdown by sexual orientation: nine novels depict heterosexual (MF) couples, ten have gay male (MM) couples, one has a lesbian (FF) couple and one has a female triad (FFF). Given that a majority of romance novels are MF, why are there relatively few in my corpus? This may be due to my sampling method: that I over-identified and/or found it easier to access non-MF novels. Nonetheless, it is worth noting that gay men are more vulnerable to EDs than straight men (Hospers and Jansen), and a large study of U.S. college students found the prevalence of self-reported ED diagnosis to be significantly higher among cisgender sexual minorities than cisgender heterosexuals for both men (2.1 percent compared to 0.6 percent) and women (3.5 percent versus 1.9 percent) (Diemer et al. 147).

Eating Disorder Types

The *Diagnostic and Statistical Manual of Mental Disorders*, fifth edition (DSM-5) (American Psychiatric Association) recognizes eight types of feeding and eating disorders. Three of these—pica, rumination disorder, and avoidant/restrictive food intake disorder—do not appear in my corpus and a fourth (unspecified feeding or eating disorder) is used as a catch-all if the clinician cannot or chooses not to specify another type. Therefore, in this essay I focus on the remaining four: anorexia nervosa (AN—which can manifest as either restricting or binge-eating/purging forms), bulimia nervosa (BN), binge-eating disorder (BED), and other specified feeding or eating disorder (OSFED, known as Eating Disorder Not Otherwise Specified [EDNOS] in previous DSM editions). Diagnosing between these four types follows a hierarchical schematic from AN to BN to BED to OFSED, with clinicians ruling out one before considering the next. ED types lower in the hierarchy are diagnosed more frequently, with estimates of lifetime prevalence in an American sample of 0.5 percent for AN (0.9 percent in women; 0.3 percent in men); 1.0 percent for BN (1.5 percent in women; 0.5 percent in men); and 2.8 percent for BED (3.5 percent in women; 2.0 percent in men) (Hudson et al.).

However, ED prevalence in my corpus does not match the pattern found in real populations, with anorexia over-represented. Fifteen of the twenty-one characters have been formally diagnosed with an ED by a health professional—nine with anorexia, one with bulimia, and five with an unrevealed diagnosis—while among the six undiagnosed characters, three display behaviors associated with anorexia, one with bulimia, and two have disordered eating and are (presumably) below the threshold for a formal ED diagnosis. It is particularly striking that although BED is more prevalent than either AN or BN, no character in this corpus had BED. Moreover, while both AN and BN can present with recurrent episodes of binge eating, no novel narrates the minute-by-minute lived experience of the feelings and behaviors of a binge and its aftermath, and the word "binge" only appears in four novels. Although some characters mentioned feeling as if they had eaten too much and then compensated by not eating for a period, or by excessive exercise, or purging, only one novel alludes to a binge episode. In *Heavyweight*, high-school wrestler Ian is with his friends at a football game:

> We cart our feast up the bleachers and chow down while waiting for the game to start again. I find I'm ravenous but try to have restraint. It's hard when Jules keeps shoving more food into my hands. I resign myself to eating everything. I know he'll have something to say if I don't.
>
> By the end, my stomach is distended and feels like it's ready to erupt. I hate the binge part as much as I hate the purge. It's so uncomfortable. Not only am I full of empty calories, but I'm full of guilt and self-loathing and disappointment in myself [Mulhall 62].

Although the over-representation of anorexia in my corpus is out of step with prevalence statistics, it mirrors the cultural hierarchy of EDs, whereby restricting AN is perceived by patients (and society) to be morally better and of higher status, followed by binge/purge AN, then BN, then BED. In a study of former ED patients, "[p]articipants associated AN with virtues such as self-control, strength, diligence, resilience, perfectionism, and hard work, whereas BN and BED were associated with morally bad character traits (or vices) such as laziness, greed, weakness of will, and lack of self-discipline" (Mortimer 371). It may be that authors believe readers can more readily identify with a disciplined, self-sacrificing hero/ine since Western society valorizes such behavior in terms of food and body image as well as more broadly.

Living with an Eating Disorder

If ED romances do not accurately show ED reality at a corpus level, individual books nonetheless portray some of the reality of living with an eating disorder, including triggers, the recovery journey, and long-term consequences.

ED Triggers

All these novels mention factors that contributed to the appearance of a character's ED, including causes also identified among real world patients, such as sociocultural factors, family factors, and body dissatisfaction (Polivy and Herman).

Sociocultural contributors to EDs include an idealization of slim physiques in societies such as the U.S. and the UK, where all of these novels are set. For many of the characters in ED romances, this idealization is compounded by the pressures of their professions—including modeling (Albert; Hayward; Kasey; Kenny), playing a theme park princess (Cozzo), and being a porn model (Witt)—or sporting/physical activities such as ballet (Locke, *Second Position*), figure skating (Blake), cheerleading (Ricci et al.), ice hockey (Gale, *Empty Net*), or wrestling (Mulhall).

Family factors include positive reinforcement about the desirable physical results of an eating disorder, which can then translate into coercive parental control. In *The Best Man's Baby* (James), *The Divorce Party* (Hayward) and *Three Times the Charm* (Ricci et al.), mothers pass their own food and appearance issues on to daughters. In the latter two novels, these issues were influenced by the mothers being dumped or cheated on by men, leading them to believe that only by maintaining a perfect physical appearance can they—and their daughters—attract and keep a man. The main character's own divorce can also spur an eating disorder, as in *Fast Women* (Crusie) although this is more due to post-divorce depression than appearance concerns. In *Empty Net* (Gale), a former hockey star pressures his son to emulate his sporting success through rigorous control over his son's physical fitness, enforced by years of physical abuse when his son fails to measure up. Familial factors can also come into play through abuse or trauma. This manifests as a pivotal moment in *Foxes* (Fleet), when Micky is rejected by his oil baron father for being queer. It can also be ongoing abuse: in *Unicorns and Rainbow Poop* (Kadence), Dane was used as a sexual favor for his mother's countless stream of friends, beaten by his homophobic father, and was punished with food: "A horrible memory flashed through Dane's head of someone putting tabasco sauce in his pancakes and making him eat them with nothing to drink, forcing them into his mouth until he gagged and vomited" (41).

Body dissatisfaction is a key risk factor for EDs in gay men, with the idealized body compounding muscularity onto the slimness prized for women (Hospers and Jansen). While the argument should not be distilled to a facile link between gay men and perceived "femininity," in two ED romances, gender confusion plays a role in the character's ED. In *The Impossible Boy* (Martin), gender-fluid Stan didn't understand how he felt about his body as he was growing up and going through puberty so tried to "fix" it through anorexia. In the "Haven Investigations" trilogy by Lissa Kasey, Ollie modeled women's clothing and presents an androgynous appearance.

Stage of ED

Within my corpus of twenty-one novels, twelve open with the character in recovery, eight are in denial, and in only one book does the ED begin during the narrative: *There You'll Find Me* (Jones) follows eighteen-year-old Finley's journey into and through disordered eating. Experiencing grief from her brother's death and stress from an upcoming audition for a prestigious New York conservatory, she escapes to Ireland, meeting on the plane Hollywood heartthrob Beckett. Faced with emotional turmoil, food, exercise and weight loss become factors within her control: "It had started out so simple. To lose a few pounds. And then the weight started flying off when I began riding my bicycle, and it had become something I could count on, control. I liked it. I did" (Jones 235). Even before her disordered eating, she had a history of weight cycling: "My ability to rattle off nutritional information was one of my few talents, learned when I'd need to lose some quick weight each year for cheerleading tryouts. I couldn't remember a single math formula, but the nutritional breakdown of a chalupa? Embedded forever" (Jones 27). Her host family worries about her weight loss, but she brushes it off, as she does initially when Beckett mentions his concerns, before she finally admits it to him:

> "I don't know that I have an eating disorder, but ... something is wrong." I hadn't been able to eat breakfast again that morning, and I knew. I knew I needed help. Beckett clasped my hands in his and just listened. "I'm not who everyone thinks I am," I said after a moment passed by. "Lately I ... I feel better when I'm hungry, when my stomach hurts. When I see the scale dip, I get this rush of total joy" [Jones 243].

Eight novels begin with a character exhibiting ED symptoms and behaviors, but in denial about, or unaware of, having an ED. For example, in *The Truth About Happily Ever After* (Cozzo), a new adult romance between college students spending the summer working in a theme park, as the novel opens Alyssa already has control issues over food and exercise, but this disordered eating is exacerbated under the pressure of the physical appearance requirements of her job as a fairy-tale princess, as well as her disintegrating relationship with boyfriend Jake, until she turns to her friend Miller, and her disordered eating is cured by the love of this good man.

Trade Me (Milan) is the only MF romance with a male ED character. Twenty-three-year-old tech prodigy Blake Reynolds will inherit the huge company built up by his father, who is already pushing him to take a bigger role. However, Blake insisted on going to college, because he wants time to deal with a "problem" he barely admits to himself, let alone anyone else:

> I run harder. I'm a little hungry; maybe I should have eaten that apple after all. But here's a trick of physiology, one that I learned in high school even though the teachers didn't put it this way. The fight or flight response shuts down the parasympathetic nervous system. It's complicated, and physiology is not my bag of tricks, but it all comes down to the same thing: Your body can't digest food while you're running. If I could run all the time, I'd never get hungry.
> I can't run all the time, but I can try. I run until the ache slips from my quads, until all sense of hunger dissipates. With every step, I imagine my body searching for energy, needing to find it somewhere. There is nowhere it can draw that energy from, nowhere except my body itself. I run, and with every step I get smaller. If I run hard enough, I tell myself, maybe one day I can run myself into someone else altogether [Milan 25].

Blake eventually tells heroine Tina Chen about his problem: "'How hard is it to fucking eat more?' His voice is shaking. 'But I don't. I can't. And when I try, when I make myself—I end up going out for a run'" (Milan 198). Being a go-getter, three days later he finds a therapist specializing in athletes with eating disorders and, "By the end of the day, I don't just have a therapist. I have a nutritionist. A food diary. And I have something else from her: a promise that this has happened to other people, but that they have gotten better" (Milan 212). Finally, he admits it to his CEO father, who instead of Blake's anticipated dismissal takes it well and blames himself for pushing his son.

Heavyweight (Mulhall) is a young adult MM romance about closeted Ian—a high-school wrestler who develops an eating disorder to preserve his weight class and secure a college scholarship—coming to terms with his attraction to fellow student Julian. Desperate to remain at the top of a wrestling weight class without tipping into the next, Ian controls by not eating and/or binging and purging, hiding this behavior from family and friends. After one wrestling match, Ian spends a night in the hospital with concussion and malnutrition. Seeing acid burns on his fingers from purging, the doctor warns about potential heart damage and talks about body dysmorphia, not buying Ian's explanation that "I don't care how I look; it's about staying in a weight class and competing in my sport" (178).

The majority of the ED characters are already in recovery when the novel opens, meaning they have acknowledged a problem, have taken steps toward recovery, and have decided that they do not want to slide back. In some cases, this trajectory included time in residential treatment, while others have outpatient support perhaps including a therapist and nutritionist. However, beginning the book in recovery does not preclude sliding back into ED behaviors and the need for medical intervention, which can become the "point of ritual death," one of the eight narrative elements Pamela Regis (14) identifies as common to the romance novel form.

If these fictional rollercoaster trajectories mirror the lived reality of ED recovery, there is one major way in which fictional narratives depart from reality: the cost and availability of ED treatment. Seven novels show the (re)hospitalization of a main character. Two are adult romances, one set in London where costs are (presumably) absorbed by the National Health Service (NHS) and the other where the medical loans are paid off by the other heroine's rich family as a wedding gift. In four of the five young/new adult romances cost is never mentioned, but three are (presumably) covered by parental medical insurance and one (presumably) by the rock star patient's own resources. In the only YA romance that does mention money, initial hospitalization is again absorbed in London by the NHS before the hero's rich brother shows up from the U.S. and funds a stay in a New York inpatient clinic.

No novel shows a character unable to access healthcare. They may not want treatment, or be in denial about needing it, but if/when they accept that need, treatment is both instantly available and immediately effective. These happy circumstances are at odds with the lived experience of real ED patients, especially under the U.S.'s for-profit healthcare model:

> one in five eating disorder specialists believe that insurance companies are indirectly responsible for the death of at least one of their patients; 96.7 percent of these specialists believe their patients with anorexia nervosa are put in life-threatening situations because of health insurance companies' refusal to cover treatment [Lester 18].

In 2010, even after the Mental Health Parity and Addiction Equity Act came into effect, designed to prevent commercial health insurance plans giving less coverage to behavioral health issues than general medical care, 22.4 percent of plans excluded eating disorders (Horgan et al. 164).

ED Long-Term Prognosis and Mortality

Among mental disorders, EDs are one of the more prevalent and intractable issues and are associated with the highest all-cause mortality risk as well as being high risk for death from both unnatural (such as suicide) and natural causes (Harris and Barraclough), with anorexia nervosa having the highest ED mortality rate (Arcelus et al.). In the U.S., roughly fifty percent of ED patients recover, thirty percent make some improvement, and twenty percent remain chronically ill or die (Lester 18–19).

Given romance fiction's HEA/HFN (happily ever after/happy for now) promise, it is perhaps not surprising that no ED character dies, but they are not untouched by mortality. In two novels, ED characters are haunted by deaths of fellow ED sufferers, although their reactions are different. In *Sweet Fall* (Cole), Lexi's relapse into anorexic behaviors is partly triggered by the death of Daisy, a friend and fellow anorexic she met in inpatient treatment, who managed to hide her continuing anorexic behaviors and died of heart failure due to ED complications, but whose weight loss Lexi envied. Throughout the novel, Lexi writes diary entries to Daisy, recording her calorie intake and weight, which drops from 98 to 70 pounds before Lexi is sectioned and hospitalized. By contrast, in *The Illegitimate Tycoon* (Kenny), supermodel and recovering anorexic Leila resolves to continue her struggle against her ED after a fellow pregnant supermodel relapses into anorexia, resulting in the deaths of both woman and fetus (20). It is worth noting that both deaths occur off the page and before the novel opens so readers are not encouraged to emotionally bond.

Pregnancy and Eating Disorders

Since pregnancy is a common trope in romance fiction, it is worth examining how ED romances approach this topic. A retrospective cohort study of pregnancy and anorexia nervosa (Eagles et al.) found no significant increase in miscarriages for women with a history of AN, concluding that while there is evidence of pregnancy problems for women currently experiencing AN symptoms, and some danger for those in early remission, this was less true for those in long-term, asymptomatic remission and that pregnancy can be a goal to motivate recovery. Nonetheless, within the ED community, pregnancy remains a topic of interest.

Three novels deal with pregnancy, with two addressing associated body image issues. All three are adult MF romances with heroines who are years into recovery, two for anorexia and one for an unspecified, anorexia-like ED and mostly asymptomatic although still experiencing some ED thoughts. In *The Divorce Party*, body image issues associated with pregnancy are only briefly discussed, and dismissed, by hero Riccardo, who tells his estranged wife, Lilly:

> "You also have to accept the changes in your body. They're natural and healthy."
> "I'm getting there," she murmured. "It's just hard when it feels like my body is out of control. The control part is the hardest for me."
> He spread his hands wide. "Just hand it over to me, cara, and I'll take care of it for you" [Hayward 140].

In *The Best Man's Baby*, Claire's doctor mentions pregnancy and body image issues: "for someone who has had an eating disorder it may be very disconcerting and may trigger those insecurities again. You'll be weighed at every appointment, you'll have cravings you might find difficult to ignore, and I'm concerned you'll have feelings of guilt when you indulge" (James 76). However, Claire is not worried: "She really felt like she had put her self-esteem issues and eating disorder behind her. She really wasn't nervous about what would happen to her body, because she wasn't the same girl she was years ago. She was older, wiser, and a hell of a lot more self-confident" (James 77), and this is not an issue in the novel.

The Illegitimate Tycoon delves most deeply into pregnancy and ED. Leila and Rafael have been married for five years but drifted apart due to the pressures of their respective careers as supermodel and billionaire software tycoon. So distant are they that, despite knowing Rafael craves children, Leila doesn't tell him that she was twelve weeks pregnant and miscarried, about which she feels guilt and worries that her history of anorexia contributed: "No, I am to blame. The doctor explained it to me. There is a higher incidence of miscarriage when the mother has a history of anorexia. She said that though I was fully recovered from the disease and have been for years, I am still technically underweight" (72). Leila is also aware of issues around ED and mental health and pregnancy:

> It had taken her years to understand that she battled her eating disorder much like an alcoholic avoided strong drink. Because any number of triggers could throw her back into that vicious cycle of anorexia.
> She'd stayed strong and healthy because her career demanded it. Because she had an average weight she must maintain to stay on top of her game. She was in total control of every aspect of her life. Being pregnant would be a completely different thing, for she'd have zero control over the changes in her body.
> If she failed to cope with her pregnancy—if she was the cause of losing another baby—she'd simply lose her mind [76].

Leila has been trying to gain weight (74), hoping this will lead to another pregnancy, but has to deal with her emotional response to this "desired" weight gain (115) even before discovering she was already pregnant having used antibiotics while on the pill (116).

#ownvoices

Given that four novels in my corpus were written by #ownvoices authors with histories of eating disorders, I was interested in whether this influence would be discernible within any of these books. Within the novels' narrative arcs, the only difference I identified was that two #ownvoices novels (Hayward; Locke, *Second Position*) ended with published interviews with the ED characters about their disorder and recovery. However, #ownvoices authors included more paratextual ED information.

New adult romance *Second Position* is the debut novel of Katherine Locke, who writes in the opening acknowledgments: "To everyone who has ever struggled with an eating disorder or addiction, remember sometimes we have to spin apart to find all the pieces we need to put our lives back together. Keep up the good fight. It's worth it" (5). In a guest blog post, Locke talked about there being:

> two types of books with mental illness at their core. The first type is for readers who suffer the same or similar mental illness. The other type is for outsiders, readers who don't suffer that mental illness. The second group of readers might be curious, or pick up the book for other reasons, or have that type of mental illness in their family or friend group. But they don't personally suffer through it themselves [...]. Eating disorder books which include numbers are for outsiders/non-sufferers. Weight and numbers are a way for outsiders/non-sufferers to understand the severity of the disease and they're more tangible than the incongruous and seemingly irrational thoughts of an anorexic person. Moreover, weights and numbers are one of the most common triggers for those thoughts to an anorexic person and merely reading them on paper can damage a recovering anorexic's recovery trajectory [Locke, "#MHYALit"].

In a post on her website, Locke ("Death Masks") wrote about being in denial about her own mortality

> It's not like I wasn't aware that what I was doing was dangerous. I knew the statistics. I knew that every time I purged, I was risking death. I knew that the things I was doing to my body were dangerous. Were killing me.
> But when my college counseling center called me and said I had to set up an appointment because three professors on campus had called in concern about me. My response was, "What? Why?"
> I was at my all time lowest weight. I wasn't handing in assignments. My hair was falling out. I was manic. But I was totally fine, totally fine, what are you talking about?

In the same post, Locke admitted to googling names of friends met in the eating disorder community

> to see if they're still alive.
> You. Google. Names. To. Find. Out. If. They're. Alive.
> [...] Of the thirteen girls I was in treatment with, one is dead.
> Of the numerous girls I've met online, at least five that I know of are dead, including two friends who were (god, I wrote are there...) really good friends of mine ["Death Masks"].

The Divorce Party, Jennifer Hayward's debut adult romance, won Harlequin's 2012 "So You Think You Can Write" global writing contest.

Although not referenced in the book, in an online interview Hayward discussed her eating disorder:

> One of the biggest challenges I've faced in my life is struggling with anorexia in my teens. It is a debilitating, painful disease which affects so many young girls who struggle with the unrealistic images society puts in front of them. The day I stopped trying to live up to those standards I was transformed as a person. I try and talk about this disease as much as I can so other young women won't have to go through what I did [Khanduja].

Sweet Fall, a new adult MF romance, opens with a forward in which author Tillie Cole outlines her personal (unnamed) ED:

> When I was fourteen, I developed a disorder, which unfortunately, took me to a very dark place in my life. It stayed with me for the majority of my teens and even reared its head a few times later in life. I fell again and again, but—luckily—every time, I managed to pick myself back up.
> What I am talking of is a very insular disorder. A very secretive disorder. And it blindsided me and riddled me with issues that I still struggle with today.
> I know now it will never fully go away [Cole 4].

Empty Net (Gale) is an adult MM sports romance. In a blog post Gale ("No One Deserves an Eating Disorder") wrote about her history with anorexia, explaining that a scene where the ED character first talks to a therapist was drawn from Gale's own experience of not feeling skinny enough to be diagnosed with an eating disorder, and the response of her therapist, to whom Gale dedicated the novel. An afterword (214) gives links to ED resources.

Conclusion

Given that disordered eating is part of the lived reality of many romance readers, it is encouraging to see 21st-century romance fiction beginning to respond to the cultures and communities in which it exists by engaging with eating disorders. However, my analysis suggests that the genre has only taken the first tentative steps and it would require shifts in both the number of novels and in how EDs are portrayed in order to more closely reflect reality.

I remain skeptical that these shifts will occur. Weight stigma is one of the few remaining "socially-acceptable" forms of discrimination (Carr and Friedman), making eating and body issues a challenging topic to address in a genre that promises readers escapism. Although the "big beautiful women" (BBW) romance subgenre, which advocates for love at every size, shows that there is—some, limited (Brown)—progress toward challenging this form of discrimination, with eating disorders, the discrimination experienced by the visible affliction of being over- (or under-) weight is compounded by the invisible serious mental health issue.

Moreover, given the commercial imperatives of romance (self) publishing, it is hard to imagine financial drivers that would boost ED romance. Perhaps it could be marketed as a subset of the commercially successful "misery porn" or "misery lit"; trauma narratives that tap into intimate details of others' lives, offering readers the enjoyment of the adrenaline rush on an emotional rollercoaster, or personally relating to the depicted trauma (Ballhaus). After all, romance does not shy away from engaging with difficult topics, with characters overcoming rape or abuse. However, such misery triggers are usually externally focused on evil family members, previous intimate partners, or random strangers, leaving the main character morally blameless. But so long as society continues to incorrectly perceive mental illness as self-inflicted, ED sufferers will seem complicit in their suffering and therefore less sympathetic.

Corpus

Albert, Annabeth. *Arctic Sun*. Carina Press, 2019.
Blake, Leta. *Training Season*. Leta Blake, 2013.
Brown, Lorelie. *Far from Home*. Riptide Publishing, 2016.
Cole, Tillie. *Sweet Fall*. Tillie Cole, 2014.
Cozzo, Karole. *The Truth about Happily Ever After*. Swoon Reads, 2017.
Crusie, Jennifer. *Fast Women*. St. Martin's Press, 2001.
Fleet, Suki. *Foxes*. Dreamspinner Press, 2016.
Gale, Avon. *Empty Net*. Dreamspinner Press, 2016.
Hayward, Jennifer. *The Divorce Party*. Harlequin Mills & Boon, 2013.
James, Victoria. *The Best Man's Baby*. Entangled Publishing, 2013.
Jones, Jenny B. *There You'll Find Me*. Thomas Nelson, 2011.
Kadence, Sam. *Unicorns and Rainbow Poop*. Harmony Ink Press, 2014.
Kasey, Lissa. *Model Bodyguard*. Dreamspinner Press, 2016.
_____. *Model Citizen*. Dreamspinner Press, 2015.
_____. *Model Investigator*. Dreamspinner Press, 2017.
Kenny, Janette. *The Illegitimate Tycoon*. Harlequin Mills & Boon, 2011.
Locke, Katherine. *Second Position*. Carina Press, 2015.
Martin, Anna. *The Impossible Boy*. Dreamspinner Press, 2017.
Milan, Courtney. *Trade Me*. Courtney Milan, 2015.
Mulhall, M.B. *Heavyweight*. Harmony Ink Press, 2014.
Ricci, Caitlin, et al. *Three Times the Charm*. Harmony Ink Press, 2018.
Witt, Brandon. *The Imperfection of Swans*. Dreamspinner Press, 2016.
Witt, L.A. *Back Piece*. SMP Swerve, 2017.

Works Cited

American Psychiatric Association. *Diagnostic and Statistical Manual of Mental Disorders*. 5th ed. American Psychiatric Association, 2013, doi:10.1176/appi.books 9780890425596.

Arcelus, Jon, et al. "Mortality Rates in Patients with Anorexia Nervosa and Other Eating Disorders: A Meta-Analysis of 36 Studies." *Archives of General Psychiatry*, vol. 68, no. 7, July 2011, pp. 724–731, doi:10.1001/archgenpsychiatry.2011.74.

Ballhaus, Louisa. "What Watching 'Misery Porn' Shows Like 'The Handmaid's Tale' Does to Your Mental Health." *Bustle*, 6 June 2019, www.bustle.com/p/what-watching-misery-porn-shows-like-the-handmaids-tale-does-to-your-mental-health-17941263.

Brown, Sonya C. "Does This Book Make Me Look Fat?" *Journal of Popular Romance Studies*, vol. 1, no. 2, 2011, jprstudies.org/2011/03/does-this-book-make-me-look-fat/.

Carr, Deborah, and Michael A. Friedman. "Is Obesity Stigmatizing? Body Weight, Perceived Discrimination, and Psychological Well-Being in the United States." *Journal of Health and Social Behavior*, vol. 46, no. 3, 2005, pp. 244–259.

Diemer, Elizabeth W., et al. "Gender Identity, Sexual Orientation, and Eating-Related Pathology in a National Sample of College Students." *Journal of Adolescent Health*, vol. 57, no. 2, August 2015, pp. 144–149, doi:10.1016/j.jadohealth.2015.03.003.

Eagles, J. M., et al. "Pregnancy Outcomes of Women With and Without a History of Anorexia Nervosa." *Psychological Medicine*, vol. 42, no. 12, 2012, pp. 2651–2660. doi:10.1017/S0033291712000414.

Gale, Avon. "No One Deserves an Eating Disorder." *Goodreads*, 13 September 2016, www.goodreads.com/author_blog_posts/13932173-no-one-deserves-an-eating-disorder.

Galmiche, Marie, et al. "Prevalence of Eating Disorders over the 2000–2018 Period: A Systematic Literature Review." *The American Journal of Clinical Nutrition*, vol. 109, no. 5, April 2019, pp. 1402–1413, doi:10.1093/ajcn/nqy342.

Goodreads. "Eating Disorders in Romance Novels." *Goodreads*, www.goodreads.com/list/show/84818.Eating_Disorders_in_Romance_Novels. Accessed 11 May 2020.

———. "M/M Romance with Body Image Disorder." *Goodreads*, www.goodreads.com/list/show/78841.M_M_Romance_with_Body_Image_Disorder. Accessed 11 May 2020.

Harris, Clare, and Brian Barraclough. "Excess Mortality of Mental Disorder." *British Journal of Psychiatry*, 2018/01/03, vol. 173, no. 1, 1998, pp. 11–53, doi:10.1192/bjp.173.1.11.

Horgan, Constance M., et al. "Health Plans' Early Response to Federal Parity Legislation for Mental Health and Addiction Services." *Psychiatric Services*, vol. 67, no. 2, 2016, pp. 162–168, doi:10.1176/appi.ps.201400575.

Hospers, Harm J., and Anita Jansen. "Why Homosexuality Is a Risk Factor for Eating Disorders in Males." *Journal of Social and Clinical Psychology*, vol. 24, no. 8, 2005, pp. 1188–1201, doi:10.1521/jscp.2005.24.8.1188.

Hudson, James I., et al. "The Prevalence and Correlates of Eating Disorders in the National Comorbidity Survey Replication." *Biological Psychiatry*, vol. 61, no. 3, February 2007, pp. 348–358, doi:10.1016/j.biopsych.2006.03.040.

Khanduja, Jaideep. "Author Interview: Jennifer Hayward: Delicious De Campos Series: The Divorce Party: Winner of Harlequin 2012." *Pebble in the Still Waters*, 22 November 2014, pebbleinthestillwaters.blogspot.com/2014/11/author-interview-jennifer-hayward.html

Lester, Rebecca J. *Famished: Eating Disorders and Failed Care in America*. U of California P, 2019.

Locke, Katherine. "Death Masks and Living With Your Own Mortality." *Katherine Locke Books*, 17 February 2014, writingwithcats.wordpress.com/2014/02/18/death-masks-living-with-your-own-morality/.

———. "#MHYALit: For Whom the Book Is Written: Addressing Intended Audience in YA Novels about Mental Illness, a Guest Post by Katherine Locke." *School Library Journal*, 1 November 2016, www.slj.com/?detailStory=mhyalit-for-whom-the-book-is-written-addressing-intended-audience-in-ya-novels-about-mental-illness-a-guest-post-by-katherine-locke.

Mortimer, Rose. "Pride Before a Fall: Shame, Diagnostic Crossover, and Eating Disorders." *Journal of Bioethical Inquiry*, vol. 16, no. 3, September 2019, pp. 365–374, doi:10.1007/s11673-019-09923-3.

Polivy, Janet, and C. Peter Herman. "Causes of Eating Disorders." *Annual Review of Psychology*, vol. 53, no. 1, 2002, pp. 187–213, doi:10.1146/annurev.psych.53.100901.135103.

Reba-Harrelson, L., et al. "Patterns and Prevalence of Disordered Eating and Weight Control

Behaviors in Women Ages 25–45." *Eating and Weight Disorders—Studies on Anorexia, Bulimia and Obesity*, vol. 14, no. 4, December 2009, pp. e190–198, doi:10.1007/BF03325116.

Regis, Pamela. *A Natural History of the Romance Novel.* U of Pennsylvania P, 2003.

Smink, Frédérique R. E., et al. "Epidemiology of Eating Disorders: Incidence, Prevalence and Mortality Rates." *Current Psychiatry Reports*, vol. 14, no. 4, August 2012, pp. 406–414, doi:10.1007/s11920-012-0282-y.

Yang, Lin, and Graham A. Colditz. "Prevalence of Overweight and Obesity in the United States, 2007–2012." *JAMA Internal Medicine*, vol. 175, no. 8, August 2015, pp. 1412–1413, doi:10.1001/jamainternmed.2015.2405.

The "Grandly and Inhospitably Strange" World of Autistic Heroines in Romance Fiction

WENDY WAGNER

On May 10, 2018, Sheldon Cooper and Amy Farrah Fowler were married on the 11th season finale of *The Big Bang Theory*, one of the most popular television shows of the 21st century. In the original log line for the show, Sheldon and his roommate Leonard are described as "the kind of 'beautiful minds' that understand how the universe works. But none of that genius helps them interact with people, especially women." From the beginning, audiences read Sheldon as autistic, though the show's creator and writers disavowed the label, and his character has even been used by medical practitioners as an example of applying the new DSM-V criteria for autism spectrum disorder (Tobia and Toma). That Sheldon himself would someday find love and marriage seemed inconceivable in the first season, but the audience's adoration of Sheldon and the unexpected chemistry between Sheldon and Amy propelled this long-term storyline. Viewers were anxious to see the couple attain their happy ending.

The popularity of Sheldon is typical of the growing interest in and audience for love stories about autistic people[1] in the 21st century. Wikipedia's list of autistic fictional characters contains 156 autistic characters since 2000, and only 25 before then ("List"). Romance fiction has been no different; increasing numbers of romance novels feature main characters who are autistic and also attain the ending expected by every reader of a romance novel: finding love. However, there are some differences in the love stories of autistic characters as told by romance writers. Rarely in mainstream popular culture (television and film) do autistic love interests find love with someone who is non-autistic; Sheldon's love interest, Amy, for example, is also viewed as autistic. But in romance novels, the autistic character is more likely to find love with a non-autistic character.

Furthermore, while many early examples of romance fiction with autistic characters focused on autistic heroes, a recent trend in romance fiction is the autistic heroine. Helen Hoang's first novel, *The Kiss Quotient* (2018), was at the top of many "Best of 2018" lists and has been optioned as a movie. *The Kiss Quotient* was preceded by two other romance novels with autistic heroines: *A Study in Scarlet Women* (2016), by Sherry Thomas, and *A Girl Like Her* (2018), by Talia Hibbert, published just two months before Hoang's novel. These three novels contain markedly different portrayals of autistic characters in love stories. First, the autistic main character is a woman, which is unusual in both mainstream popular culture and romance fiction. Second, these novels make the heroines' autism significant in ways that transcend issues of representation and calls for inclusiveness.

This essay draws from the feminist disability studies perspective articulated by Rosemarie Garland-Thomson and the scholarship of Michael Bérubé on intellectual disability and narrative to show how these novels synthesize perspectives on disability, gender, and the genre of romance fiction to "confront the limits of the ways we understand human diversity, the materiality of the body, multiculturalism, and the social formations that interpret bodily differences" and "enhance how we understand what it is to be human, our relationships with one another, and the experience of embodiment" (Garland-Thomson 362–363). These three novels, in telling the love stories of autistic heroines, also interrogate patriarchal social norms. By encouraging readers to empathize with the autistic heroine (as the narratives require the non-autistic hero to do), these novels defamiliarize social behaviors that the non-autistic take for granted.

This essay explores the love stories of these three autistic heroines: Ruth Kabbah, from Talia Hibbert's contemporary romance *A Girl Like Her*; Stella Lane, from Helen Hoang's contemporary romance *The Kiss Quotient*; and Charlotte Holmes from Sherry Thomas's Lady Sherlock series of historical romantic mysteries. Each character faces challenges from internal factors (impairment of social skills and increase in sensory-regulating behaviors) and external factors (society's difficulty in accepting the characters' impairments). The development of the love story and the non-autistic hero's acceptance of the autistic heroine reveal avenues to address assumptions about what is considered normal, assumptions that have been defined by a patriarchal society. These romances demonstrate that "disability is the most human of experiences" (Garland-Thomson 363).

The visibility of characters with autism (or Asperger's Syndrome) has increased dramatically since Stuart Murray's book *Representing Autism* (2008) identified the ways autistic characters had been represented as "objects of fascination and wonder," focusing mainly on the autistic person as a savant or extraordinary person and calling for expanding the range of portrayals of autism in media, i.e., issues of representation (Murray). Similarly, Elizabeth Bartmess identifies three problem areas relating to representation of autistic people: "being described or treated as less real than non-autistic people; autism being shown as a debt we have to repay to others around us; and our being portrayed as only looking or acting certain ways" (Bartmess). Twenty-first-century novels such as Elizabeth Moon's *The Speed of Dark* (2002), Mark Haddon's *The Curious Incident of the Dog in the Night-Time* (2003), and Graeme Simsion's *The Rosie Project* (2012) challenged the objectification of autistic characters by using first-person narratives to establish the autistic character as the subject, not the object, of interpretation, and to demonstrate the diversity of the autistic community. For the non-autistic reader, these portrayals are eye-opening and increase empathy for autistic people. For the autistic reader, they are totems of representation, reflecting their experience as a person with autism and the validity of their individual perspectives.

The visibility of characters with autism has increased in romance fiction as well. Ian in Jennifer Ashley's *The Madness of Lord Ian Mackenzie* (2009) and Adam in Tracy Livesay's *Love on My Mind* (2016) are just two examples of autistic male characters in well-regarded romance novels. The focus on autistic heroes makes sense from the perspective of increasing accurate representation of autistic people in romance. Demographically, men diagnosed with autism outnumber women 4 to 1, although research suggests that autism is under-identified among women. But perhaps there is another explanation. The ways that impairment of social skills in autistic men appear as arrogance, rudeness, and need for control bear a strong resemblance to the characteristics of many romance heroes of 20th-century romance fiction. Robyn Donald, for example, writes that the heroes in romance novels are men who "admit to being difficult to live with, ... demand extremely high standards in every aspect of their lives..., [are] in control." They are described as "short-tempered, ruthless, tough, even cruel" (Donald 82). In romance novels, these characteristics also lead autistic characters to financial success, which, as men, they already have greater access to in a patriarchal society. In the novels mentioned above, autistic heroes such as Ian and Adam are less likely to be considered outsiders or shunned in part because of the power granted to them by capitalism and patriarchy: Ian is the younger brother of a duke, and Adam is the CEO of a tech company. Their economic privilege intertwines with social class privilege, so their autistic characteristics are seen as signs of success and hegemonic masculinity instead of reasons for social stigma.

The situation is much different for autistic heroines in romance fiction.

Autistic heroines generally feel like outsiders, mainly because they have difficulty enacting the social behaviors expected of women, such as emotional warmth, understanding of social cues, and focus on the interests of others (usually men) rather than their own. Autistic heroines who violate social expectations by being rude, arrogant, or inattentive are alienated from society, not held up as exemplars of success. This may present a significant obstacle to their happiness, not to mention hope of a satisfying romantic relationship.

The concept of agreed-upon "norms" of physical characteristics and social behaviors and the disabled person's deviation from these norms is foundational to disability studies. Lennard Davis suggests that disability studies should problematize the concept of "normalcy," and in terms of autism, this means questioning the normalcy of expectations about social interactions. In medical terms, autism is described as deficits in social-emotional reciprocity, nonverbal communicative behavior, and developing and maintaining relationships. It also is identified by behaviors considered socially unacceptable, i.e., "repetitive patterns of behavior, manifested by some combination of repetitive motor movements, insistence on sameness, abnormally intense interests, hyper- or hyporeactivity to sensory input" ("Diagnostic"). The idea that there is a "normalcy" against which the autistic person should be measured underlies these identified characteristics. However, what we consider to be "normalcy" may be socially constructed, hegemonic, and thus subject to interrogation (Davis 2–3).

Fiction writing provides an opportunity to explore this process of interrogating normalcy not just in terms of looking at "normal" and "not normal" side by side, but also in terms of how narrative works to reflect reality and also to influence it. One example of this approach is David Mitchell and Sharon Snyder's concept of the "narrative prosthesis." Discussing portrayals of disability in literature, Mitchell and Snyder argue that disability in a literary character serves as a crutch, a "narrative prosthesis" on which the narrative is based: "The very need for a story is called into being when something has gone amiss with the known world," they write. The disability is the problem, the deviation from the norm, that sets the literary narrative into motion (Mitchell and Snyder 209).

Mitchell and Snyder's analysis, however, is derived from their study of literary narrative, which they describe as "open-ended" narratives that foreground the "'play' of multiple meanings" (Mitchell and Snyder 205). In applying this concept to genre fiction, such as the romance novel, does the concept hold up? Genre fiction often consists of narrative structures based on elements that meet readers' expectations. In the genre of romance fiction, the problem that sets the narrative in motion is the lack of romantic love, and the resolution is the discovery and acceptance of the love relationship. The disability of one of the main characters can be part of the story, but it does not have to be. The formulaic elements of the romance genre have not always led to nuanced portrayals of disabled heroes and heroines, but they make possible a reading of disability in a romance novel that is not a version of narrative prosthesis.

Ria Cheyne's work on disability and affect in romance fiction, with its emphasis on "the representational disability encounter," i.e., the encounter of the reader with the representation of disability in a text, extends the idea of the disabled character as a narrative prosthesis but also raises the possibility of the transformative effects of disabled main characters on the romance narrative (Cheyne 11). Cheyne observes that "romance's key potential with regard to disability representation comes not just from the ways it encourages 'knowing afresh' by generating moments of recognition but from the ways it encourages disability to be *felt* afresh in ways that can destabilize habitual feelings and responses" (Cheyne 160) This, Cheyne argues, leads readers to experience meta-feelings, feelings about initial negative thoughts or assumptions about disability and/or disabled characters. The discomfort caused by these meta-feelings "can be resolved or eased in multiple ways, but one of them is through a shift in the way the reader thinks (and feels) about disability, a shift that may affect behaviours and feelings in all kinds of disability encounters" (Cheyne 152). Cheyne is thus positing that romance stories involving disabled main characters have the potential to transform not only the characters involved in the love relationship but also those around them.

The work of Cheyne and others calls attention to the fundamental sociality of the romance narrative. Built into the structure of the romance novel, as Pamela Regis has articulated it, is the idea that the story of individuals' transformation is accompanied by a form of social transformation. All romance novels, Regis argues, begin with defining a flawed society that will be re-formed (and reformed) by the end of the novel in conjunction with the success of the love relationship of the main characters. Regis derives this insight from the work of Northrop Frye, who notes comedy's "movement ... from one society to another" (Regis 28); John Morreall expands this definition of comedy when he states that tragedy is often the story of an individual and their isolation from society, but "in comedy the basic unit is the group" and the narrative moves toward social integration (Morreall). For Regis, defining the society at the beginning of the romance novel sets up "the status quo which the heroine and hero must confront in their attempt to court and marry and which, by their union, they symbolically remake" (Regis 31). In essence, what the romance novel does is establish a social norm that is specific to the novel and which is then critiqued and reformed. In this, the romance has much in common with Rosemarie Garland-Thomson's emphasis in feminist disability studies on "integration and transformation":

"Integration suggests achieving parity by fully including that which has been excluded and subordinated. Transformation suggests reimagining established knowledge and the order of things" (Garland-Thomson 362). Integration and transformation are also characteristics of the romance novel, as the main characters of a romance novel invite and integrate the ethos of love into their lives and in doing so inspire transformation of the social order.

An approach to using disability studies in concert with textual and narrative analysis comes from scholar Michael Bérubé. Bérubé moves away from representation as a goal for disability narrative and instead looks at appearances of disability in literature as possible "strategies, devices for exploring vast domains of human thought, experience and action" (Bérubé 2). The specific aspect of intellectual/cognitive disability/autism that intrigues him is the way that "literary works depict systems of sociality in part by including characters who either are or are presumed by their fellow characters to be constitutively incapable of understanding or abiding by the social systems by which their worlds operate" (Bérubé 21). Bérubé is moving away from both the individual model of disability (disability as personal tragedy) and the social model of disability (disability as socially constructed restrictions and labels) (Shakespeare 197) to something far more complex. For Bérubé, the autistic character is neither the subject narrating their own tragedy nor the object victimized by socially constructed restrictions and labels but instead a way of examining the nature of social systems. He writes that one of the ambitions of *The Secret Life of Stories* is "to use the study of intellectual disability in narrative to ask what the 'real' and the 'normal' consist of, and to lay bare the crafty procedures that go into the cultural production of artifacts we now take to be ordinary, straightforward, unproblematic representations of the world" (Bérubé 55). Bérubé is examining literary narrative, but his focus on the idea of normalcy and the ways that narratives about characters with autism can disrupt that understanding is relevant to a study of autistic characters in romance fiction.

In the following discussions of romance novels featuring autistic heroines, I will use these insights from feminist disability studies and disability narrative studies to show how these novels develop alternatives to patriarchal social norms through telling stories about building and maintaining love relationships. In particular, these novels explore ideas about consent in intimate relationships, gossip and "slut-shaming," and women and work.

Stella Lane

The Kiss Quotient, by Helen Hoang, is about Stella Lane and Michael Larsen, who meet when Stella hires Michael from an escort service to teach her how to become better at sex and then, later, to become better at being a girlfriend. Stella self-identifies as autistic. However, she resists identifying herself as autistic to others because she does not want to be labeled. Stella's autism is signaled to the reader early in the novel and reinforced through her need for routine, her lack of comfort in social situations, her directness of speech, her displeasure with being touched, and her tactile sensitivity—all characteristics shared by many autistic people.

Stella's story begins with pressure to conform to social norms epitomized by her mother's expectations about Stella marrying. Stella approaches this pressure by deciding to change herself, to learn social skills and behaviors that will make her more acceptable to the non-autistic. She knows that she is autistic and does not fit in, but she will try to adapt so that she can pass as non-autistic. The novel ends with Stella's realization that she does not have to change herself: "She wasn't broken. She saw and interacted with the world in a different way, but that was her. She could change her actions, change her words, change her appearance, but she couldn't change the root of herself. At her core, she would always be autistic." In this way, Stella's story is one of self-acceptance through love.

However, this novel also positions autism in another way. Instead of focusing on Stella's need (or lack of need) to change to fit into society, her story also addresses an issue of great concern in the romance fiction community: consent. In her 2018 keynote speech to the Romance Writers of America annual convention, Kate Cuthbert spoke of the need for romance fiction to resist remaining static and instead continually adapt to social change, citing the #MeToo movement as an example and romance writers' inclusion of "active, informed consent in all aspects of sexuality" in their novels as a desired outcome (Cuthbert).

Hoang foregrounds the issue of consent with reference to Stella's feelings about being touched, one of the characteristics that marks Stella as autistic. In other words, in this novel, autism is not just a characteristic of Stella, but it is also acting "as a trope, a critical and underacknowledged thread in the social fabric, a device for exploring the phenomenon of human sociality as such" (Bérubé 21). Early in *The Kiss Quotient*, we find out that Stella's mother thinks of touching people as something Stella needs to get used to. Hoang writes, "Uninvited touches irritated [Stella], and her mother knew it. She did it to 'acclimate' her." Mrs. Lane sees Stella's aversion to touch as a sign of not fitting in, and she tries to make Stella adapt to social norms of touch, putting her hand over Stella's when they are out to dinner, when Stella has not invited it or agreed to it. But Stella is quick to point out later that "she didn't mind touching when she initiated it or had time to mentally prepare for it." In other words, Stella does not fit a stereotype of autistic people as having an aversion to touch. She just wants to control the situation, to be aware of touch before it happens.

Stella's feelings about being touched are thus presented in the context of consent. The response of Michael, her non-autistic love interest, is to respect her need to give permission and consent before being touched. Michael's acceptance of Stella is contrasted to the behavior of another possible love interest, Philip, who tells Stella, "You just have to get used to me, Stella. You acclimated to that bastard" (i.e., Michael). Both Philip and Stella's mother believe Stella needs to adapt to others and change herself. In contrast, Michael either allows Stella to initiate touch or asks permission, even to kiss her: "At her small nod, he crushed their mouths together and kissed her deeply." The idea that forcing physical contact on another person is necessary, romantic, or sexy has been the norm in both romance fiction and society as a whole, but Stella and Michael's relationship undercuts the seeming necessity of women accepting touch without consent and instead makes consent seem positive and sexually arousing, for Stella and Michael and, therefore, also for the readers.

Ruth Kabbah

Ruth Kabbah of *A Girl Like Her*, by Talia Hibbert, identifies herself as autistic almost from the beginning of the novel. Her self-identification happens not through narration of her inner thoughts (as was the case with Stella Lane), but in her desire to describe and explain herself to Evan Miller (the non-autistic love interest). Before she labels her autism, the book's narration gives the reader hints: Daniel Burne (her ex-lover) describes her as "slow"; Ruth refers to her own "fractured mind that can't think" and notices "that she was rubbing her own hands—wringing them, people said—and made herself stop, even though the action was calming." But Hibbert allows Ruth to speak the words and name herself to other characters.

This is not a radical moment in a novel featuring a POV character who is autistic, but it is central to Hibbert's deployment of autism in her novel. *A Girl Like Her* is not a romance novel about an autistic woman who finds love with a non-autistic man so much as it is a romance about two people finding love amid a community (the town of Ravenswood) that is inherently corrupt in terms of what it values. Like present-day society at large, this community overvalues social class status and beauty, and it is structured around social interactions that maintain these values through shared narratives that objectify and silence those who do not meet the community's standards.

Ruth's disability contributes to her problems with her community, but it does not cause these problems. Her problems with Ravenswood residents are also inflected by her race, gender, social class, and body size. But as the book's title, *A Girl Like Her*, suggests, the main culprit is gossip and the community's need to enforce in-group/out-group boundaries through talking about others. Ruth is the subject of gossip, and she has trouble making her voice heard. "A girl like her," the community thinks, is not worth hearing.

Most of what happened to Ruth before the novel begins is hinted at but never fully told until Ruth discusses it with Evan. In high school, Ruth and a classmate, Daniel, began a sexual relationship in secret. Daniel, good-looking and popular, did not want the community to know of his relationship with Ruth, who is African-British, fat, and autistic. The relationship became emotionally abusive, as Daniel frequently "negged" Ruth and coerced her into sex. Meanwhile, he was dating and proposed marriage to another woman.

Eventually, Ruth's sister Hannah found out and confronted Daniel at his engagement party, revealing the relationship to everyone present. Subsequently, the people of the town (who valued Daniel for his good looks and high social status) took his side and scapegoated Ruth. At the beginning of the novel, the non-autistic hero, Evan, is ignorant about what the town knows about Ruth. There are stories about her that clearly exist (intimated by Daniel's derisive comment about "a girl like her" and a storeowner's comment about "that Kabbah girl"). Evan is literally an outsider to the town, moving to Ravenswood to take a job and then learning of the community's shared values as part of his integration into the community. Gossip is, of course, a way to convey these values.

Communications scholars define gossip in multiple ways. It can be characterized by casualness, informality and social knowledge. It is talk, and it is a social skill. It also demonstrates the values and norms of a community. Philip Esler, in his work on the Biblical Ruth, synthesizes the work of several scholars on gossip, noting that gossip can serve functions including social control, information management, and the development of friendship and intimacy. Esler observes that "One aspect of the social-conformity dimension of gossip is that, if it is to be influential, those involved must agree on the prevailing norms of acceptable behavior and gossipers frequently articulate those norms" (Esler).

For autistic people, gossip and small talk are challenging social skills to learn. It is difficult for Ruth to participate in gossip, nor can she evade being the subject of it. So, she simply allows the stories to circulate around her and about her, telling herself that she doesn't care, even though doing so isolates her further from her community and prevents her from doing activities she enjoys, such as going to the pub or volunteering at the local library. Ruth assumes that her future is one of isolation, so the stories about her become ways of avoiding social interaction. To Evan she claims she is the Town Jezebel: "You know; a harlot. A terrible, ungodly slut and misleader of men, etcetera, etcetera." When this confession fails to deter him from engaging with her, she wonders whether "having heard of her reputation, he was on a mission to try the town bicycle for himself." Her relationship with Daniel and the subsequent gossip about her sexual relationships with other men has changed her: "Being around people who were supposedly 'normal' made her feel abnormal. She'd never had that problem, before. Her life was split in two like that: before [Daniel] versus after." Ruth's isolation comes in part from her resistance to and/or difficulty in telling her own story, a trait that is directly connected to her autism. The consensus among experts is that many autistic people struggle with telling stories about themselves due to weak intrapersonal theory of mind (Westby). It is much easier for her to allow others to tell stories about her and for her to adjust to the consequences (being shunned).

As she and Evan develop their love relationship, Ruth's acceptance of the status quo (her isolation from her community) becomes untenable not just on a social level but on a relationship level. Because Ruth does not talk to him about her experience, Evan is left to figure it out on his own, leading Ruth to believe that Evan has sided with the community: "Because what you hear is so important. Why should I bother saying anything if gossip is all you need?" This moment of conflict between Ruth and Evan is the "point of ritual death"[2] of Hibbert's novel, the moment at which Ruth and Evan's relationship is at risk because of her weakness in talking about her own experiences and feelings and Evan's failure to understand. The relationship will prevail because Evan quickly identifies his mistake and indicates that he will wait for her to tell her own story, but while the relationship goes through this step, something else is happening. Daniel's obsession with Ruth, triggered by Ruth's relationship with Evan and her growing defiance of his attempts to control her, begins to affect his relationship with his wife and leads his father to confront Ruth. These two crisis points create the conditions for Ruth to be able to advocate for herself and to tell her story to Daniel's disapproving father, forcing Mr. Burne to recognize that his social power made it difficult for her to speak about her experience:

"I...." His voice was hoarse. "I wish you'd said all this earlier. I wish you'd explained this to me."

"When?" Ruth asked. "When I was eighteen years old and in love with a man who told me you were the devil incarnate? When I was twenty-two and you called me a gold-digging slut? When I was twenty-five and you gave your police statement?"

Ruth's lack of social power and her autism combine to create a situation in which she is the subject of negative, mostly untrue gossip in her community. In the past, when a friend asked Ruth about what happened, Ruth clammed up; Evan correctly guesses, "Someone asked you what was going on, and you very helpfully told them to fuck off." She begins to understand, though, that speaking about herself is not weakness but strength and self-understanding: "It was as if the act of speech cleared the murky waters of her mind, finally allowed her to see herself." It is Evan's patience and willingness to hear her story that create the conditions in which she can speak her truth.

Ruth's experience is another example of the way that autism can be used as a trope to explore human sociality. The difficulty of telling one's own story to counter gossip is not limited to autistic people. Gossip relies on social power and social skills, which provide opportunities for one story to be heard over another. Ruth's autism is a factor in her inability to counter the gossip about her with her own personal narrative, but so are her gender, her race, her economic class, her body size, and her overall disenfranchisement from the source of social power. Ruth's autism stands in for the myriad ways that people can be silenced and objectified by those with power.

Charlotte Holmes

Charlotte Holmes is the "Lady Sherlock" of Sherry Thomas' series of romantic mystery novels that are a feminist retelling of the Sherlock Holmes stories written by Arthur Conan Doyle. In these books, Charlotte Holmes is the youngest daughter of a baronet, and thus a member of the upper class of British society. But Charlotte has always been different, rejecting the social norms that call for her to marry and have children. In the first novel, *A Study in Scarlet Women*, Charlotte pursues a future not of marriage but of work, and she does so by losing her virginity to a man she knows so that she will be considered unmarriageable. Unfortunately, Charlotte's plan goes awry, and instead she is blackballed in society and cut off from her family. In order to re-establish herself, she connects with Mrs. Joan Watson and begins a career as a "consulting detective," but due to the social stigma against an upper-class woman working, she devises a plan to hide behind the identity of "Sherlock Holmes" and poses as Sherlock's sister and amanuensis. The novels in this series all involve Charlotte's work on various cases along with a romance storyline (with long-time friend Ash, aka Lord Ingram Ashburton), family drama (her involuntary separation from her beloved sister Lydia and cognitively disabled sister Bernadine), and the ongoing involvement of the nefarious Moriarty in the lives of her and her loved ones.

According to Thomas,[3] Charlotte is meant to be read as autistic, but Charlotte neither names herself as autistic or is identified as such in these novels because the term "autistic" and an understanding of the disorder were not used in her time. However, Thomas does a thorough job of calling attention to characteristics of Charlotte that lead readers to understand she is on the autism spectrum. Charlotte exhibits several behaviors and responses to the world that indicate not only her significant intellectual gifts but also traits common to autistic people: she does not speak until she is four years old, and when she does, she speaks in complete sentences; she does not enjoy fiction or imaginative stories and prefers information and logic; and she does not understand social norms or human emotions easily and must learn many of the social conventions that others take for granted.

But one passage that stands out to mark Charlotte as an autistic character is an anachronism, a modern-day reference that clues in the reader to Charlotte's disability:

> Sometimes, as Livia stood beside her, perspiring on her behalf and making every attempt to convey the correct response via telepathy, it struck her how much Charlotte resembled a foreigner who found native customs baffling and, on occasion, patently ridiculous. One time, in the middle of reading a magazine article about the possibility of life on Mars, it occurred to Livia that Charlotte was more akin to an interplanetary alien: It wasn't only the habits and conventions of the English she found perplexing, but that of all humanity.

This comparison of Charlotte to a visitor from Mars is striking because autistic people frequently use the analogy of feeling like an alien to describe how they understand their own autism.[4] Like a visitor to a strange place, Charlotte has had to adapt to a world she finds difficult to understand. Interestingly, most of the work Charlotte has done to navigate society has happened before the timeline of the novels, and what the novels focus on instead are the ways other people adapt to Charlotte, changing their worldviews as a result of their relationships with her. In this essay I'll focus on one example: Inspector Treadles, the Scotland Yard inspector who often consults with Charlotte and Ash on difficult cases.

Robert Treadles is married to Alice, the daughter of a business owner who is from a higher social class than him. By the end of *A Study in Scarlet Women* (the first book in the series), Treadles realizes that the Sherlock Holmes he has consulted with on cases and whom he admires greatly is actually Charlotte herself, a fallen woman who has been ostracized because of her unacceptable behavior. This discovery forces Treadles to question his cherished beliefs about the intellectual differences between men and women. It is around this time that Treadles learns that his wife, Alice, had hopes of taking over her father's business (before it was given to her brother, the more socially acceptable choice). The combination of learning that Sherlock is Charlotte and that Alice would like to run a business rocks Treadles' world, and not in a good way. In *A Scandal in Belgravia* (the second novel in the series), Alice must take over the business, leading to a growing distance between Treadles and his wife explored in *The Hollow of Fear* (the third book in the series). A confrontation with Charlotte's sister Livia and a conversation with Charlotte (who, to his shock, is disguised as a man) lead him to reconsider his disapproval of his wife's new job. Charlotte tells Treadles that to women like herself and Livia, Treadles is "the personification of the larger world they have known, the one that has thwarted them at every turn." Treadles eventually takes these words to heart, wondering if his own wife has felt this way: "Frustrated with her father…, she had fallen in love with a man she believed to be different, only to realize that of the two, her father had, in fact, been far more broad-minded. When had she realized that?" This story arc of Treadles reaches closure in *The Hollow of Fear* when, at breakfast, he asks his wife about her work for the first time, signifying his acceptance of it.

Inspector Treadles does not become magically "woke"; this is Victorian England after all, and he still holds onto many of his socially conservative values. But his interactions with Charlotte have changed some of his assumptions about the way the world works, and the measure of their effect on him is that he is able to apply these new insights to his relationship with the wife he loves dearly. Treadles' ability to change is especially important when you consider that he is a genuinely nice man. In fact, Charlotte points out that it is precisely his pleasant and friendly demeanor that makes his negative judgment of violation of social norms so difficult to accept. In romance fiction, social change does not happen in a burst of revolution, but in small moments of adaptation to new understandings prompted by love and respect for others.

In Thomas's third Lady Sherlock novel, *The Hollow of Fear*, the hero, Ash, is questioned by a police detective about Charlotte: "Lady Avery and Lady Somersby characterize her as odd, grandly odd. What do you think?" Ash responds with this observation: "If I were to think of it at all, I would be struck by how grandly and inhospitably strange the world must appear to Charlotte Holmes." What is interesting here is the repetition of certain words, calling back to previous uses in the Lady Sherlock novels. First, within this passage, Ash takes the detective's description of Charlotte as "grandly" odd and re-uses it in his response to emphasize Charlotte as a subject, that she herself sees the world as "grandly" strange. The word "strange" is also a callback to the first novel as the reader meets Charlotte for the first time, when she is found naked (having just lost her virginity) by Lady Shrewsbury, her paramour's mother. Lady Shrewsbury "had the distinct sensation that of the two of them, Miss Holmes considered Lady Shrewsbury the far stranger specimen." These novels reverse the readers' attention, in a way, directing the readers to see the "oddness" or "strangeness" of the world and its people from Charlotte's perspective. In the process, we learn more about our own grand strangeness, the ways we make the world inhospitable for others.

It is a sobering realization, but it is also an optimistic one because romance novels can instill in readers a desire to reform society and imagine a pathway to do so: to see the world from another person's perspective. Rosemarie Garland-Thomson applies Eve Sedgwick's formulation of the "universalizing/minoritizing" view of sexuality to feminist disability studies to argue that feminist disability theory's constituency extends beyond the boundaries of the disabled community, or the feminist community, but instead affects everyone (Garland-Thomson 363). The intersectionality is the point; the interconnectedness of humans' experience provides multiple points of identification with others who do not fit into the socially constructed idea of "normalcy." These multiple identifications encourage us to rethink "normalcy" and consider the possibility that it is not the autistic person who is "strange" but instead the social norms that exclude them.

Notes

1. In this essay I will use identity-first language except in sentences structured to make person-first language more appropriate. In addition, I will use the terms "autistic" and "non-autistic" rather than "neurodiverse" or "neurodivergent" and "neurotypical." Like the scholars whose work I cite, I would like to challenge readers' ideas about what is "normal."

2. "Point of ritual death" is a term used by Pamela Regis in *A Natural History of the Romance Novel* to describe the lowest point of the romance narrative, the moment when the union of the love interests seems impossible (35).

3. In April 2019, I presented an earlier version of this essay at the Popular Culture Association's national conference. A conference-goer tweeted about my suspicion that the author intended Charlotte to be read as autistic, and Thomas herself replied "She intended that. :)"

4. Oliver Sacks' profile of Temple Grandin, an animal behavior specialist and noted spokesperson for autism, quotes Grandin, who is autistic, as saying that among other people, she feels like "an anthropologist from Mars" (Sacks). The children's television show *Arthur* echoes this comparison in the 2010 episode "When Carl Met George," in which a non-autistic character makes friends with an autistic character.

Works Cited

Ashley, Jennifer. *The Madness of Lord Ian Mackenzie*. Kindle ed. Berkley, 2011.
Bartmess, Elizabeth. "Autistic Representation and Real-Life Consequences: An In-Depth Look." *Disability in KidLit*. 18 December 2015, http://disabilityinkidlit.com/2015/12/18/autistic-representation-and-real-life-consequences/.
Berubé, Michael. *The Secret Life of Stories: From Don Quixote to Harry Potter, How Understanding Intellectual Disability Transforms the Way We Read*. Kindle ed. New York UP, 2016.
Cheyne, Ria. *Disability, Literature, Genre: Representation and Affect in Contemporary Fiction*. Liverpool UP, 2019.
Cuthbert, Kate. "Consenting Adults: Kate Cuthbert on the Romance Novel and Representations of Sexuality after #MeToo." *Books + Publishing*. 12 September 2018, https://www.

booksandpublishing.com.au/articles/2018/09/12/115350/consenting-adults-kate-cuthbert-on-the-romance-novel-and-representations-of-sexuality-after-metoo/.

Davis, Lennard. "Introduction: Disability, Normality, and Power." *The Disability Studies Reader*, 5th edition, edited by Lennard Davis, Routledge, 2017, pp. 1–14.

"Diagnostic Criteria." *Centers for Disease Control and Prevention*, 29 June 2020, www.cdc.gov/ncbddd/autism/hcp-dsm.html.

Esler, Philip F. "'All That You Have Done ... Has Been Fully Told to Me': The Power of Gossip and the Story of Ruth." *Journal of Biblical Literature*, vol. 137, no. 3, 2018, p. 645. EBSCOhost, doi:10.15699/jbl.1373.2018.348544.

Garland-Thomson, Rosemarie. "Integrating Disability: Transforming Feminist Theory." *The Disability Studies Reader*, 5th edition, edited by Lennard Davis, Routledge, 2017, pp. 360–380.

Haddon, Mark. *The Curious Incident of the Dog in the Night-Time*. Vintage, 2004.

Hibbert, Talia. *A Girl Like Her: A Small Town Romance*. Kindle ed. Nixon House, 2018.

Hoang, Helen. *The Kiss Quotient*. Kindle ed. Berkley, 2018.

"List of Autistic Fictional Characters." *Wikipedia*, 1 October 2020, en.wikipedia.org/wiki/List_of_autistic_fictional_characters.

Livesay, Tracy. *Love on My Mind*. Kindle ed. Avon Impulse, 2016.

Mitchell, David, and Sharon Snyder. "Narrative Prosthesis." *The Disability Studies Reader*, 5th edition, edited by Lennard Davis, Routledge, 2017, pp. 204–218.

Moon, Elizabeth. *The Speed of Dark*. Kindle ed. Ballantine, 2004.

Morreall, John. *Comedy, Tragedy, and Religion*. State U of New York P, 1999.

Murray, Stuart. *Representing Autism: Culture, Narrative, Fascination*. Liverpool UP, 2008.

Regis, Pamela. *A Natural History of the Romance Novel*. U of Pennsylvania P, 2003.

Reid, Penny. *Neanderthal Meets Human: A Smart Romance*. Cipher-Naught, 2013.

Roberts, Nora. *The Witness*. Kindle ed. Berkley, 2012.

Sacks, Oliver. "An Anthropologist on Mars." *New Yorker*, 27 December 1993. https://www.newyorker.com/magazine/1993/12/27/anthropologist-mars.

Shakespeare, Tom. "The Social Model of Disability." *The Disability Studies Reader*, 5th edition, edited by Lennard Davis, Routledge, 2017, pp. 195–203.

Simson, Graeme. *The Rosie Project*. Kindle ed. Penguin, 2013.

Thomas, Sherry. *The Hollow of Fear*. Kindle ed. Berkley, 2018.

_____. *A Scandal in Belgravia*. Kindle ed. Berkley, 2017.

_____. @sherrythomas. "She intended that" Twitter. 11:53 AM · 19 April 2019.

_____. *A Study in Scarlet Women*. Kindle ed. Berkley, 2016.

Tobia, Anthony, and Annmarie Toma. "Rethinking Asperger's: Understanding the DSM-5 Diagnosis by Introducing Sheldon Cooper." *Journal of Communications Disorders, Deaf Studies & Hearing Aids*, vol. 3, no. 4, December 2015, https://www.longdom.org/open-access/rethinking-asperger-s-understanding-the-dsm5-diagnosis-byintroducing-sheldon-cooper-2375-4427-1000146.pdf.

Westby, Carol. "Personal Narratives of Persons with High-Functioning Autism." *Word of Mouth*, vol. 26, no. 4, March 2015, pp. 6–9, doi:10.1177/1048395014566122a.

PART FIVE

Romance Tropes and Social Status

Women Policing Whiteness
Deviance and Surveillance in Contemporary Police Procedural Romance

Nattie Golubov

> *"Tough. Brass balls. Ice princess. Damn good at her job.
> Mercy wouldn't mind the descriptions for herself."*
> —Kendra Elliot, *A Merciful Silence*

> "As long as white people are not racially seen and named,
> they/we function as a human norm.
> Other people are raced, we are just people."
> —Richard Dyer, *White*

The fraught relationship between whiteness and the models of society implicit in the subgenre of the contemporary romance police procedural originates in the contradiction shaping the experience of the figure of the white professional female investigator, which "simultaneously depends on both the embracement and denial of whiteness" (Moon 179): in other words, female cops are rendered as white women through the creation of the illusion of a naturalized white social realm, while the novels simultaneously drain that whiteness of any mark of historical and structural embeddedness. The female cop is an empowered woman battling everyday sexism in a male-dominated institution, yet she is complicit in the definition and policing of social deviance: specifically the surveillance of boundaries between acceptable and undesirable varieties of whiteness. The female plainclothes detective is a representative of the state who believes in the efficacy and legitimacy of the law to represent and protect her particular social milieu against criminals who rupture the everyday fabric of this world: judicial and moral codes coincide to protect communal life. Yet as a woman negotiating the gendered power dynamics of hierarchical and patriarchal organizations, the heroine shares with the criminal a certain exceptionality, though unlike the murderer whose "abnormality" is coded as dangerous to the stability and coherence of the social order, her "weirdness" (Force, *Accusation* 129) is a heroic trait. Both figures are departures from a norm: while the criminal deviates from the standard for what is human (the white middle class embodied by the hard-working, upstanding citizen), the heroine challenges cultural assumptions about gender roles and abilities. However, her individualism and the assumption that her professional reputation is the result of her work ethic and determination, rest upon her possession of "an invisible package of unearned assets" (McIntosh 1) available due to her unacknowledged white privilege.

The complicity between white feminism and racism has been contested for over forty years, the subject of classic texts by bell hooks, Kimberlé Crenshaw and Moraga and Anzaldúa among many others, yet more recently, in the U.S., the discussion has reached a much wider audience by pointing to white women's wielding of white privilege. Media coverage of several social movements has prompted a critique of the whitewashing of the #MeToo phenomenon (Tambe, 2018), white women's roles in white supremacist movements such as the "Alt-Right," and the use of a rhetoric of victimization by white women policing public space (Mann, 2018). Framed by this contemporary moment, this essay takes up Dreama Moon's effort to "particularize white experience" (1998) so as to better understand the fictional depiction of the material and social effects of discourses that reproduce the conceptual and symbolic frameworks of white racial formations in romance procedurals. This "particularizing" of whiteness calls for the analysis of the specific social locations and power relations in which whiteness is enacted by specific bodies. The two contradictory yet interrelated discourses which work to create the figure of the bourgeois "good (white) girl" (181) studied by Moon are applicable to the contemporary white female cop and her world: "white solipsism" (the belief that whiteness is normative, pervasive and general rather than positioned and particular), and "whiteness-evasion" (the notion that whiteness and issues of race are not connected) (Moon 179). In procedural romance, the heroines' battles against both crime and sexism rely upon their loyalty to a (white) male-dominated institution to which they gain access because they are white women who reproduce and uphold the values, expectations, aspirations and morals of their class: their whiteness is disavowed as the bedrock of their race and class loyalty and solidarity (Moon 195), although their whiteness is manifestly inscribed in their bodies and classed habits.

The power of the heroines' whiteness is instantiated in the color of their "investigative, and knowledgeable gaze," coded as an act of "visual transgression [because of] their desire to see and know" (*Dangerous* 209); Jeffrey Brown argues that contemporary female investigators are, by virtue of their profession, active lookers in command of the dominant narrative view who refuse to be simply objects of male visual pleasure, so have claimed for themselves the "right to look" (*Dangerous* 213). The challenge of this commanding look, often remarked upon in the narratives, does not go unpunished, however: in all three series under consideration here, the heroines become targets of violence for meddling. Samantha (Sam) Holland is punched in the face by an irate married colleague whose family life unravels when, in the course of one of her inquiries, she discovers his infidelity. Mercy Kilpatrick is captured and beaten by white militia men: "*The things I do for justice. And my own curiosity*" she thinks to herself (Elliot, *Secret* 169). Thus, their active looking, which is ultimately an "epistemological quest" (Brown, *Dangerous* 227) to accumulate knowledge by *looking for* and *through* evidence, motives and deceit, sets them up for reprisal because they cross a gendered line when their inquiring gaze is turned upon men's actions, thus upsetting the conventional structure of looking.

Brown suggests that action heroines are also "lookers," objects of male desire, and these heroines are no exception. Though their sexual desirability is downplayed in public (all three dress for the comfort required by their daily routines), their beauty is remarked upon in passing by other characters. Lacey Sherlock's eyes are "blue as a June sky" (Coulter, *Insidious* 102), she is described as a "sweet-as-a-daisy woman with her vivid red hair and beautiful blue eyes" (*Whiplash* 107); Sam's "pale blue eyes" (Force, *Affair* 21) command "perp" and "cop" (*Justice* 232) stares, and Mercy's green-eyed gaze is described as "probing and measuring" (Elliot, *Truth* 52) as well as "penetrating" (169). Sherlock in particular acquires an almost otherworldly status: "The woman was tall, dressed in black pants, a crisp white shirt, black boots on her feet. She looked like a sprite or a redheaded fairy princess with blue eyes, a lovely smile, and no hard edges to her" (Coulter, *Power* 74).

In the white imaginary, blue and green eyes are identified as long-standing markers of a whiteness associated with moral and spiritual values such as purity, honesty, innocence and transparency, while darkness is coded as black and masculine. Thus it is no coincidence that, although Dillon Savich, Sherlock's husband, initially has "soft summer-sky blue" eyes (Coulter, *Maze* 20), they darken as the series progresses; Nick Cappuano, Sam's husband, has hazel eyes and is "Olive-toned" because of his Italian mother (Force, *Affair* 42) and Truman Daly has "honest" brown eyes (Elliot, *Death* 41). Anger and desire deepen the darkness of their gazes, a transformation that underscores the potency of the heroes' masculinity. Richard Dyer notes that white men are seen as divided between their powerful sex drives (coded as dark and dangerous) and great "will power" (27), often exercised to control their desires. As a result of this internal division, personal struggles involve "not being able to resist the drives or with struggling to master them" (Dyer 27); that is, darkness is an integral element of whiteness and must be dominated: "Nick's expression darkened, but he held his tongue" (Force, *Deception* 222). Here there need not be an explicit reference to race for darkness to acquire meaning within a racialized regime of representation; indeed, as Dyer notes, it is precisely because of the presence of darkness in the white man that he can assume the "position as the universal signifier for humanity. He encompasses all the possibilities for human existence, the darkness and the light" (28). Consistent with this regime, descriptions of white heroines also use "racially encoded language" and imagery (Burley 21) as noted above, reinforcing the association of darkness with (white) male desire. As we shall see, in contrast to white heroes, the generally white criminals are incapable of self-control.

The popularity and volume of romantic suspense are overwhelming, encompassing other subgenres driven by intrigue and featuring many types of protagonists and storyworlds. Here I will focus on series by three seasoned romance authors, based upon two criteria: they can be categorized as police procedurals because of their detailed descriptions of the "investigative processes, of command and communication structures, and the way knowledge is shared and institutional resources used" (Messent 175) and the protagonists are professional law enforcers. Catherine Coulter's ongoing FBI series, which she began to publish in 1996, Marie Force's Fatal series, starting in 2010 (and continued as the First Family series as of 2021), and Kendra Elliot's completed Oregon-based series illustrate the diverseness of the subgenre, yet they are similar in that whiteness is an unmarked normative identity. In other words, race usually means nonwhiteness while whiteness is a "non-color, the absent presence or hidden referent, against which all other colors are measured as forms of deviance" (Ahmed, "Declarations" 1).

In these series, class and race reinforce each other to produce white privilege (Sullivan, *Good* 7), which comes with "education, money, and the lifestyle and personal appearance that both of those provide" (Sullivan, *White* 17). White "middle-class goodness" is entangled with class privilege, and "moral badness" (Sullivan, *Good* 5) becomes attached to an undesirable whiteness, which is often—though not exclusively—either lower-class and rural or, at the other extreme, a property of the extremely wealthy or powerful: the American professional middle class is depicted as "normative, and average, also ideal, so that when [they] work to benefit others, this is seen as work which will allow 'them' to be more like 'us'" (McIntosh 1).

Irrespective of their specific institutional and geographical environments, the normative social milieu is predominantly white and middle-class: in the Fatal series the rich and powerful are capable of unspeakable evil, while it is the socially and culturally marginal in the Mercy Kilpatrick novels who commit atrocities. Privilege is established by the description of habits that are constitutive of the white self, ranging from "ontological expansiveness" (Sullivan, *Good* 20) to lifestyles, aspirations and expectations, including a sense of social obligation and public service. Sullivan explains that habits are "the mental and physical patterns of engagement with the world that operate without conscious attention or reflection. They fly under one's radar, so to speak, and are all the more effective precisely because they tend to function unnoticed" (*Revealing* 4). Habits are environmentally constituted, so they are located in "both the individual person and the world in which she lives" (*Revealing* 4), socially reproduced and individually practiced. White privilege, she argues, is the effect of these non-conscious habits, a predisposition to perceive the self, her possibilities and place in the world in particular ways.

The ideologies of meritocracy, familism and equal opportunity sustain white privilege. Characters of any color other than white are few in Coulter's novels and those that recur are a Latina housekeeper together with the black owner and employees of a jazz club in DC where the hero sings country westerns. Racialized others are altogether absent in Mercy's rural landscape, though there is a concerted effort to dignify that easily ridiculed social group identified as "white trash." Sam is a DC Metro cop whose homicide team includes three Hispanic people, one Italian and one African American woman (white men are the brass in the department), yet their individual stories of upward mobility and their hard-earned membership to the cop family reinforce the symbolic power of middle-class whiteness. From this it would be wrong to conclude that the characters are racist, or that there is a denial of racism, though it may be read as a strand of well-meaning, middle-class white liberal anti-racism (*Good* 5): these narrative worlds are marked by color blindness, the belief that "people are just people, and to treat them as raced is to treat them unfairly and even discriminate against them" (*Good* 85).

Race or ethnicity does not significantly shape the identity of non-white characters or in any way affect their assimilation into the police family: indeed, there is an implicit suggestion that "diversity involves a degree of assimilation to white middle-class/upper-middle-class norms" (Doane 19), facilitated by the rhetoric of equal opportunities in the workplace and a belief in meritocracy. Federico (Freddie) Cruz and Tommy "Gonzo" Gonzales embody this process: Cruz, Sam's partner, is initially a religious "virgin hero" (Allan 2011) whose Swedish love interest has "white blond hair, icy blue eyes" (Force, *Affair* 153), while Gonzo marries a petite, blonde, blue-eyed deputy chief of staff (*Affair* 68). If whiteness can be "attached" to non-white bodies because it is a form of "property with prosthetic qualities" (Preston 332), Gonzo and Freddie integrate into "the family in blue" (*Reckoning* 17) by attenuating their cultural difference and marrying into whiteness.

Police procedurals place the responsibility of crime fighting on the "right persons with visible authority," a legitimate authority materialized in the "badge and the revolver" (Primasita and Ahimsa-Putra 36). These emblems bestow upon female cops power over civilians, mediating between the authority of abstract law and the social order it upholds. But the symbolic force of gun and badge relies upon the confidence and conviction with which they are wielded, a bodily disposition that has become second nature as a result of training and experience. For example, Sherlock has a "no-nonsense stride" (Coulter, *Backfire* 15); Mercy "exude[s] focus and intensity" (Elliot, *Silence* 349). The heroines are secure in their ability to protect themselves against the physical and verbal aggression to which they are routinely exposed: Sam's mouthiness and Sherlock's comebacks are weapons. Yet their fearlessness and secure sense of self are enabled by their "ontological expansiveness," a term used by Sharon Sullivan to name the white habit "of assuming and acting as if any and all spaces—geographical, psychological, cultural, linguistic, or whatever—are rightfully available to and open for white people to enter whenever they want" (*Good* 20).

Although their authority is hard-earned, it is also inherited: they begin their careers in law enforcement and thus obtain their success in part due to their "unearned assets." First of all, both Sherlock and Sam are "surrounded by father figures who aid them in their adventures and ensure their sovereignty in the symbolic realm of paternal law enforcement" (Brown, *Dangerous* 14). The "police in the family" trope is typical of cop novels (Panek, *American* 38) and figures in different ways in the Fatal and FBI series. Sherlock prefers to be addressed by her surname. As characters comment upon the reference to Holmes, she invariably invokes her father, Cormac Sherlock: "My dad's a federal judge; it suits him even better. Criminals and defense lawyers do a double take" (Coulter, *Nemesis* 24). Sam chooses to retain her paternal surname at work and use her husband's surname when she navigates his domain. She lives to fulfill her father's desire for a son, "trying to fill that void for him" (Force, *Reckoning* 45), so when she talks about her "balls" she is metonymically appropriating phallic power: "'We get to stand around and sweat our balls off while the ME does her thing,' she tells her partner Freddie. 'I hesitate to point out, Lieutenant, that you don't actually have balls to sweat off.' 'You know what I mean!'" (Force, *Threat* 9). Mercy may seem to be an exception to this rule because she has been banished from the family circle for challenging her father's "patriarchal core" (Elliot, *Death* 238), yet she too inherits his symbolic power (he is respected in his community) together with the practical knowledge that translates into wealth in her social milieu: Mercy is a prepper because of him, and her "deep-boned philosophy" (*Secret* 43) that teaches "self-reliance" (Death 95), makes her an outstanding agent: "Good preparation. It's like gold" (*Death* 95).

Family connections are the mainspring from—and with—which the heroines orient their lives, are embedded in whiteness and learn to inhabit it, embody it as an array of habits, affective dispositions and possibilities. The trope of the precinct as family extends the dynamics of familism beyond the personal world into the workplace. The ideology of familism sustains a "model of social organization, based on the prevalence of the family group and its well-being placed against the interests and necessities of each one of its members. It is part of a traditional view of society that highlights loyalty, trust, and cooperative attitudes within the family group" which, by analogy, characterizes other forms of organization and sociality anchored in group-interest and well-being (Garzón 546). Not only does shared whiteness carry material advantages such as wealth and property, employment opportunities, prestige and different types of capital, it is a habitus, to use Pierre Bourdieu's concept; it naturalizes racial privilege (Pinder 2015). Here family is more than an ideal form of social organization, it is also the environment in which the heroines learn to be white and, as mothers, pass the habit down, thus proving the effectiveness of "family familiarity" (Sullivan, *White* 33) in inculcating white habits.

Each series will serve to illustrate a particular point. I have mentioned that recent representations of female investigators emphasize the command of the gaze as an act of empowerment. In Coulter's series it is through the trained gaze of FBI agents that the loving gaze and the controlling "electronic eye" of contemporary forms of vigilance, a "looking *after* and looking *over*" (Lyon 3), become part of a continuum linking the realm of the intimate with public life, if we define surveillance as "the focused, systematic and routine attention to personal details for purposes of influence, management, protection or direction" (Lyon 14). The Fatal series explores the gendered dynamics of the police procedural; of the three writers, Force foregrounds the tensions between private family dynamics and working public life as well as the gendered experience of corporeal boundaries and sexual violence (Sam miscarries when a suspect punches her abdomen [*Consequences* 292]). Elliot's six-book series delves into a world that is largely absent in romance: Eagle's Nest is a tiny, remote, less than idyllic town, poverty-stricken and "packed with characters" (*Death* 39), a location in stark contrast to the pastoral towns more frequent in "Main Street" romance (novels by Robyn Carr and Linda Howard immediately come to mind). This series best illustrates how "poor white trash is a boundary term that speaks equivocally and ambivalently to the question of belonging and membership in the category white, and one that mobilizes a wide array of social differences to do so" (Wray, 139). The "bad" whites who disrupt small-town life fail to live up to "middle-class expectation of white behavior" (Sullivan, *Good* 30).

Coulter describes how the middle-class norm becomes hegemonic. The FBI novels have at least two strong plot lines: one unites a new couple and another develops the relationship between the nuclear pair of agents, Lacey Sherlock and Dillon Savich, her husband and boss, an MIT graduate who creates and leads the Criminal Apprehension Unit specialized in the use of "databases and data-mining programs to help catch criminals" (*Blindside* 80). His delocalized form of information gathering mediated through Max, Savich's laptop, is not the all-seeing eye of a panoptical Big Brother which concentrates data in one fixed location, but a mobile node in a dense network of flows. By collecting information from a wide variety of databases, routine investigative work, personal information retrieved from dataveillance and biometric technology, Savich's software makes visible those details of citizens' lives that are otherwise dispersed or hidden. Transparency here is a means to sort people into the good and the bad as they take shape based upon the intelligence gathered about them.

Hence civilians are presented as bundles of data that become evidence of criminality when interpreted with suspicion and assembled with reference to taken-for-granted assumptions about criminal behavior. A "regime of the norm" in which "normalized and normalizing perceptions, prescriptions, and sanctions" (Miller vii) separates the good from the morally questionable, thus defining deviancy and affirming the moral authority of the norm, embodied by the federal agents and the social milieu to which they belong. The overarching message of the series is that "good people (i.e., trustworthy figures of authority) are watching" (Steenberg and Tasker 132).

One social sorting technique is the "surveillant gaze" (Bell 1). As a result of their training, Coulter's agents develop the skill to regulate their voices and gaze in such a way that these may be deployed as techniques for intimidation, as weapons (they are all very good marksmen) and a form of control: whenever she looks over a crime scene, Sherlock puts "it all together in her mind, using her special gift to picture what few people could see at a crime scene" (*Backfire* 195). The disciplined attention required of them is contrasted to what I will call the loving eye, following Marilyn Frye. The private lives of suspects are monitored and publicly exhibited, their body language examined for signs of guilt or duplicity. Murderers' eyes are uniformly described as "a fathomless void" (*Enigma* 187) or "flat as a stagnant pond" (*Backfire* 568), so unreflective that they communicate nothing because the "blackness inside" (*Maze* 292) absorbs all light. Criminals are often either dehumanized "monsters" or simply objectified: Sherlock refers to the serial killer known as the Toaster as "it" in *The Maze* (53). Significantly, the surveillant gaze reads the criminal as a member of a group: this is the work of profiling.

In contrast, the eyes of the beloved are expressive, brimming with emotion for the attentive loving gaze that lacks the "presupposition that the other poses a constant threat or that the other exists for the seer's service" and does not simplify the other by assimilating it to what is already known and expected (Frye 74). The agent who gazes with a loving eye acknowledges the independence and separateness of the beloved, accepts the other's complexity and is generous to this object because s/he recognizes the boundaries of the self in that s/he does not seek to assimilate the other but learns to know the individual other as different. There is no desire to define, control, or slot the beloved into a category, which is precisely how the vigilant FBI gaze identifies deviants. However, in both scenarios the gaze is used to unveil what is hidden beneath the surface of everyday normality, making the invisible visible so as to give meaning to and normalize individual behavior by embedding the other's story in a familiar narrative, precisely the task of any detective in crime fiction. Thus, the gradual process of discovering and understanding the beloved and resolving a puzzle in order to punish evil emerge as parallel journeys of discovery which involve professional investigative ways of seeing. Their concern for the protection of civilians and public space becomes coextensive with the safety of the family, loved ones and domestic space.

Profiling individuals according to their family history is a way of mapping the social world onto class distinctions and geographies. The lifestyle and social world represented by the Savich and Sherlock marriage are exhibited as a cultural and social norm, set up as *background*, to use Luc Boltanski's (3) concept to refer to a stable reality of habitual, pre-established forms, practices, meanings and relatively predictable causal relations. Against this background, generally depicted as unproblematic, crime fiction presents a mystery as a singularity whose character can be identified as *abnormal* because it "breaks with the way things present themselves under conditions that we take to be normal" (Boltanski 3).

Of particular interest here is that in crime fiction reality is a network of causal relations that holds together the events with which experience is confronted; in other words, a network that makes it possible to give meaning to events that are produced by identifying the entities to which these events must be attributed. For example, in Coulter's novels serial killers are entities invariably portrayed as monstrous psychopaths who are incapable of controlling their pathological hunger for violence because it is genetic, and it is through psychological profiling that their extremely violent crimes—usually of a sexual nature—are given meaning.

In contrast to the faulty genetics inherited from deviant parents and grandparents, the FBI agents are personally connected to a stable social order buttressed by representatives of the worlds of finance, politics, the military, industry, media, arts and the judiciary. When one of their own turns to crime it is often because of a single-minded pursuit of strictly individual objectives with no consideration for the common good, as is expected of them because of their class allegiances. They are asocial rather than monstrous because they are overcome by their passions, no threat to the public at large as their grievances are personal rather than nonspecific.

The FBI social milieu has a "socially agreed morality" (Evans 22) and is offered as a desirable world presented as a national network of middle-class nuclear families that are mutually interconnected through consanguinity and friendship. Marriage integrates individuals into this network, so all newly formed couples join the privileged socio-professional milieus, often welcomed into the fold by a symbolic meal at the Sherlock and Savich home while, in a contrary move, the irruption of evil in the fragile fabric of the everyday is expressed as the devastation of family, the community destroyed by a "perturbation of a 'normal,' peaceful state of things" and subsequently restored (Zizek 2). For the purposes of plot, the bad guys are always punished, the motives for crime explained as particular rather than social (Evans 2), but the serial format and the multiple plot lines suggest that the battle is never won, although state power, continuously operating through its authorized agents and the technologies they command, penetrates beyond appearances to the evil that lies within civil society.

This is not a faceless state power but one in which authority is invested in individuals who have particular characteristics: white, college-educated, able-bodied, heterosexual, socially conformist and politically conservative, their daily domestic routines and consumer behavior are representative of middle-class whiteness. Clearly these agents are not outsiders: for the members of the Unit, the social order is worth defending and indeed constitutes reality itself, although clearly allegiance to the nation translates into loyalty to a particular class with easy access to places, people and resources, often with inherited economic, cultural and social capital. Savich's father was a notable FBI agent, his grandmother a famous painter from whom he inherits an artistic sensibility, a house and works of art worth millions; Sherlock is a talented pianist who turned away from a musical education at Berkeley and Julliard to earn a B.S. in Forensic Science and a Master's in Criminal Psychology from Berkeley. The portrayal of female agents registers the general equalizing shift in crime fiction (Evans 114), yet their hypermasculine male partners are feminized (Savich is artistic, intuitive, vegetarian, does not swear), perhaps another strategy to deflect the association of violence with the agents of law enforcement and a criticism of certain types of masculinity.

Coulter's social world is divided into three groups: the good, the traitors, and the monsters. The first two belong to the professional urban middle and upper middle classes. The good adhere to a "general order that is indissolubly legal, moral and economic" (Boltanski 109), whereas the traitors commit crimes against their own class, implying that privilege must be tempered by a moral code that expects them to take on their communal responsibilities and patriotic loyalty. Monsters generally come from rural areas and deviant families, the parent-child relationship corrupted by mental illness. In Coulter's world killers are born, not made (Evans 125): Ted Bundy's daughter features in *Split Second*.

Murderers are placed outside the boundaries of normality and become a social threat when they move from the isolation of rural areas to urban space; on a few occasions their cultural dislocation explains their evil intent: for example, in *Power Play* one of the aggressors is the son of a British aristocrat who has converted to Islam, in *Double Take* Xavier Makepeace is a professional assassin whose father was white and his mother a black Jamaican, in *Backfire* Xian Xu is Chinese-American who passes as Caucasian and is a Chinese spy. Simultaneously, their deviancy reinforces our sense of the ordinariness represented by the private lives of FBI agents and the network radiating out from the central hub of Savich's (family) unit in Washington.

The novels are conservative in this respect, because the state is recognized as the only entity with the power to ensure order throughout the country, suggesting also that we are dealing with a polity that is governable, that the sanctioned surveillance of individual privacy is in the national interest, and that the agents have the training as well as the social and cultural capital to move between social milieus and understand their internal dynamics sufficiently to be able to identify a break with the norm that governs them. Sherlock explains early on that "The FBI is a group, not an individual. Loyalty is to the Bureau, not any single person" (*Maze* 100); yet this "corporate hero" (Winston and Mellerski 6) is also a model of society based on a "utopian vision of cooperation between the police and society" (Winston and Mellerski 7).

Marie Force's series also individualizes detectives and foregrounds teamwork, yet the driving force behind the fast-paced plots is fast-talking lieutenant Holland. Each novel allots equal narrative time to the investigative processes involved in the resolution of a case and Sam's personal life, reflecting the major themes explored in the series: the struggle to balance responsibilities at home and at work, the challenge of "being of both professionally strong and romantically feminine" (Brown, *Beyond* 19), life-affirming when death is her trade (Jackson 3). Since fictional female detectives are no longer a novelty, Force's portrayal focuses on the challenges of Sam's power as a lieutenant in an institution harboring an old boys' network and the tension between her roles as non-traditional daughter, mother, sibling and wife, defined by her work rather than by her looks or marriage: "She loved being Nick's wife, but on the job she preferred being known for her own accomplishments rather than who she'd married" (*Mistake* 78).

The serial form allows for more nuanced understanding of how the habits of whiteness are enacted. Although emphasis is placed on the fact that Sam, her squad, and her family are solidly middle-class good white people, Sam's white privilege enables her behavior on the job, aggressively interviewing suspects, threatening liars, fearlessly confronting powerful men and women and forcefully tough-talking against sexist abuse. Her boss, Uncle Joe, lets her "get away with everything except murder itself in running her investigations and her division" (*Mistake* 23). Sam also relies upon an extensive support system, including an efficient housekeeper/cook/nanny/personal assistant, family members, and staff at the White House when she becomes the vice president's wife: "We're very lucky to be able to have a family and two demanding careers. I'm under no illusions that we could do it without our village" (*Accusation* 205). Sam can work a case around the clock and also nurture her personal relationships because her "village" solves the practicalities of her everyday domestic life. Not having a double workday is privilege, not "luck." Needless to say, her husband (like Savich and Daly) admires, accommodates, and facilitates her single-minded dedication to the job and repairs its emotional and psychological toll.

Indeed, her class origins and upward mobility grant her access to the world of White House politics as a cop and the wife of the vice president (and later president) of the United States; she is morally equipped to weed out corruption and unethical activity. In her world, many criminals belong to the "one percent" (*Invasion* 167): one running joke is Sam's dislike of their "obnoxious" doorbells (*Mistake* 185). Their conviction that they are untouchable, above the law that she is sworn to enforce, is morally objectionable and an affront to the value system she represents: "Entitlement and all the things Sam hated most about rich people who thought they owned the world" (*Mistake* 145). Criminals are self-interested, overbearing and treat people as commodities; incapable of controlling their impulses, in their pursuit of wealth and power they overstep the boundaries of socially acceptable behavior.

Whiteness is lived as a "background to experience" (Ahmed, "Phenomenology" 150), a set of givens including lifestyles, life choices, worldviews and subjective positions which are also the basis of investigative work: the inferences and speculation required in police work are often achieved through Sam's famous "gut that never let her down" (Force,

Accusation 191). Boltanski suggests that cops have split personalities in that their identities, practices and moral dispositions are divided between the properties conferred upon them by their status as civil servants and their own personal properties, inasmuch as they are like any other person—an ordinary person although not just anyone (74). Sam's divided nature means that her power of interpretation is located at the point where both sides coincide: her roles in the home and upbringing foster her "gut" recognition of suspicious behavior on the job, a causal attribution that signals a break from a normalcy which she strives for and embodies:

> "She's too nervous for my liking. I feel like she knows something else that she's not telling us."
> "Could she be nervous after having found her boss strangled?"
> "Sure, but I sense this is something more. She's too skittish."
> "I'll call Green and tell him to get everyone on it."
> "Tell him the lieutenant is having one of her feelings" [*Accusation* 192].

Likewise, when a woman is found dead and in the course of the investigation Sam discovers that she has had several sexual partners, she applies a form of discernment that is moralistic, despite her awareness that she should not be judgmental:

> Sam tried not to judge other women for the choices they made. God knows, she didn't want anyone judging her. But this was a tough one. Tara had slept with the most high-profile man in the world [*Accusation* 93].

Although Sam explicitly states that the victim should not be remembered solely as a woman whose sexual choices may have been misguided, if we apply Anita Harris' distinction between "can-do" and "at-risk" girls (Harris 2005), there is an unarticulated assumption that although certain practices do not in any way justify male violence, they place women at greater risk of becoming victims of male violence, a lesson learned by her niece, who sneaks out of boarding school and ends up being drugged and gang-raped (*Jeopardy* 62).

Emphasis is placed on the fact that blame is never on the victims, yet there is a recognition that in a world where gender violence is ubiquitous, certain femininities will be punished while others will be rewarded:

> Someone like Ramsey expected promotions and awards to come his way for just showing up and doing the bare minimum each day. It infuriated him that Sam had made lieutenant over him when he'd had more years on the job, but he hadn't used those years as productively as she had. She'd taken full advantage of every opportunity that had come her way and had busted her ass for the rank she now held. To hear him tell it, the only reason she still had a job, let alone the rank of lieutenant overseeing one of the most critical divisions in the department, was because her dad was the chief's best friend [Accusation 196].

Harris points out that many of the aspirations and ideals of the middle class are "fundamentally associated with whiteness" (102). "Can-do" femininity is identifiable by key motifs, including a commitment to exceptional careers and planning for them, a belief in women's capacity to invent themselves and succeed because they are self-actualizing, driven and resilient and display a consumer lifestyle (Sam has a vast wardrobe, loves her Louboutin heels, her wedding dress is designed by Vera Wang). In contrast, the victim of the novel places herself "at-risk" because she deliberately leaks her affair with the President of the Unites States in an effort to regain his attention (*Accusation* 296), lying about the paternity of her child.

Sam is a privileged "can-do" white woman who can choose where to live, has the freedom of movement authorized by her badge as she boldly performs police routines in public and private spaces. She and Nick corroborate the myth of a meritocratic social order: he comes from "humble beginnings" and is familiar with "the struggles of regular people" (*Accusation* 126), a scholarship student at Harvard from a broken home who has earned his reputation through hard work, integrity, and good behavior. Yet they both partake of the legacies of whiteness expressed in the conviction that they can achieve—and deserve—whatever they desire so long as they do not betray their own class origins. Thus, in tune with popular concepts of self-improvement and self-fulfillment (Dolby 21), Sam overcomes her dyslexia to obtain a graduate degree in criminal justice from George Washington (and incurring debt), her dream to become a mother despite her endometriosis comes true through her adoption of three children, and she prevails in a sexist hostile workplace when she unearths police and political corruption while searching for the shooter who ultimately causes her father's untimely death.

Although she hates "the way her world and Nick's continued to overlap. In a perfect world, her professional and personal lives would be entirely separated. Sadly, she didn't live in a perfect world" (*Jeopardy* 110), the further Nick rises in the political world the more popular she becomes, a notoriety that hinders her performance at work, but an interesting blurring of boundaries that confirms their middle-class authenticity:

> "The two of you are what the rest of us aspire to be. When I first met you, I wondered whether your public persona was too good to be true. But after spending time with you and getting to know you both, I tell everyone who asks that you guys are every bit the real deal that you appear to be" [*Accusation* 173].

Not only are they the "real deal," that is, they are what they seem, there is no deception, but they are also down to earth: "We try to keep it real. I can't imagine either of us getting caught up in the nonsense that goes along with his job'" (*Chaos* 63). They both remain "true to themselves" (*Chaos* 63), suggesting that celebrity, status, or wealth need not be corrupting influences if they remain loyal to their origins. Criminals are infrequently what they seem; they feel unfairly treated or aspire to something to which they feel entitled. They are inauthentic, and their true identities are finally revealed.

Kendra Elliot's series illustrates Sharon Sullivan's claim that liberal white anti-racism shores up the racial goodness of white liberals by "expelling white trash from the realm of proper whiteness" (*Good* 8). To be fair, Elliot describes a poverty-stricken rural landscape and resists stereotyping poor whites: Mercy, a returning insider, interprets the area's impoverishment for outsiders as a conflict between regional realities and federal policies: "The mill was a victim of poor economics, federal policies on tree harvests, and increased conservation measures" (*Death* 26). Subsequently, the sheriff explains the source of local anti-government feeling:

> "It's like a line of dominoes. Usually the first domino is tipped over by having their homes foreclosed on. Something personal happened ... either they got ill and racked up huge medical bills or they lost their job and couldn't find another. They have to choose whether to feed their kids or pay the mortgage. Guess which is going to come first? (...) Suddenly the home that's been in their family for decades is ripped from under them and their credit rating is destroyed. They need a place to live. They need a job and they need their pride restored" [*Death* 81].

Among the "families, retirees, ranchers, farmers, cowboys, millennials, and business professionals" inhabiting the city of Bend, "farther out (...) the population drastically thinned and tended toward ranchers and farmers.... Some wanted to live on their own terms without relying on the government for their safety or food supply. Sometimes they were called preppers; other times they were called unpleasant names" (*Truth* 36). These are the "good" whites whose lives border with those of other types of survivalists, militia men, patriots and sovereign citizens, shown to be "bad" whites.

"Good" preppers are not "hoarders" (*Death* 96) as Daly describes them before he fully grasps the purpose of stockpiling and survival-skill development. In his study of survivalism, Philip Lamy claims that at "one end of the spectrum" of this subculture are the "'boy scout' survivalists, who aim to be 'prepared' for potentially difficult times; at the other end are white supremacists, anti-government zealots, and apocalyptic cults" (14). Elliot's series resists the idea of a continuum by exploring secular survivalism exclusively as disaster preparedness divested of anti-government feeling. Mercy is neither a religious fanatic nor a millenarian, she does not believe in militarism, conspiracy theories, white supremacism, or extreme-right messianism. Rather, it is as a female FBI agent born and bred on a farm that she frames her need for preparedness, ensuring the long-term availability of "nutrition, hydration, shelter, security, hygiene, and medicine" (Mills 1).

Initially, Mercy is described as extremely reserved and very professional. The intensity of her fear of "TEOTWAWKI. The end of the world as we know it" (*Death* 18) eases somewhat as she sheds her skittishness to assemble a family with Truman Daly, the sheriff who exudes "stability, integrity, and honor" (*Secret* 137), his protégé Ollie, Mercy's niece Kaylie, and their pets. The significance of her secluded cabin shifts accordingly. If at first it "was her lifeline. Her center. Her balance" (*Secret* 29), by the end she is centered by her family. The fifteen-year rift with her father is repaired and the wedding which closes the series attests to her integration into the social world of Eagle's Nest. The house she has rebuilt with Truman is no longer the post-apocalyptic, isolated, self-enclosed bunker for one but becomes a sheltering family home.

Her underlying anxiety about future disasters is assuaged when her reclusive life becomes populated by family and friends: "she suddenly had a small crowd to care about. It hadn't weakened her foundation. She was stronger" (*Secret* 82). Mercy learns that preparedness need not be "*a selfish philosophy*" (*Secret* 118) when she realizes that the prepper model of community is ideal: "Her father had a small circle of people who subscribed to his beliefs, ready to have one another's back in time of need. Each person brought a valuable skill to the exclusive community. Midwifery, livestock health, plumbing, electronics, medicine" (*Secret* 118). Truman, in turn, learns to appreciate Mercy's survival skills when he escapes the sovereign citizens who have kidnapped and tortured him only to endure the outdoors with the help of Ollie, a self-sufficient adolescent who has lived alone in a shack in the woods for several years.

"She was one of the most driven people he'd ever met. She set goals and smashed the hell out of them. College on her own? She graduated top of her class. Get accepted into the FBI? Again, she graduated at the top of her class. Give her orphaned niece a home? Boom ... done. Find a killer? She didn't hold back" (*Secret* 215). Mercy's strong, independent spirit is a habit learned from her father's model of fiercely independent selfhood and the sociality of an autonomous prepper community. Her prepper habits facilitate her adjustment to the dynamics of the police precinct and FBI field office, which showcase new forms of policing (Panek, *American* 39) dependent upon the coordinated efforts of more specialized departments ranging from K-9 units to forensic experts and SWAT teams, among many others. She skillfully adapts her prepper skills to the workplace, thus severing the association between the backward "boonies" (Elliot, *Secret* 60) and a "can-do" ideal of womanhood, becoming whole by connecting the private "dirty little secret" (*Death* 222) of her survivalism to her life as an agent.

"Bad" whites are militaristic, self-aggrandizing, deluded misogynists motivated by greed, who imagine themselves to be strong leaders, or murderous heirs of pathologically deviant parents: in the first novel, the murderer is a ranch-hand seeking to ingratiate himself to his prepper boss and inherit his kingdom by stockpiling stolen weapons; in the second, the killer leads an anti-government militia, a "society formed by fear, paranoia, and isolation, not formed from freedom" (*Truth* 286). In the third novel, the wrongdoer is a deranged son who murders his own father and the mother of his illegitimate half-sister, his rage triggered by his betrayed mother's hatred and motivated by avarice. In the fourth novel, the serial killer is the son of a "falling-down, shit-faced, hateful angry drunk" (*Silence* 126), an abusive father and husband, while sovereign citizens do not hesitate to kill to protect their forgery scam. In the fifth novel, the criminals are an abusive ex-husband, the greedy participant of a notorious heist and a corrupt ex-FBI agent. The final tyrannical culprit leads a group of sexist patriotic militiamen, "America's Preserve," who traffic illegal weapons. In this context, law enforcers provide security to a community that feels abandoned by the state while they police the boundaries between different sorts of whiteness: not all survivalists are bad. Mercy's father hates militias, "he viewed them as a crude attempt at government, a masquerade of representing the little guy, usually led by someone with a big ego who simply wanted power" (*Truth* 306).

"Bad" white people are aberrant exceptions that fail to live up to the "middle-class expectation of white behavior" (Sullivan *Good* 30) by exhibiting undesirable traits: they are uneducated and stupid, like the anti-government sovereign citizens who spout nonsense in *A Merciful Silence* and believe themselves to be legitimately exempt from the law of an illegitimate U.S. government, or the Patriots who refuse to provide prenatal care to women and education to children (*Promise* 87); their bodies are problematic because they are "unclean" (Sullivan, *Good* 30), unwashed, alcoholic, as unkempt as their dwellings, and they breach proper white social etiquette (30): they shoot at anyone who approaches their hidden, dilapidated homes, for example, in contrast to the "salt of the earth people" (*Fate* 53) who look out for each other.

Procedurals emphasize the institutional and systemic framework of police work (Messent 177), but because of the centrality of the romance plot there is a happy ending that attenuates the critical potential of the genre, extending the utopian impulse of romance to encompass a "utopian vision of cooperation between the police and society" (Winston and Mellerski, 7). Indeed, Peter Messent suggests that the procedural focused on the team as extended family is less likely to question the dominant social system (181) than series which self-consciously reflect upon systemic corruption and "barely controlled chaos" (Winston and Mellerski 2) or problematic aspects of policing and surveillance, not least their systemic racism.

When Coulter, Elliot and Force individualize the members of a "corporate squad" (Winston and Mellerski 6), the faceless bureaucratic state apparatus becomes an engaging tightly knit community of like-minded individuals who restore and validate a particular social order. Leroy Panek points out that the single most enduring theme of the police novel has been the solace provided to the individual by belonging to the extended family of police officers whose solidarity rests upon the shared purpose to serve society in the struggle of good versus evil ("Post-War" 170). In Coulter's and Force's series the family is connected to the state, political power with economic power, society with the police in such a way that together they hold reality together (Boltanski 49). Elliot amplifies law enforcement's benevolent power in a white social context marked by a deep mistrust of the federal government when the survivalist central couple is as eccentric as their neighbors.

Romance and crime fiction are driven by a search for knowledge: as Sue Turnbull suggests, in the romance this knowledge is about the self and the other and closure is achieved at the level of the personal; in the crime story knowledge is about the crime and closure is achieved at the level of the social (75). The notion that these novels are restorative because the ordinary course of things is re-established (Evans 19) works well with the romance novels' redemptive impulse, although the "sense of normality" (Evans 49) is no longer grounded exclusively in private feeling but sustained by the institutional power of the state in a dominant social-moral order.

Works Cited

Ahmed, Sarah. "A Phenomenology of Whiteness." *Feminist Theory*, vol. 8, no. 2, August 2007, pp. 149–168, doi.org/10.1177/1464700107078139.

_____. "Declarations of Whiteness: The Non-Performativity of Anti-Racism." *Borderlands e-journal*, vol. 3, no. 2, 2004, pp. 1–14.

Allan, Jonathan A. "Theorising Male Virginity in Popular Romance Novels." *Journal of Popular Romance Studies*, vol. 2, no. 1, October 2011. www.jprstudies.org/2011/10/theorising-male-virginity/.

Bell, David. "Surveillance Is Sexy." *Surveillance & Society*, vol. 6, no. 3, 2009, pp. 203–212. ojs.library.queensu.ca/index.php/surveillance-and-society/article/view/3281/3244.

Boltanski, Luc. *Mysteries and Conspiracies. Detective Stories, Spy Novels and the Making of Modern Societies*. Polity, 2014.

Brown, Jeffrey A. *Beyond Bombshells: The New Action Heroine in Popular Culture*. UP of Mississippi, 2015.

_____. *Dangerous Curves: Action Heroines, Gender, Fetishism and Popular Culture*. UP of Mississippi, 2011.

Burley, Stephanie Carol. *Hearts of Darkness: The Racial Politics of Popular Romance*. U of Maryland, PhD Thesis, 2003.

Coulter, Catherine. *Backfire*. G.P. Putnam's Sons, 2012.

_____. *Blindside*. Jove, 2004.

_____. *The Cove*. G.P. Putnam's Sons, 1996.

_____. *Double Take*. Penguin, 2007.
_____. *Enigma*. Gallery Books, 2017.
_____. *Insidious*. Gallery Books, 2016.
_____. *The Maze*. Berkley Books, 1997.
_____. *Nemesis*. G.P. Putnam's Sons, 2015.
_____. *Paradox*. Gallery Books, 2018.
_____. *Power Play*. G.P. Putnam's Sons, 2014.
_____. *Split Second*. G.P. Putnam's Sons, 2011.
_____. *Whiplash*. G.P. Putnam's Sons, 2010.
Crenshaw, Kimberlé. "Demarginalizing the Intersection of Race and Sex: A Black Feminist Critique of Antidiscrimination Doctrine, Feminist Theory and Antiracist Politics." *Feminism and Politics*, edited by Anne Phillips, Oxford University Press, 1998, pp. 314–342.
Doane, Ashley ("Woody"). "Shades of Colorblindness: Rethinking Racial Ideology in the United States." *The Colorblind Screen: Television in Post-Racial America*, edited by Sarah Nilsen and Sarah. E. Turner, New York UP, 2014, pp. 15–38.
Dolby, Sandra K. *Self-Help Books: Why Americans Keep Reading Them*. U of Illinois P, 2005.
Dyer, Richard. *White*. Routledge, 2017.
Elliot, Kendra. *A Merciful Death*. Montlake Romance, 2017.
_____. *A Merciful Fate*. Montlake Romance, 2019.
_____. *A Merciful Promise*. Montlake Romance, 2019.
_____. *A Merciful Secret*. Montlake Romance, 2018.
_____. *A Merciful Silence*. Montlake Romance, 2018.
_____. *A Merciful Truth*. Montlake Romance, 2017.
Evans, Mary. *The Imagination of Evil. Detective Fiction and the Modern World*. Continuum, 2009.
Force, Marie. *Fatal Accusation*. Harlequin, 2019.
_____. *Fatal Affair*. Carina Press, 2010.
_____. *Fatal Chaos*. Harlequin, 2018.
_____. *Fatal Invasion*. Harlequin, 2018.
_____. *Fatal Jeopardy*. Carina Press, 2014.
_____. *Fatal Justice*. Carina Press, 2011.
_____. *Fatal Mistake*. Carina Press, 2013.
_____. *Fatal Reckoning*. Harlequin, 2019.
_____. *Fatal Threat*. Harlequin, 2017.
Frye, Marilyn. "In and Out of Harm's Way: Arrogance and Love." *The Politics of Reality: Essays in Feminist Theory*, edited by Marilyn Frye, The Crossing Press, 1983, pp. 52–83.
Garzón Pérez, Adela. "Familism." *International Encyclopedia of Marriage and Family*, edited by James J. Ponzetti, Jr., Thomson Gale, 2003, pp. 546–549.
Harris, Anita. *Future Girl: Young Women in the Twenty-First Century*. Routledge, 2005.
hooks, bell. *Ain't I a Woman. Black Women and Feminism*. South End Press, 1981.
Jackson, Christine A. *Myth and Ritual in Women's Detective Fiction*. McFarland, 2002.
Lamy, Philip. *Millennium Rage. Survivalists, White Supremacists, and the Doomsday Prophecy*. Springer, 1996.
Lyon, David. *Surveillance Studies. An Overview*. Polity, 2007.
Mann, Justin Louis. "What's Your Emergency? White Women and the Policing of Public Space." *Feminist Studies*, vol. 44, no 3, 2018, pp. 766–775. JSTOR, www.jstor.org/stable/pdf/10.15767/feministstudies.44.3.0766.pdf.
McIntosh, Peggy. "White Privilege: Unpacking the Invisible Knapsack." *Peace and Freedom*, July/August 1989.
Messent, Peter. "The Police Novel." *A Companion to Crime Fiction*, edited by Charles J. Rzepka and Lee Horsley, Wiley-Blackwell, 2010, pp. 175–186.
Miller, D.A. *The Novel and the Police*. University of California Press, 1988.
Mills, Michael F. "Obamageddon: Fear, the Far Right, and the Rise of 'Doomsday' Prepping in Obama's America." *Journal of American Studies*, June 2019, pp. 1–30. Cambridge Core, 10.1017/S0021875819000501.
Moon, Dreama. "White Enculturation and the Bourgeois Ideology. The Discursive

Production of 'Good (White) Girls.'" *Whiteness: The Communication of Social Identity*, edited by Thomas K. Nakayama and Judith N. Martin, Sage Publications, 1998, pp. 177–197.

Moraga, Cherríe, and Gloria Anzaldúa, editors. *This Bridge Called My Back. Writings by Radical Women of Color*. Kitchen Table: Women of Color Press, 1983.

Panek, Leroy L. "Post-war American Police Fiction." *The Cambridge Companion to Crime Fiction*, edited by Martin Priestman, Cambridge UP, 2003, pp. 155–171.

_____. *The American Police Novel*. McFarland, 2003.

Pinder, Sherrow O. *Colorblindness, Post-Raciality, and Whiteness in the United States*. Palgrave MacMillan, 2015.

Preston, John. "Prosthetic White Hyper-Masculinities and 'Disaster Education.'" *Ethnicities*, vol. 10, no. 3, 2010, pp. 331–343. Sage Journals, doi.org/10.1177/1468796810372299.

Primasita, Fitria Akhmerti, and Heddy Siri Ahimsa-Putra. "An Introduction to the Police Procedural: A Subgenre of the Detective Genre." *Humanoria*, vol. 31, no. 1, February 2019, pp. 33–40. jurnal.ugm.ac.id/jurnal-humaniora/article/view/15309, doi.org/10.22146/jh.15309.

Steenberg, Lindsay, and Yvonne Tasker. "'Pledge Allegiance': Gendered Surveillance, Crime Television, and Homeland." *Cinema Journal*, vol. 54, no. 4, Summer 2015, pp. 132–138. Project Muse, 10.1353/cj.2015.0042.

Sullivan, Shannon. *Good White People. The Problem with Middle-Class White Anti-Racism*. SUNY Press, 2014.

_____. *Revealing Whiteness. The Unconscious Habits of Racial Privilege*. Indiana UP, 2006.

_____. *White Privilege*. Polity, 2019.

Tambe, Ashwini. "Reckoning with the Silences of #MeToo." *Feminist Studies*, vol. 44, no.1, 2018. pp. 197–202. JSTOR, doi.org/10.15767/feministstudies.44.1.0197.

Turnbull, Sue. "'Nice dress, take it off': Crime, Romance and the Pleasure of the Text." *International Journal of Cultural Studies*, vol. 5, no. 1, January 2002, pp. 67–82. Sage Journals, doi.org/10.1177/13678779020050010501.

Winston, Robert P., and Nancy C. Mellerski. *The Public Eye: Ideology and the Police Procedural*. Palgrave Macmillan, 1992.

Wray, Matt. *Not Quite White: White Trash and the Boundaries of Whiteness*. Duke UP, 2006.

"I'm a *mehfil*, I'm a gathering to which everyone is invited"
Reading "Outcast" Romances in Arundhati Roy's Fiction

Lucky Issar

When Arundhati Roy's novel *The Ministry of Utmost Happiness* (2017) appeared, many readers thought its title to be an ironic one. The title is reminiscent of George Orwell's novel *1984*, in which ministries do the opposite of what they claim they do. Orwell's "Ministry of Love" is an armed fortress surrounded by "barbed-wire entanglements, steel doors, and hidden machine-gun nests" (6) in which the novel's central characters Winston and Julia are tortured for falling in love. Since Roy's *The Ministry of Utmost Happiness* engages with extreme situations involving blood, violence, and state-sanctioned torture, some of Roy's western readers thought that she used "magic realism" to tell "extreme stories" of present-day India.[1]

The novel opens with one such story. Anjum, a hijra (intersex) person, when left with no option, goes to live in a graveyard (after leaving her parental home, she joins the hijra house, Khwabgah, but later when she is compelled to leave Khwabgah, she has no place to go). Soon afterwards, the graveyard becomes a dwelling place for others who share Anjum's situation as society's outcasts; they call their abode in the graveyard the Jannat (Paradise) House. Despite their traumatic pasts and bleak presents, these outcast characters start afresh; they sing, laugh, and some of them fall in love. The seemingly realistic novel erupts with tiny signs of regeneration. Drawing upon the interplay of caste and romance tropes in a caste-based society, citizenship theory, and contemporary Indian culture, I will examine Roy's *The Ministry of Utmost Happiness* (2017), and compare it briefly with her first novel *The God of Small Things* (1997) to underscore that *The Ministry of Utmost Happiness*, despite its ultra-realistic mode, contains significant romance tropes. On the surface, the novel engages with caste violence, tribal unrest, and Kashmir conflict, but underneath, romance works in ways that challenge the dominance of a single brahminic narrative that emphasizes heteronormativity to retain caste-order.

Since the task of defining romance or listing romance tropes seems to be an ongoing process, I rely on tropes of "arranged marriage," "boy meets girl," "fatal attraction," "forbidden love," and "tragic love affair" in the context of caste that gives these romance tropes a radically different aspect. Caste, for instance, by its very nature is anti-desire because caste society compels its members to act in caste-appropriate ways; men and women are expected to marry within their caste community so that caste purity is maintained. Thus, such a society not only limits desire to heterosexual desire, it recognizes and validates heterosexual marriages only when they are mediated by caste norms. Seen in this light, the idea of arranged marriage in the context of caste has very little to do with romance or love.

Since arranged marriages are common and compulsory in India, they suffocate all those who want to marry for love and pursue desire on their terms. By defying caste-appropriate "arranged marriage," one shows daring and courage, often associated with romance. The imagination that one can transcend or mold caste norms, especially when chances of doing so are bleak, is at the heart of romance. By referring to the trope of "arranged marriage" in the context of caste society, I want to highlight that we not only need to extend the romance-trope list but also recognize that they are culturally specific and that they acquire new characteristics and uses when transposed to different locales. By considering the specificity of caste, I seek to examine in what ways romance tropes emerge in Roy's fiction, and how they illuminate the social beliefs that caste society holds about who is deemed worthy of love and happiness.

Unlike *The Ministry of Utmost Happiness,* Roy's first novel, *The God of Small Things,* deals with a story of cross-caste, transgressive love that is consummated spectacularly in a lush green tropical landscape, but it's a "closed" novel at its core; it chokes its main characters to death. Caste hovers and envelops the story of cross-caste lovers. The novel's inviting landscape, its strikingly sensuous imagery, and its fascinating central characters, upper-caste Ammu and "Untouchable" Velutha, cannot save themselves from the clutch of caste. Despite its overt romance tropes, the novel is essentially the story of caste's resilience that overpowers individual desire.

In contrast, *The Ministry of Utmost Happiness* engages with urban violence and regional conflicts and insurgencies, but within this "hyper-realistic" mode the novel is grounded in hope; its marginalized characters transcend societal restrictions. Unlike Ammu and Velutha who meet in the dark only to return to their abodes at daybreak, in *The Ministry of Utmost Happiness*, characters go out in broad daylight, and if they decide to leave their home or their native place they do not look back. Implicit in their leaving home is their hope to find a better life elsewhere. Despite societal odds, the novel's marginalized characters—a hijra, an "Untouchable" man, and other minority figures—undertake their own journeys. Without ignoring or undermining the epistemological violence that hijras and other outcast figures endure, Roy's narrative humanizes their stories, and offers other ways to imagine a more inclusive and equal society.

From Aftab to Anjum: Coming Home

Does romantic love always require the other? Is the act of romancing in a normative way a sign of privilege? Can one read or represent the love lives of non-normative people through popular, recognizable romance tropes? For instance, anyone born with an undefined biological gender in a rigidly heteronormative, conservative Indian society with its attendant complexities of caste, is placed in a peculiar relation to the world. I suggest that while neat, normative romance tropes can reveal and constitute normative realities, such tropes take on other features and meanings for someone who is placed queerly in the world in a very fundamental sense. Anjum's life is a good case in point. Unlike pursuing a lover, she seeks herself, and once she finds herself, she begins a life-long romance with herself, and others, in both literal and figural ways. Before I explore her life through romance tropes, I wish to comment on the circumstances that place her in an oblique relation to the world.

When she is born, her hijra (intersex) body is marked as undesirable. Even before she opens her eyes, her mother, Jahanara Begum, shrieks with horror at what she has "created." She is terrified to discover "nestling underneath her baby's boy-parts, a small, unformed, but undoubtedly girl-part" (*Ministry* 7). She contemplates killing herself and her child. The world ceases to make sense to her. Everything in her world has a gender—"all things—carpets, clothes, books, pens, musical instruments [...]. Everything [is] either [...] man or woman. Everything except her baby [...] she knew there was a word for those like him—*Hijra* [...] *Hijra* and *Kinner*. But two words do not make a language" (8). The child is real bodily, but it cannot be narrated in the Urdu language. "Was it possible to live outside language? Naturally this question did not address itself to her in words, as a single lucid sentence. It addressed itself to her as a soundless, embryonic howl" (8). One can argue that her howl is the collective voice of caste society that rejects "unruly bodies."

Although the child's body is of indeterminate sex, Jahanara Begum raises the child as a boy and calls him Aftab, which shows the societal preference for male sex.² Also, in this case, everyone expects her to give birth to a male child for she already has given birth to five girls. What follows is a series of measures that are employed to "fix" the child. She hides him from others, and wishes for a miraculous change in his body. She carries the burden of his intersex status for years, which demonstrates not only society's obsession with male children but also the extreme pressure it exerts on women to produce only certain kinds of bodies.³ At one point, when she cannot hide it anymore and tells her husband about Aftab's "unruly" body, this information renders him mute, and his grand ideas about his distinguished genealogy take a huge blow. Her husband, a *hakim*—a doctor of herbal medicine—by profession but a poet by passion, who has a couplet ready "for every illness, every occasion, every mood and every delicate alteration in the political climate" (15) is speechless at this revelation. He rebukes his wife for not telling him earlier, for he believes that doctors can "fix" their child. When they take the child to a doctor's clinic, they have already invented lies as to the where-and-why questions that their neighbors might ask, which shows the strength of caste-norms in everyday life (16).⁴

Roy's text continually stresses Indian society's immense fear of non-normative bodies. Although Jahanara Begum raises Aftab lovingly, his ordeal begins when he starts going to school. The mother's shriek at his birth and father's speechlessness on knowing Aftab's intersex status begin to make sense. The outside world shows its contempt for Aftab. At school he shows talent for music and is admired by his teachers and others, but this does not save him from harassment. Other children call him names, and he is harassed to such an extent that he gives up music. Other boys make ditties to ridicule him. "*He's a She. He's not a He or a She. He's a He and a She. She-He, He-She Hee! Hee! Hee!*" (*Ministry* 12), and this is one of his first real, traumatic encounters with the world outside home. Consequently, he stops going to school. The adult world's prejudices toward non-normative bodies seamlessly leak into children's play.

Despite these culturally specific limitations, and contrary to "abject" brahminic discourse on hijras, Roy's narrative shows hijra lives in a positive light. Anjum pursues her dreams with the same zeal a lover chases his beloved. Once, when Aftab sees an attractive hijra on the street "wearing bright lipstick, gold high heels and a shiny, green satin salwar kameez buying bangles" (*Ministry* 19), he follows her. There is an instant attraction. He wants to be her:

> Like her he wanted to shimmer past the meat shops where skinned carcasses of whole goats hung down like great walls of meat [...]. He wanted to put out a hand with painted nails and a wrist full of bangles and delicately lift the gill of a fish to see how fresh it was before bargaining down the price. He wanted to lift

his salwar just a little as he stepped over the puddle—just enough to show his silver anklets [19].

This desire to become a hijra on seeing one comes from nowhere—everything around him is gendered, including things, as we have already been told, and yet Aftab wants to be an ungendered person when he sees one. At age 17, he leaves home in search of a "home," and joins the hijra community household called Khwabgah, the House of Dreams (19). Although Khwabgah is not far from his home, stepping into it feels like entering another world.

On becoming one of Khwabgah's permanent residents, Anjum "wears the sequined, gossamer kurtas and pleated Patiala salwars […] silver anklets, glass bangles and dangling earrings. She had […] outlined her eyes with kohl and blue eye shadow and gave herself a luscious, bow-shaped Madhubala mouth of glossy-red lipstick" (26). With her exaggerated kind of femininity, she "made real, biological women look cloudy and dispersed" (27). While she enjoys this space, this romance with self also has its tragic side. All hijras treats her like a new bride and she feels like one, but her body fails her:

> That night she dreamed she was a new bride on her wedding night. She awoke distressed to find that her sexual pleasure had expressed itself into her beautiful new garment like a man's [...] the humiliation she felt had never been so intense. She sat in the courtyard and howled like a wolf, hitting herself on her bed and between her legs, screaming with self-inflicted pain [27].

All the feelings of intense pleasure experienced earlier are followed by intense pain. Also, her pleasure and pain show that Aftab's "girl-part" that his family tried to fix by replacing it with the "boy-part" was not merely an "appendage" (19). Rather, it was central to her being. Passion, desire, dream, and pain all emerge in Aftab's romance with Anjum.

While in conventional romance novels, men and women pursue each other, in Aftab's case, the object of desire is trapped within his own body. In order to free himself of bodily constraints, he undertakes an unusual path, thus showing his agency.[5] His transition from his biological home to his chosen home shows two things: First, the clutch of the normative home that marks him an outsider; he cannot participate in everyday life rituals that gradually prepare children for heterosexual marriage and procreation. Second, society with all of its institutional power cannot regulate individual desire. Aftab shows his agency by leaving home, by pursuing his desire, and by becoming Anjum. What one associates with a typical romance is at work here except that male and female actors are not two independent entities; they reside in one body.

As Anjum, she finds home in a place that not only supports but celebrates Aftab's new life as Anjum. Whereas normative society (Aftab's birth home) suffocates his freedom, a queer space (the hijra house) gives him freedom. (Roy's *The God of Small Things* does not allow any such escape to its central characters.) Once in the community of hijras, Anjum becomes the all the rage in Delhi society. It is not that by becoming hijra, Anjum suffers no indignities on the streets, and that she faces no problems within the hijra community, but as Anjum she is in sync with herself. She lives on her terms, and expresses herself without constraints. Societal indifference frees her from societal norms.

Much later in life, when someone tells Anjum that her name when written backwards reads Majnu, a male name, Anjum laughs because she contains both Romeo and Juliet. But afterwards the same man tells Anjum that when her name reads backwards, it reads Mujna, which is no name at all. Anjum tells him, "It doesn't matter. I'm all of them, I'm Romi and Juli, I'm Laila and Majnu. And Mujna, Why not? Who says my name is Anjum? I am not Anjum, I'm Anjuman. I 'm a *mehfil*, I'm a gathering. Of everybody and nobody, of everything and nothing. Is there anyone else you would like to invite? Everyone's invited" (Roy, *Ministry*, 4). Anjum's understanding of herself is radically different from how mainstream society frames hijras.[6]

If the word "romance" indicates "an excess of passion, yearning and bliss leading to conflict and drama" (Vanita 36), then surely Anjum has romanced. However, by calling herself a *mehfil* (a commune, a gathering in which people assemble for social interaction and entertainment), she also seems to have transcended sexual love, and thus the personal in a way that enables her to "love" by imaginatively putting herself in the place of "another and many others" so that the pleasure and pain of the "species" become her own (Shelley 759).

Roy shows how dominant brahminic narratives on hijras conceal the complexity of hijra lives by tending toward "closure of meaning," thus denying them humanity. Without bypassing the everyday violence that hijras face, the novel shows hopeful aspects of hijra lives. Although brahminic discourse frames and archives narratives of violence against hijras in such abject ways that reinforce violence against them, nowhere does Anjum appear to be an abject figure in the text. Unlike real women from the so-called respectable upper-caste families, Anjum lives a tough but fiercely independent life.[7] She transcends society's deeply-held prejudices by turning the graveyard into a guest house. She calls it Jannat (Paradise) Guest House—a commune, a *mehfil*, where everyone is welcome.

Anjum's *mehfil* has members, both dead and alive, whose life journeys echo Anjum's. Like her, they find themselves in an odd relationship with the world on account of either their caste or sexuality. Since a caste society is driven by heteronormativity, it resents non-normative ideas, people, and behavior. Anyone who counters these norms and creates a "safe" space for oneself is assigned negative meanings, even when such a person charts a path full of daring and romance.

By following Anjum's life, the novel tells the story of hijras; likewise, by following the life of one Dalit man, Dayachand, the novel shows the full horror of caste. Like hijras, Dalits are marginal figures in society.[8] They are treated as "Untouchables" because they do the "dirty" work that upper caste people avoid. In addition to the practice of untouchability, the upper-caste people brutalize Dalits in different ways.[9] Before looking at his typical romance story that leads to marriage, I would like to detail his life as an "Untouchable" man because that will show how his typical romance story involves an atypical journey. Dayachand calls himself Saddam Hussain in the city, but at one point, he reveals his real name and his Dalit identity, and narrates his traumatic past to Anjum:

> "We found the dead cow easily," Saddam said. "It's always easy, you just have to know the art of walking straight into the stink. We loaded the carcass on to the Tempo and started driving home. On the way we stopped at the Dulina police station to pay the Station House Officer—his name was Sehrawat—his cut. It was a previously-agreed-upon sum, a per-cow rate. But that day he asked for more. Not just more, for *triple* the amount [...] when they said they didn't even have that much money on them. He arrested them on the charge of cow slaughter and put them in the police lock-up [...] I waited, assuming that they were just doing some hard bargaining and would soon come to an agreement [...]" [*Ministry* 87–88].

Not only do Dalits work in extreme life threatening situations for meager money, they are tortured by brahminic forces. In this case, it is the upper-caste Police Inspector, Sehrawat.

Soon the cow's carcass begins to stink. A mob returning from the Dussehra celebration event (a Hindu festival) gets a hint about the dead cow and its assumed killers, they drag the Dalit men out of the police station and kill them. Dayachand silently witnesses the death of his own father by the mob. "I was part of the mob that killed my father" (*Ministry* 89). He promises himself that he would kill Sehrawat who instigated the mob to kill his father. He leaves his native village, comes to live in the city, adopts a Muslim identity to hide his Dalithood, finds a job, and awaits the right opportunity to avenge his father's murder. In the meantime, he lives in the Jannat house.

Like Anjum, who becomes Anjum by negating Aftab, Dayachand becomes Saddam Hussain—to quell the curse of caste. However, the Jannat house frees him from his obsession for revenge when he falls in love with Zainab, Anjum's adopted daughter; and thus emerges as a more hopeful, real representation of the "Untouchable" Velutha from *The God of*

Small Things. Unlike Velutha, who is squashed by brahminic forces so that caste-order continues, in *The Ministry of Utmost Happiness* caste is transcended so that Dayachand can live. Also, whereas Velutha hardly speaks, and floats as an unreal but perfect figure in the novel (Khair 138), in *The Ministry of Utmost Happiness* Dayachand speaks, marries, and remains an everyday Dalit. Although there are obstacles of caste and religion between Dayachand and Zainab's love, their story ends in marriage.

However, not all stories that the novel tells end happily like Dayachand's because, like him, not everyone is straight, seeking a union that can be recognized as normative. The novel tells stories of two queer romances without emphasizing their queerness. Both intersect with Anjum's life. One is the story of Hazrat Sarmad Shaheed, a 17th-century sufi saint, and the other is the story of Anjum's aunt, Begum Zeenat Kauser, whose grave lies in the graveyard. Hazrat Sarmad Shaheed comes into the story when Jahanara Begum (Anjum's mother) visits his Dargah to cure her intersex child. (While the stories about his saintliness and spirituality are well known, few know about his homosexuality.) The narrator says, "Most knew he was a Jewish Armenian merchant who had travelled to Delhi from Persia in pursuit of the love of his life. Few knew the love of his life was Abhay Chand, a young Hindu boy he had met in Sindh" (Roy 2017, 9). His "'unrequited'" love for the Hindu boy led him to madness; he lived on the streets of Shahjahanabad as a naked fakir before being publicly executed. The text stresses that he was beheaded not for his nakedness in public but for his apostasy; it can be argued that it was his nakedness that drew the negative attention of the Muslim ruler. Although this same-sex love story ends in Sarmad's "beheading" (9), I argue that this tragic story has a happy ending in an unconventional sense because it has gained a kind of afterlife and permanence in the popular culture one associates with prototypical romance stories—such as the stories of Romeo and Juliet, Shirin and Farhad, and Leila and Majnu. However, by turning Sarmad Shaeed into a saint, the same-sex desire that Sarmad had for the Hindu boy is effectively erased.

The story of Begum Zeenat Kauser, Anjum's aunt, is a queer story that involves the unromantic, or rather suffocating, aspect of arranged marriage in a society hinged on caste, but she finds romance in her own way. Her story has to go unremarked so that caste society can keep its heteronormative order. The narrative summarizes Begum Zeenat Kauser's life thus:

> [She] settled down in Shahjahanabad in a tiny room with a kitchen and a view of her beloved mosque. She shared it with a widow roughly her own age. She earned her living by supplying mutton korma to a restaurant in the old city where foreign tour groups came to savour local food. She stirred the same pot every day for thirty years and smelled of korma the way other women smelled of ittar and perfume [*Ministry* 58].

This somewhat monotonous narration of Begum's life, when seen in its "proper" cultural context, gives a very different picture that hides the exceptional forays this woman made to be with her lover. While understandably she leaves Delhi for Lahore at the time of partition, she returns to India ten years later, leaving her husband and children behind in Pakistan.

This seems like a perfect case of an arranged marriage that has gone wrong. Her return to Delhi does not make sense. She says, "she was unable to live anywhere except in the immediate vicinity of Delhi's Jama Masjid. (For some reason Lahore's Badshahi Mosque did not work out as a substitute.)" (58). Roy's parenthetical remark reflects, perhaps unconsciously, societal phobia against queerness, but it could also be her way to hint at Begum's queerness to the unsuspecting reader.

Begum's life in a tiny room on a crowded street, her embracing of "korma smell," and disregard for the "ittar and perfume" that other women cherish, suggests her opting-out of the normative order that society imposes on women. Her leaving the normative role, tied to husband and children, carries the tropes of queer desire, forbidden love, imagination, daring, conflict, and even secrecy that society does not recognize because recognizing them as such means validating them, which, in turn, means destroying the caste order on which Indian society stands. While the narrative does not explicitly state the queer dimension of Begum's story, it alludes to it. Begum does not leave her children and husband to meddle with "cooking pots" and prepare food for foreign tourists to satiate their hunger and please their palates. she spends thirty long years with a woman who is her age, and, like her, free from societal restraints. Interestingly, while Begum's story disappears into nothingness (as it remains firmly in the domain of the unspeakable), Sarmad Shaheed's publicly displayed queerness meets the same fate, as its ultra visibility makes it unseeable.

Despite caste's grip on the lives of these outcast characters and the myriad limitations that society imposes on them, in one instance, the text engages with the clash between passion and reason, wildness and order, queerness and normativity, and romance and realism when Anjum wants to adopt an infant that someone has left on the street to die, and an upper-caste politician questions her. They cannot be more different from each other:

> He, who filled in forms and ticked boxes. She, who never knew which box to tick, which queue to stand in, which public toilet to enter [...]. He, who believed he was always right. She, who knew she was all wrong, always wrong. He, reduced by his certainties. She, augmented by her ambiguity. He, who wanted a law. She, who wanted a baby [*Ministry*, 122].

Whereas the novel engages with the theme of queerness, here we see how the male, upper-caste, *realistic* politician obstructs the queer, outcast, and *romantic* hijra from fulfilling her desire. Here we see the clash between Anjum's inclusive, romantic approach and the politician's belief in "order" that demands exclusion and suppression. Anjum wants to adopt the child, but the "reasonable" politician wants her to follow the "proper" procedure.

An argument follows between the male, upper-caste, mainstream, *realistic* politician and the queer, outcast, marginal, and *romantic* hijra. The realistic politician gets in the way of the hijra's desire. In a brahminic society, epistemologically, it is the reasonable (brahminic) mind that creates caste hierarchies and marks some bodies as outcasts. Seeing in this way, Anjum is the byproduct of the politician's brahminic mind that classifies human beings into categories of high/low, touchable/untouchable. The narrative invites the reader to ponder on the hijra-politician negotiation in which, through the use of reason, the politician tries to contain the hijra. However, when Anjum's genuine desire is quashed by "brahminic" logic and she fails to defend her position, she answers the politician with a hijra *taali* (clap)—the wordless hijra taali is a resounding response to the "brahminic" reason that seeks to denigrate a hijra's desire of raising a child. More than her argument, it is the sudden onslaught of Anjum's taali and dance, and the overall illegibility of her performance that baffle and make the politician retreat. In everyday life, hijras use taali to deflect insults that people hurl at them.[10]

Whereas Indian society shows its contempt toward hijras openly, it curbs the desire of gay, lesbian, and other non-hijra groups in more strategic ways. In its essence, the upper-caste politician's "articulations" about how things should be are the very things that either behead—that is, erase—queer romances as in the case of Sarmad Shaheed or keep them in the domain of the "unnameable" and "unspeakable" as in the case of Begum Zeenat Kauser. Whereas these outcast figures such as Anjum, Dayachand, Begum Zeenat, and Sarmad Shaheed enter in the domain of romance in their own ways, society deromanticizes their romance stories by placing their stories into the non-human realm of "sainthood" or "untouchability," and when such placings are not possible, society empties out these stories of their meaning or buries them in the overpowering smell of "korma dish."

Despite the hurdles that these outcast characters face, they dare, and succeed in building the Jannat house in the graveyard. Over a period of time, all kinds of people, also birds and animals, come to live in the Jannat House. In the graveyard, the members of the Jannat House not only bury unidentified bodies, they grow "brinjals, beans, chilies, tomatoes, and several kinds of gourds" (*Ministry* 339); their vegetable garden seems to suggest "fulfillment" (Toth 197)—a new beginning and phase that lovers enter once their love is consummated; it is here that the Untouchable Dayachand marries Anjum's adopted daughter, Zainab. When Tilottama, an educated, upper class woman, joins the Jannat house, she teaches children. The narrative voice observes, "So all in all, with a People's Pool, a People's Zoo, a People's school, things were going well in the old graveyard. The same however could not be said of the Duniya" (*Ministry* 400). Outcasts that caste society mark as undesirable create their own space; they sing songs, cook food, and some fall in love.

Also, whereas each member has a tragic story, they are not assailed by guilt. On the other hand, the text alludes to the guilt that the city's elite may experience. We see how the rich would stop at traffic signals, and momentarily, how they pull down the window to buy a newspaper and then quickly shut it to avoid dust, hot air, and the urban poor. They seek to learn new ways to "cleanse" themselves. Indirectly, indulgence in such "cleansing" rituals indicate a brahminic epistemological approach to assuage guilt by bathing in the Ganges (Harper 151–97).

When *The God of Small Things* ends, Ammu and Velutha promise to meet each other the following day, Ammu says to Velutha, "'Naaley'—tomorrow" (Roy, *Small Things*, 340). But that tomorrow has always been answered in the novel's shifting timeline; they are both already dead. However, in *The Ministry of Utmost Happiness*, despite extreme situations in cities and hinterlands, the novel does not cave to violent forces. In the national capital, it is the Jannat house in the graveyard that resists violence in its way while in Kashmir, by dying, Kashmiris resist state force: "Dying became another way of living. Graveyards sprang up in parks and meadows, by streams and rivers, in fields and forests glades" (*Ministry* 314). Also, in the novel, when the body of Mumtaz Afzal Malik, the young taxi driver whom Amrik Singh (an Indian Army Officer) has killed, is recovered and delivered to his family, his clenched fists have earth in them and "mustard flowers growing through his fingers" (437). Without mitigating the reality of contemporary India, Roy's novel weaves together stories of grief and violence, of hope and small successes. "Over the course of the novel, Anjum's graveyard home comes to function as a secular, or at least multifaith, sanctuary, protected by willpower from the turbulent outside world" (Clark). Despite society's violent dismissals, these outcast figures chart their own unique romances, thus creating their own spaces of "utmost happiness."

Notes

1. Arundhati Roy mentioned this while presenting the novel *The Ministry of Utmost Happiness* at Kaaitheatre in Brussels on 15 June 2017.
2. Sidney B. Westley and Minja Kim Choe, "How Does Son Preference Affect Populations in Asia?" *AsiaPacific Issues*, no. 84, September 2007.
3. See "More than 63 million women 'missing' in India, statistics show," *The Guardian*, 30 January 2018.

4. See Kalpana Lajmi's film, *Darmiyan: In Between* (1997). A story of an effeminate, intersex child who is raised as a boy by his (actress) mother. The mother disguises the intersex status of her child to protect him from hijra groups as well as from society at large.

5. In a rare story, when Gazal Dhaliwal, born as a boy in a middle-class Sikh family, underwent sex reassignment surgery and started living as a woman, many criticized her, saying that she changed her sex because as a transgender woman she can have more sex with men, to which she replied that it has never been about men, nor about sex: she wanted to love herself. Implicit in critiquing her choice is queerphobia of Gazal Dhaliwal's nonnormative body and desire. By owning both, she is transcending the normal, and thus making her desire illegible in a way that exceeds or falls short of what is recognized as proper romance in caste-society (see Dhaliwal 2014).

6. Since hijras cannot reproduce, and nor can they participate in religious rituals because participation requires one to be either male or female, they are seen as abject. However, they are also seen as auspicious because in Hindu mythology it is believed that they can bless the fertility of others. Simply put, by constructing them as abject and auspicious, brahminic (upper-caste) society frames them as the Other (see Nanda 5–6).

7. Ruth Vanita, *Dancing with a Nation: Courtesans in Bombay Cinema* (Bloomsbury, 2017), pp. 100–128. Like Oldenburg's essay, Vanita's book engages with the representation of courtesans in Indian cinema; the book shares striking similarities with hijra lives that are seldom given attention in Indian literary and visual texts.

8. Khuswant Singh, "Brahmin Power," *Sunday*, 29 December 1990.

9. Arundhati Roy, "The Doctor and the Saint," *Annihilation of Caste* (1936) (Verso, 2014), pp. 27–37. In recent years, because of the rise of Hindu supremacists, incidents of violence against Dalits have substantially increased in India. See, S. Dutta, "Dalits, Lynchings and Democracy," *www.youthkiawaaz.com*, 4 June 2019.

10. Kira Hall, *Hijra hijrin: Language and Gender Identity* (Doctoral dissertation, University of California, Berkeley, 1995).

Works Cited

Clark, Alex. "A Patchwork of Narratives." *The Observer*, 11 June 2017.
Dhaliwal, Gazal. "Accepting Alternative Sexualities: Born Again." YouTube, uploaded by Satyamev Jayate, 19 October 2014. https://www.youtube.com/watch?v=ZOicQppaqnk&t=884s.
Harper, Edward. B. "Ritual Pollution as an Integrator of Caste and Religion." *The Journal of Asian Studies*, vol. 23, June 1964, pp. 151–197.
Khair, Tabish. *Babu Fictions*. OUP, 2001.
Lajmi, Kalpana, director. *Darmiyaan: In Between*. Pan Pictures, 1997.
Nanda, Serena. *Neither Men nor Women: The Hijras of India*. Wadsworth, 1999. https://petervas.files.wordpress.com/2013/03/serena_nanda.pdf.
Oldenburg, Veena Talwar. "Lifestyle as Resistance: The Case of Courtesans of Lucknow, India." *Feminist Studies*, vol. 16, no. 2, Summer 1990, pp. 259–87.
Orwell, George. *1984* (1949). Penguin, 1990.
Roy, Arundhati. *The God of Small Things*. Flamingo, 1998.
_____. *The Ministry of Utmost Happiness*. Penguin, 2017.
Shelley, Percy Bysshe. "A Defense of Poetry." *The Norton Anthology of the English Language*, vol. 2, Norton, 1962.
Toth, Sara. "What Does Literature Say?: The Problem of Dogmatic Closure from Romanticism to Northrup Frye." *ESE*, vol. 37, no. 2, June 2011.
Vanita, Ruth. *Dancing with a Nation: Courtesans in Bombay Cinema*. Bloomsbury, 2017.
_____. "The Romance of Siblinghood in Bombay Cinema." *Journal of South Asian Studies*, vol. 36, no. 1, 29 May 2013.

PART SIX

Romance Tropes in Online Spaces

The System That Loves Me
The State of Human Existence in Web-Based Romantic Fiction from Post-Socialist China

Jin Feng

An epidemic breaks out. The deadly virus passes from person to person at lightning speed. At the epicenter, the healthcare system is quickly overwhelmed. Doctors and nurses work around the clock with no hope of catching up with infections. Patients die or kill themselves in despair. The military takes over and enforces emergency rule. The government orders millions of people to have their temperatures taken constantly, self-isolate, and wear face masks outside the home. Gated residential communities impose curfew and deny entry to anyone not residing inside. The police forcibly take away those suspected of having contracted the virus and refusing to cooperate with quarantine orders. Schools are closed, and factories shut. Ordinary citizens take the law into their own hands, blocking roads and turning away cars with plates issued at the epicenter. They are also told to inform on anyone from out of town, and neighbors turn against neighbors.

This is not the plot from a tale of the apocalypse. In late January 2020, just before the Chinese New Year holiday, the truth was finally out, but not before weeks of official cover-up of the lethal spread of COVID-19 by the local government of Wuhan, Hubei Province in central China. Wuhan was sealed; all means of transportation by land, water, and air out of the city were banned. People in other parts of China gradually learned of the terrible details described above, and also came to experience the pandemic that would claim thousands of lives, cause tens of thousands of infections, and wreak untold economic and social damage in China alone.

This public health crisis provides the perfect background and metaphor for my exploration of Chinese web-based romantic works that feature an "operating system" (OS) or xitong, a commanding intelligence that metes out justice while inhabiting a human host, an eerie albeit unintended echo of viral infection. The coronavirus outbreak generates materials and inspirations for both producers and consumers of OS fiction. It also reveals that Chinese web novels offer much more than innocuous diversion or even a pressure valve for releasing citizen discontent. As will be shown, OS fiction challenges traditional morality and existing power structures, experiments with different modes of governance and self-governance, and questions the state-sanctioned myth that nationalism, modernity, and technology can bring prosperity and happiness to all.

Crystallizing a trend existing in Chinese web-based romantic fiction from earlier years (Feng 2013), OS fiction produces *Bildungsroman* under extreme circumstances while deploying romantic relationships as just one of many tools of identity exploration. Thus, it not only brings to sharp relief the collective psyche underlying the unique aesthetics of the reversal that attracts Chinese readers, but also once again reminds us of "the fundamental interdependence of romance and *Bildungsroman*. Common to both genres is the vision of life as a series of quests, tests and challenges for which the brave are duly rewarded" (Pearce 2007, 33).

In this essay, I examine a group of OS works published at the Colony of Ants (Mayi Shequ), a Bulletin Board System (BBS) forum catering to worldwide Chinese-speaking audiences with the server based in China. Following a brief description of this forum, I focus on the themes and devices shared by these works. Categorized as either "heterosexual romance" (*yanqing*) or "male-male homoerotic tales" (*danmei*) in Chinese web literature, they are infused with romantic elements, and authored and read mostly by women, even while not adhering strictly to the definition of "romance" promulgated by the Romance Writers of America (RWA). The trope of an operating system reflects public interest in new technologies such as holographic computer games and artificial intelligence, and the rising popularity of new media platforms including those featuring live-stream (*zhibo*) broadcast in contemporary China. Yet these works also reveal women's anxieties about an alien outside world and the willingness to rely on external forces for discipline, survival, and success, for the system recalls the Chinese patriarch, the party-state, and deities, whose "tough love" supposedly motivates growth and ensures success. At the same time, they investigate the relationships between humans and non-humans, and discuss whether the development of science and technology could contribute to human freedom and progress. Although not all of them represent anti-anthropocentric or feminist thoughts, most challenge the Enlightenment idea that "Man" represents the universal human being and occupies the center of the known universe.

Just like the zombie apocalypse genre popular in the West since the 1990s, which describes zombies as humans infected by a virus that eventually takes over its human hosts (Luckhurst 2015), OS fiction pushes at the boundaries of the known human world through the inclusion of an "other." By staging liminal experiences that challenge the existing human order in both "realist" and fantastical settings, these works employ depictions of romantic relationships to explore alternative social orders, unveil the blurred boundaries between life and nonlife, and examine what it means to be human and be a woman under a totalitarian regime in multivalent manners.

The Colony of Ants

The Colony of Ants (CA) was founded in 2004 with its server based in the United States, but moved to a server in China in 2009. It has no claim to ownership of most of the works available through the site. These serialized genre fiction works have mostly been transferred here by users from sites where they were initially published, although a link to the original web publisher is provided in the very first posting of each work, together with its title and a plot summary. The works discussed in this essay were mostly first published at Jinjiang Literature City, the largest Chinese-language, creative literature website for women, with a small number of them from Starting Point (Qidian), the largest male-oriented Chinese web literature site and the first to adopt the "VIP," pay-per-view system for web novels in China.

Like U.S.-based Yaya Bay (Feng 2013), which also transfers Chinese web literature, CA fosters a participatory culture through a variety of interactive features. For instance, readers can send "meal tickets" (*fanpiao*) or "ant beans" (*mayi dou*)—purchased with web coins they have accumulated through participation at the forum—to those whose postings they like. In turn, the more meal tickets or ant beans a certain work receives, the more followers it will attract. However, compared to Yaya Bay, web administrators at CA must adhere to rules of censorship to which all China-based sites are subject, such as the prohibition of sexually explicit content and politically sensitive topics. As a result, they police the forum vigilantly and intervene to delete postings, bar users, or move discussions that appear unrelated to the novel to another space. Moreover, CA users must take care when transferring works published elsewhere to the site, in case the original author or publishing site finds out. Thus, CA membership is by invitation only, and users need to receive a unique QR code to register.

In contrast to what happens at the two literature sites that publish creative works, the authors of novels circulated at CA are usually not involved in the posting and commentary process, since their works have often been transferred to the site without their knowledge or authorization; the authorial monitoring and manipulation of reader response common at Jinjiang or Starting Point is absent here. Moreover, transfers and web administrators at CA have no stake in the commercial success of the works. The egalitarian structure of the forum, its relative freedom from commercial concerns, and its reader-centered, participatory culture not only foster tightknit reading communities, but also allow readers to reveal their desires, fears, and fantasies all the more freely.

Chinese web readers share several interpretive practices. They instantaneously incorporate elements lifted from contemporary, global sociopolitical life into their comments. They tend to use their own life stories to vouch for or question the plausibility of the plot, and to agree or disagree with their fellow readers. They also frequently post apparently unrelated comments under a web novel, if the plot rouses their curiosity about topics ranging from how to make candies at home to historical battles between nations.

These reading habits also play out in their consumption of OS works. After the pandemic erupted, authors immediately incorporated plots about epidemics into their works. Some also described immense stress after displaying flu-like symptoms in postscripts to chapters (Taiji Yu #16). Readers meanwhile complained of boredom after being cooped up at home for weeks with no school or work to go to, described panic at the sight of deserted streets, and expressed concern for an author's wellbeing when she failed to update her novel. They also voiced gratitude that they could read web romance to while away time, and became all the more enthusiastic about posting comments and recommending novels to each other.

During this public health crisis, readers especially gravitated toward works that describe struggles of ordinary people amid wars, famines, and other natural and man-made disasters, and sounded inspired by tales of regular people's unlikely victory against all odds, such as in their responses to *All My Family Time-Travelled Here* (*Wo quanjia doushi chuanlai de*) by YTT Taotao. Revealingly, readers favored plot-driven works that feature fantastical elements, such as time-travel, and privilege action over contemplation, while undoubtedly feeling helpless and vulnerable in the meantime. That OS works have been transferred and drawn large followings at CA alone has proven their attraction. Further, the narrative features that resonate with readers reveal the collective psyche and cultural landscape of post-socialist China in especially distinctive ways during this emergency.

The "Golden Finger"

In recent Chinese web romance, human beings increasingly time-travel into the narrative universe armed with an operating system. It provides resources, rewards satisfactory performances, and penalizes failures according to its own rules after making itself at home in the human mind. Rewards by the system occupy a wide spectrum but can be roughly divided into two categories according to their use: to strengthen the protagonist's physical or mental advantages or manipulate other people's psychological and emotional responses.

For example, in *The Little Secretary System* (*Xiao mishu xitong*) by Qing Hou, Ju Li, administrative assistant to the CEO of a multibillion-dollar media company, receives a variety of prizes for completing tasks assigned by the system. Ordinary though much desired prizes include salary raises, promotions, cars and houses, luxury goods such as name-brand handbags and watches, a driver's license, and the household registration (huji) that allows people from other parts of China to live and receive social benefits in Shanghai. But there are also magical cosmetics that instantly boost the heroine's physical beauty, ranging from mascara, shampoo, eyebrow pens, eye drops, and facial cream to weight loss pills and breast-sculpting bras. There are even wonder foods and drinks that can boost energy, increase alcohol tolerance, enhance mood, help people withstand cold, or make them speak the truth.

The system offers tools that help with her work as well, such as a pen that writes excellent speeches and playscripts, a barometer that forecasts her boss's emotional state, a CV that reveals anyone's past experiences, and a schedule for anyone's future activities as long as she writes down the person's name. As a result, Ju Li skyrockets from the position of a contract worker to vice-president of the company within one year, wins the love and admiration of her boss, colleagues, and subordinates, and ends up in a happy marriage to her handsome, talented, and rich boss.

Highlighting the rise of a heroine from humble origins to wealth and fame, this work produces a Cinderella story in the guise of a modern office romance. It resembles Western reworkings of the classic fairy tale by offering "emotional justice" through liberating recasting of the heroine (Crusie 1998), though she receives help from the system rather than a fairy godmother in this twenty-first-century Chinese version. Yet it also repeats the narrative arc of "from rags to riches" typical of Chinese web romance, where romantic entanglements pale in comparison to career and personal successes, and romance turns into a woman's *Bildungsroman*.

Chinese web romance set in premodern patriarchal societies, with women constrained by gender segregation and oppressive feminine codes, often relegates the hero to the periphery after the nuptials, like a trophy won and put aside, whereas the heroine claims center stage in "household fights" (*zhaidou*), and shines in her own milieu, in contrast to the classic Western popular romance that ends with a happy betrothal or wedding. Web novels with modern settings allocate even more space to the heroine's growth than to romance. To be sure, *Little Secretary* gives voice to the desires and fantasies of many a female office worker, such as physical beauty, a successful career, and happy marriage, and outlines what a successful heroine should look like in contemporary Chinese culture. Yet in emphasizing Ju Li's efforts and career achievements, it also makes the hero less central to the heroine's fate. The marriage is no longer the primary goal that gives meaning to her identity and purpose to her life. Although the hero sometimes provides help as a sidekick, the heroine ultimately wins him as one reward on the way to proving her true mettle.

As such, the heroine sets and keeps the plot in motion by her quest, and defines her identity through action rather than beauty and passivity. But her relationship with the system remains complicated even after dislodging the hero from the central position of power and importance. Time-travel romance by definition must equip the protagonist with some form of fantastical advantage, or "a golden finger" (*jin shouzhi*) in Chinese web lingo, so that he or she can accomplish spectacular feats and fulfill readers' vicarious desires and pleasures. However, compared with the first wave of Chinese time-travel romance, recently protagonists more often than before rely on external forces rather than on their modern knowledge and wits alone for successes in the world they newly enter. Female-authored OS fiction follows this trajectory, and illustrates women's increasing uncertainties and anxieties about the present and the future, and also the further disintegration of the master narrative of national revival pushed by the state.

In recent web romance the public prominence and success typical of the first generation of time-travelers gives way to more domestic concerns, where familial relationships as well as economic production become the focus of the plot. Novels featuring a magic space, a metaphor for the protagonist's "inscape," mark a further retreat into the sanctity of the interior self. This magic space can be collapsed into a piece of jewelry or simply conjured up in one's mind's eye, and is only visible and accessible to the protagonist. Although a magic space can supply great wealth, lost cultural artefacts, or magical plants and animals, it also exposes protagonists' dependence on magic powers that are neither of their own choosing nor, at least initially, the fruits of their labors. It thus reveals their lack of autonomy even while adding fantastical appeal to the plot.

A commanding system, by all accounts an upgrade of a magic space in terms of power and intelligence, shows how protagonists yield to external forces even more and at the expense of true emotional and romantic fulfillment at times. Compared with a usually helpful but insentient magic space, a system functions more like an artificial intelligence. It has its own inner logic and will, and can act in ways that are benevolent, malicious, or indifferent toward the human it commands. The protagonist often cannot ascertain its true intentions in the beginning. In best case scenarios, the system uses rewards to incentivize the protagonist to practice tirelessly and advance quickly in career and life, as is the case with a female live-stream broadcaster named Yun Jin in *I Have Acquired a Life-Skills System* (*Wo bangding le shenghuo xitong*) by Song Hanghang. However, the protagonist may end up finding him- or herself deceived by the system. The heroine in *Daji's Task* (*Daji de renwu*) by Zhang Dingding, for instance, is ordered by the system to make at least one man of great wealth, talent, and beauty fall in love with her in three years or face elimination. Engineered by the system to pursue romantic conquests, she faces the peril of losing her true love in the end, despite initial successes with different men by relying on culinary skills and physical beauty granted by the system.

Works featuring a magic space or system incorporate elements from new media products such as live-stream broadcast and computer games. More importantly, they manifest a collective consciousness "that is attempting to reconstruct the self as an individual in a postrevolutionary society" (Kong 2005 104) by experimenting with new ways of storytelling. Novels featuring a magic space spin off the notoriously popular game "Happy Farm" (Kaixin Nongchang), which allows players to cultivate their own piece of virtual land while also rising in the ranks by spending time online. OS fiction likewise deploys a game-like system as a narrative device for Chinese women to experience the unique aesthetics of the reversal while exploring the meanings of individuality and humanity.

The Devices and Aesthetics of the Reversal

The aesthetics of the reversal are enacted at three different levels in OS fiction. First, the narrative unfolds from the perspective of a previously minor or even villainous character, who nevertheless claims the limelight and achieves amazing feats after a time-traveler takes over. Villains have become more popular than traditional heroes in web fiction perhaps because, as the heroine claims in *The System Forced Me to Become a Saint* (*Xitong bi wo zuo shengmu*) by Luo Qingmei: "They can do whatever they like with no regard for moral values or social pressure" (#2). Yet female authors and readers share admiration for antiheroes not only because of their powers of action, but also because they challenge conventional wisdom and morality for the purpose of restoring justice and protecting the vulnerable.

Further, these "refitted" characters can succeed by taking advantage of loopholes to "game the system" as well as by completely overthrowing existing power structures. In *Everyone Knows I Am a Good Man* (*Suoyou ren dou zhidao wo shi hao nanren*) by Tang Zhong Mao, for instance, the time-traveling protagonist corrects his predecessor's moral transgressions by words and by deeds. Acting as savior of wronged women in all the worlds he travels into, he whitewashes the malicious conspiracies cooked up by his predecessor, which could have (and indeed had in an alternate universe) destroyed the innocent, and acts to right wrongs only after rebuilding his moral authority. Thus, end seems to justify means, and the villain turns into a superhero that transcends traditional moral values such as authenticity and integrity with the help of the system, as long as he takes care of women and does good for humanity.

Second, the narrative structure highlights *nixi*, or counterstrike, which tells the miraculous rise of an initially powerless protagonist; devoiced due to origin, race, class, gender, ability, appearance, disposition, or any combination of the above, he or she fights back from a position of marginalization, and eventually overpowers the original oppressors. Most web novels, especially male-oriented fantasies published at Starting Point, utilize this narrative arc to execute tales of revenge and redemption. Extracting emotional satisfaction from these stories of the reversal of fortunes and the victory of the small people, readers have identified them as having established "the Starting Point Model" (Shao Yanjun 2019). This narrative model gives voice to a collective unconscious dislodged from the rigid social structure of Maoist China and disconcerted by fast economic development and social transformations in the wake of the Reform and Opening Era of the late 1970s. Yet authors also face the challenge of sustaining reader interest after capturing their attention and inducing identification with the initially downtrodden protagonist. Since authors need to update their serialized works over months and years, they often have to adopt a "string-of-pearls" narrative structure, and devise endless new quests for their protagonists in order to retain readers jaded by their multi-million-word works.

OS fiction is uniquely suited to deploy this narrative model through the aesthetic experience of detached amusement. For Chinese women, it also grants them emotional distance that generates a sense of security as well as entertainment. OS fiction originates from and adopts the narrative style of role-playing games (RPG), and thus creates a third reversal in terms of the definitions of human and non-human. Just as players of RPG must obey game rules and play different characters in different settings, protagonists in OS fiction act on orders issued by the system. Moreover, OS works narrate protagonists accomplishing tasks of increasing complexity and risk, the same way that players of online games advance by accumulating "experience" (XP) through "farming," or accomplishing lower-level tasks. Authors often have their protagonists enter into different worlds through a series of "short time-travel trips" (*kuaichuan*), and develop sequential narratives along distinct storylines without having to describe the inner growth of the protagonist, for he or she essentially faces a completely new setting with a new cast of characters, and can act the same way as before in different time-travel trips.

In this way, character development can be kept at the surface level while the plot hurtles from one climax to the next. In *Everyone Knows I Am a Good Man*, for example, the protagonist carries out a consistent mission to restore justice in different worlds, always by using his amazing powers of persuasion to spin tales. The settings change from premodern to modern to doomsday worlds, but the time-traveling protagonist can always smooth things over without any inner struggles or changes in consciousness.

Since protagonists lack psychological and moral complexity in OS works, they can work as "placeholders" for readers to take a step back and reflect on the logics and ethics of game culture, precisely because of the detachment it induces. *Suffering Financial Losses to Become the Richest Person: Starting from Games* (*Kui cheng shoufu cong youxi kaishi*), by Jue Bu Xianyu, tells the story of Pei Qian (punning on "to lose money"), a college student who has suddenly acquired a system, and must try his best to lose money in business ventures in order to accumulate wealth, thanks to the perverse accounting methods of the system. The author dissects the inner workings of industries in game, cell phone, film, and amusement parks one by one, and pokes fun at consumers as well, while delivering his critique through light-hearted satire.

In the same vein, the integration of live-stream broadcast and talent shows (that are similar to "American Idol") into plot development, on the one hand, showcases widespread fan culture in contemporary China, and attracts readers who have grown up with and are insiders of this culture. On the other, it also sheds light on the symbiotic relationships between media stars and their fans, and exposes the underlying business model premised on attention-seeking and time consumption. Protagonists in OS fiction often depend on audiences for their success and survival. The heroine in *The Imperial Concubine Time-Travelled Back to Become an Internet Sensation* (*Guifei niangniang chuan huilai baohong le*) by Song Hanghang must earn enough "popularity points" through live-stream shows to summon her family from the premodern world. OS works thus both appeal to insider-readers and expose the underbelly of contemporary fan culture.

More importantly, while protagonists with superhuman powers sans emotional complications generally attract those feeling powerless in real life, this way of characterization resonates with female readers especially. It allows them to withdraw from intense emotional engagements, which can make them feel vulnerable, the same way that consuming male-male homoerotic tales gives them leeway to pose as "androgynous reader" and therefore feel less bounded to a feminine gender position (Feng 2009). OS romance thus makes it possible for women to probe into what it means to be human in post-socialist China in unique ways.

In *Becoming Immortal by One Stroke of the Sword* (*Yi jian feng xian*) by Zhijian Shang de Yongtan Diao, a seasoned hacker happens upon a conspiracy to hijack human brains to use as non-character players (NPC) in the game. At once a male-male homoerotic romance and crime drama that also does some soul-searching, this work uses reckless, mindless, and superficial gamers not only as comic relief, but also as tools. The protagonist announces a quest in the game whenever he needs labor for his own agenda. In turn, the human players with real life stories in reality are turned into cardboard characters who care only about amassing XP to rise through the ranks, with a total disregard for human life in the game since they can "die" countless times and "be reborn" as long as they endlessly pay and play online. In contrast, the NPCs involved in romantic and other relationships with the player-protagonist develop real emotional lives in the game, and are eventually revealed to represent hijacked human brains. This work not only exposes a game culture that can desensitize players and strip away ethical considerations, it also challenges the very basis of what it means to be human. In ostensibly depicting romantic relationships between men for women's consumption, it illustrates how female-authored OS romance pushes at the boundaries between human and non-human while experimenting with diverse gender positions.

The System and Me

The narrative characteristics, such as featuring antiheroes rather than conventional heroes, privileging plot over psychological depth, and incorporating popular cultural products, illuminate the psyche of a generation growing up with the culture of animation, comics, and games (ACG). While playfully dismantling the officially sanctioned master narrative of collective struggle for national salvation, OS fiction also explores what it means to be human and be woman in post-socialist China. Indeed, how the system looks and how it interacts with its human host (*suzhu*) reflect how Chinese women understand the current state of human existence.

Expressing a desire to shake off social constraints facing women and the female gender, human beings in OS fiction take on remarkable fluidity in shapes and identities. In works with time-travel or other fantastical elements, they enter into different worlds and become humans, animals, fairies, spirits, or aliens, can be of male, female, or some other gender, and can even appear as characters in online games and TV shows. Even in works with contemporary settings, humans are frequently described with animal metaphors. In hospitals, doctors become "lions" and "dogs" in a workplace ruled by the law of the jungle (Zhi Niao Cun). In a romantic relationship between the boss and his assistant, he becomes the fierce "dog" and she the cute "cat" (Qing Hou).

Meanwhile, the system can be bodiless and issue orders in the host's mind only, it can be a ball of energy or aura visible only to a chosen few, or it can take on human or animal forms. Sometimes it appears as a cuddly companion. In *My Medical Skills Shock the World* (*Wo de yishu zhenjing shijie*) by Tian Miao, the system first appears as an orange cat and later turns into a human infant to be adopted by the protagonist and his male lover. In *Every Travel into a Book I Am Forced to Make a Startling Turn* (*Meici chuan shu dou bei po shen zhuanzhe*) by Yu Xiao Guaiguai, the male protagonist who travels into each book and takes over the original hero's body and life must fulfill his unrealized wishes as well. His partner-in-crime in every book world happens to be the same system that takes on different men's bodies, as does he. Even when appearing in human form and eventually forming a romantic relationship with the protagonist, though, the system is described as unable to read nuances in human interactions. Thus, it is shown to be at once not-quite-human in terms of emotional intelligence, and superhuman with regard to the capability to search, memorize, calculate, and provide resources.

Not all systems lack human affects, though. They can act out human hubris without taking human forms. Authors also often endow the system with negative character traits such as anger, jealousy, greed, and arrogance, modeled on human dispositions as they devise ways for the host to take advantage of the system's weaknesses. The relationship between the system and its human is usually fraught with tensions and contradictions, and rarely peaceful and collaborative, since authors often have the human fight with the system for control of the host's body, life, and destiny. As a "golden finger," a device that provides supernatural assistance, the system always supplies the human with abundant and fantastical resources. It can act kindly toward its host as well, such as the one growing up together with a young girl who wants to become a doctor in *The Lucky Farm Girl* (*Nongjia xiao funü*) by Yu Yuzhu. Here the system offers science and technologies much more advanced than available in the heroine's premodern world through a platform for her to conduct transactions of knowledge and goods with intelligent beings from other universes. It can even act paternally toward the host, such as the one in *The Little Secretary*, where it appears protective and caring toward the heroine, but is also hard to please, strict, and stingy with kind words.

When their goals line up, the system helps its host to achieve career, romantic, and family successes, and the human becomes a renowned chef, surgeon, CEO, a good mother, or a good father. The heroine in *I Acquired a Life-Skills System*, for instance, changes from a "lazy, fat, asocial, and depressed" (Song Hanghang, #1) twenty-something white-collar worker to a renowned host of web shows and successful businesswoman, accomplishing amazing transformations of appearance, skills, and romantic fortune aided by the system. Inasmuch as the system helps its host to become a better version of him- or herself, its function resembles a cell phone app that can supervise, discipline, and encourage the human to push forward. Yet a benevolent system not only provides inspiration for self-improvement like self-help literature, it also hands out wealth, beauty, and skills as rewards for obedient behaviors, attempts to co-opt the human into a certain regime, and does some dehumanizing as well. Thus, it turns out that every golden finger has clay fingernails, so to speak.

Whatever form the system takes, it illustrates Chinese women's imagination of external forces controlling their lives, such as modern technologies and dominant socio-political forces. Whether benevolent, hostile, or indifferent, and whether stronger or weaker than human will, the system compensates for what they find lacking in their lives, such as wealth, status, power, paternal love, self-discipline, skills for emotional management, or powers of action. Yet the human host also seeks ways to turn the tables, whatever the form and function of the system, and no matter how dystopian the imagined world.

The humans may not always win in the numerous battles of will and wits they wage against the system, either. But if they do, they must resist the temptation of "a free lunch," or to achieve success without effort, as can be seen from the following three male-male homoerotic romances. In *The Aggressive Life-Skills System* (*Jinji de shenghuo liu*) by Qing Zhuye, the author has a variety of systems use different pitches to tempt their host and coerce him into obeying orders, but he sees through all their tricks. To overpower the system, the human must also think outside the box and find unexpected ways to subvert its rule. In *After a Minor Character Went Bankrupt* (*Dang nanpei pochan hou*) by Chun Feng Yao, the hero repeatedly ignores the system's temptations and finds new ways to earn his freedom, such as by publishing bestselling works online rather than by becoming involved in complicated romantic relationships. In *The Daily Life of A Charming Student of Immortality* (*Xiuxian dalao wanrenmi richang*) by Muhan Gongzi, the protagonist even succeeds in turning the system against its boss, a chief system (*zhu shen*), by raising its consciousness to fight for workers' rights. The power structure among the corps of systems thus portrayed, interestingly, resembles those of human bureaucracy, and recalls similar depictions in tales of gods and aliens. At times, the human in OS fiction also experiments with different governing models and social systems in different worlds while fighting the system (thaty).

In OS romance humans, especially women, can only survive and triumph by overcoming character flaws and emotional weaknesses, including but not limited to greed, laziness, impetuosity, and self-delusion, wherein also lies the downfall of the system. As both web authors and readers show impatience with human frailties, they explore alternative ways to "beat the system," and deal with the perennial struggle between agency and dependency in search of the meaning of existence.

The Post-Socialist Self

In testing the boundaries between human and non-human existences, OS romance provides a kind of identity workshop for its female producers and consumers, allowing them to move back and forth between premodern, modern, and post-modern conceptions of personhood, and to traverse uncharted and potentially dangerous territories together in relatively safe, game-like worlds. Authors find pleasure in innovative storytelling, and readers gravitate toward tales that empower those oppressed by existing power structures. Together they try out different ideas of what it means to be human, challenge traditional wisdom, and derive emotional satisfaction from reading in the company of other women in virtual space.

Anthropologist Alasdair MacIntyre (1984, 33) contrasts the modern "emotive self" to the traditional "heroic self": the latter is wholly defined by one's membership in a variety of social groups such as family, lineage, local community, and political institutions. In the heroic society, a man is what he does; he has no hidden depths. Moral judgments are formed on the basis of the ethics of action, not on a hermeneutics of intention. The modern emotive individual, in contrast, prides themselves on being an autonomous moral agent free from the hierarchy of traditional society. Their moral authority resides squarely within themselves rather than in the external authorities of traditional morality. Historian Lynn Hunt demonstrates that novels published in eighteenth-century Europe, such as Samuel Richardson's *Pamela* (1740), generated "torrents of emotion," making readers empathize with the heroine's moral struggle across the boundaries of gender and class. These texts served as a foundation for the

Enlightenment ideal of individual autonomy: people thinking and feeling for themselves.

The modern emotive self is conspicuously absent in OS romance, as it privileges a more "heroic" version of the self: playing many social roles as well as possessing extraordinary or even superhuman attributes. Rather than the sympathetic, sensitive, but ultimately vulnerable modern individual, Chinese women tend to root for resilient protagonists with powers of action rather than contemplation. Yet they also favor tales of human protagonists rebelling against the system, and challenge traditional definitions of female virtue, including those disseminated by the party-state, such as women's selfless sacrifice for the family and the nation, by commandeering the stage for themselves rather than waiting to be pursued by men. Seen against the background of the coronavirus pandemic, which has provided only one, albeit an especially apt, example of overwhelming political and social forces against individual rights, their cheering for those struggling against the system by whatever means is nothing short of heroic.

OS romantic works of course do not universally or always embrace feminist, progressive, or democratic values. Yet in their complex ways, female web authors and readers have found tools to cope with a deadly pandemic and an oppressive regime, while creating a peculiar form of hybrid identity in postmodern Chinese cyberspace. OS fiction not only reveals the many dilemmas facing women in post-socialist China, it also cross-pollinates with genres such as fantasy and science fiction to develop the genre of popular romance. Just like the zombie who would always live on in our imagination, it ultimately shows that portrayals of romantic relationships can interrogate the very processes in which identity is formed and social order is produced, maintained, and reinforced, with the system signifying the dominant political structure, patriarchy, deity, virus, technology, or even the mythical other whose exclusion is foundational to human civilization.

Works Cited

Chun Feng Yao. *Dang Nanpei pochan hou* (After a Minor Character Went Bankrupt). http://bbs.55ab.com/forum.php?mod=viewthread&tid=3786805. Accessed February 25, 2020.

Crusie, Jennifer. "This Is Not Your Mother's Cinderella: The Romance Novel as Feminist Fairy Tale." *Romantic Conventions*, edited by Anne Kaler and Rosemary Johnson-Kurek, Bowling Green Press, 1998. pp. 51–61. http://www.jennycrusie.com/for-writers/essays/this-is-not-your-mothers-cinderella-the-romance-novel-as-feminist-fairy-tale/. Accessed January 3, 2013.

Feng, Jin. "Addicted to Beauty: Web-based Danmei Popular Romance." *Modern Chinese Literature and Culture*, vol. 21, no. 2, 2009, pp. 1–41.

_____. *Romancing the Internet: Producing and Consuming Web-based Chinese Romance*. Brill, 2013.

Hunt, Lynn. *Inventing Human Rights: A History*. Norton, 2007.
Jue Bu Xianyu. *Kui cheng shoufu cong youxi kaishi* (Suffering Financial Losses to Become the Richest Person: Starting from Games). http://bbs.55ab.com/forum.php?mod=viewthread&tid=3768096. Accessed February 25, 2020.
Kong, Shuyu. *Consuming Literature: Best Sellers and the Commercialization of Literary Products in Contemporary China*. Stanford UP, 2005.
Luckhurst, Roger. *Zombies: A Cultural History*. Reaktion Books, 2015.
Luo Qingmei. *Xitong bi wo zuo shengmu* (The System Forced Me to Become a Saint). http://bbs.55ab.com/forum.php?mod=viewthread&tid=3116272. Accessed February 25, 2020.
MacIntyre, Alasdair. *After Virtue*, 2nd ed. U of Notre Dame P, 1984.
Mayi Shequ. http://bbs.55ab.com/forum.php. Accessed February 25, 2020.
Muhan Gongzi. *Xiuxian dalao wanrenmi richang* (The Daily Life of a Charming Student of Immortality). http://bbs.55ab.com/forum.php?mod=viewthread&tid=3571754. Accessed February 25, 2020.
Pearce, Lynne. *Romance Writing*. Polity Press, 2007.
Qing Hou. *Xiao mishu xitong* (The Little Secretary System). http://bbs.55ab.com/forum.php?mod=viewthread&tid=3736744. Accessed February 25, 2020.
Qing Zhuye. *Jinji de shenghuo liu* (The Aggressive Life-Skills System). http://bbs.55ab.com/forum.php?mod=viewthread&tid=3839362. Accessed February 25, 2020.
Shao Yanjun. "Wangluo wenxue de 'duandai shi' yu chuantong wangwen de 'jingdian hua'" (A Short History of Internet Literature and the Canonization of 'Traditional Web Novels'). *Zhongguo xiandai wenxue yanjiu congkan* 2 (2019), pp. 1–18.
Song Hanghang. *Guifei niangniang chuan huilai baohong le* (The Imperial Concubine Time-Travelled Back to Become an Internet Sensation). http://bbs.55ab.com/forum.php?mod=viewthread&tid=3858237. Accessed February 20, 2020.
———. *Wo bangding le shenghuo xitong* (I Acquired a Life-skills System). http://bbs.55ab.com/forum.php?mod=viewthread&tid=3590557. Accessed February 25, 2020.
Taiji Yu. *Fugui shunü* (Rich and Noble Lady). http://bbs.55ab.com/forum.php?mod=viewthread&tid=3890123. Accessed February 25, 2020.
Tang Zhong Mao. *Suoyou ren dou zhidao wo shi hao nanren* (Everyone Knows I Am a Good Man). http://bbs.55ab.com/forum.php?mod=viewthread&tid=3809831. Accessed February 25, 2020.
thaty. *Zhen hai yiwei zhishi gu chuan jin* (We Thought It Was Only Time-travel from Premodern to Modern Worlds). http://bbs.55ab.com/forum.php?mod=viewthread&tid=3801595. Accessed March 1, 2020.
Tian Miao. *Wo de yishu zhenjing shijie* (My Medical Skills Shock the World). http://bbs.55ab.com/forum.php?mod=viewthread&tid=3571015. Accessed February 25, 2020.
Toscano, Angela. "What is Romance?" https://teachmetonight.blogspot.com/p/romance-novel.html. Accessed April 4, 2020.
Turkle, Sherry. *Alone Together: Why We Expect More from Technology and Less from Each Other*. Basic Books, 2011.
YTT Taotao. *Wo quanjia doushi chuanlai de* (All My Family Time-Travelled Here). http://bbs.55ab.com/forum.php?mod=viewthread&tid=3748840. Accessed February 25, 2020.
Yu Xiao Guaiguai. *Meici chuan shu dou bei po shen zhuanzhe* (Every Travel into a Book I Am Forced to Make a Startling Turn). http://bbs.55ab.com/forum.php?mod=viewthread&tid=3757649. Accessed February 25, 2020.
Yu Yuzhu. *Nongjia xiao funü* (The Lucky Farm Girl). http://bbs.55ab.com/forum.php?mod=viewthread&tid=3555322. Accessed February 25, 2020.
Zhang Dingding. *Daji de renwu* (Daji's Task). http://www.huarenv5.com/forum/viewthread.php?tid=242917. Accessed February 25, 2020.
Zhi Niao Cun. *Da Yi Ling Ran* (Big Doctor Lin Ran). http://bbs.55ab.com/forum.php?mod=viewthread&tid=3020655. Accessed February 25, 2020.
Zhijian Shang de Yongtan Diao. *Yi jian feng xian* (Becoming Immortal by One Stroke of the Sword). http://bbs.55ab.com/forum.php?mod=viewthread&tid=3785922. Accessed February 25, 2020.

Original Slash, Romance, and C.S. Pacat's *Captive Prince*

Maria Alberto

The meteoric rise and massive commercial success of E.L. James's 2011–2013 *Fifty Shades of Grey* series drew considerable media coverage and critical attention, with the former tending to focus on the shock of "discovering" mommy porn, BDSM erotica, and the large market of women readers interested in such subgenres, while the latter more often explored how *Fifty Shades* had begun as fanfiction of the also wildly successful *Twilight* series and so reinvigorated questions of genre and authorship (see Jamison; Morrissey). Taken together, though, *Fifty Shades* and the conversations surrounding its publication provided a productive occasion through which "to revisit past conversations regarding the connections and disconnections between romantic fanfiction and commercial romances" (Morrissey "Fifty Shades of Remix" 1)—an opportunity that transpired in close conjunction with commercial publishers scrambling to capitalize on a slew of *Fifty Shades*-inspired titles.

This, however, was far from the only romance series to prompt re-evaluations of common assumptions about the many connections between fanfiction and romance. C.S. Pacat's 2008–2012, 2014–2016 "original slash" series *Captive Prince* achieved its own surprising, if more modest, commercial success soon after *Fifty Shades*, drawing accolades and attention as both a romance series and a "fan object," or cultural product that attracts sustained fan engagement (Williams 25), in its own right. Although the two series represent very different subgenres of romance, they are also distinguished by the rhetorical and cultural positionings instantiated by the term "original slash," as well as by the ways in which *Captive Prince* drew a fandom of its own while *Fifty Shades* more drew from fandom. Thus, where

Slash, Romance, and Pacat's Captive Prince (Alberto)   217

Fifty Shades serves as a reminder that the differences perceptible "between categories [of fanfiction and romance] can be shaped as much by networks of production and distribution as they are by story content" (Morrissey "Fifty Shades of Remix" 2), *Captive Prince* reiterates and complicates this idea by offering a more self-conscious model of "the networks that circulate slash" (Rambukkana 71).

Captive Prince is an erotic M/M romance series that consists of three novels (*Captive Prince*, *Prince's Gambit*, *Kings Rising*) and several short stories, all set in the fantasy kingdoms of Vere and Akielos. The trilogy follows Damen, crown prince of Akielos, beginning when he is captured and sent to Laurent, prince of Vere, as an unnamed pleasure slave after Damen's illegitimate brother usurps power in Akielos. As the books progress, Damen's initial plan to escape and return home to fight for his own kingdom is complicated by his growing attraction to Laurent and his conviction of Laurent's right to lead Vere. As even this brief summary suggests, then, the *Captive Prince* series deals with power dynamics, questions of consent, and other complex themes, albeit in a completely different vein than *Fifty Shades* does as a heterosexual BDSM romance with a contemporary setting.

Parts of *Captive Prince*'s road to success, though, might initially seem to reveal surface similarities between the two series, particularly regarding their online origins. The first two *Captive Prince* books were published on LiveJournal from 2008 through 2012 in serial updates that readers could access and comment on freely, in a model much like writing fanfiction: Pacat has reported that this direct interaction "absolutely" affected how she wrote, supporting her decision to tackle difficult issues and utilize unreliable narration (Von para. 4–6). While online, Pacat's work racked up over 15 million hits through word-of-mouth, in-community promotion, which eventually encouraged Pacat to self-publish on Amazon, and from there even higher numbers eventually sparked "a bidding war between U.S. publishers" (Bartlett par.2). As the novels were re-released through first Gatto and then Penguin, and drew reviews in industry venues such as *Publisher's Weekly*, readers often reported that the *Captive Prince* series was their first introduction to the possibilities of M/M romance and also that it revised certain expectations of romance itself as a genre (see Wynne; yourlibrarian). Meanwhile, an active fan community created reading resources and held discussions on LiveJournal, posted meta and fanart on Tumblr and DeviantArt, and published fanfiction on the Archive of Our Own (Ao3) (Romano), and several pockets of *Captive Prince* fandom still remain active as of this writing.

My project here is not to conflate, or even to compare, romance as a genre with slash as a maybe-genre, given both the longstanding critical conversation surrounding this comparison as well as the ways in which attempting such assessments can inadvertently reify the stigmas surrounding women's authorship and reading practices more generally, let alone fanfiction and romance specifically ("Fifty Shades of Remix" 2). However, the *Captive Prince* series also offers a great deal to consider on the other side of this phenomenon: that in which both reading communities and "slash writers themselves actively debate and theorize their practices" (Willis 298). In this essay, then, I will explore how the *Captive Prince* series draws from the modes, conventions, and networks of original slash—itself already a contentious term—and examine how this has impacted both the series' own production and readers' impressions of it.

The Terminology at Hand: Slash and/as/vs. Romance

The term "slash" originated with fandom, drawing its name from the back-slash punctuation mark in "Kirk/Spock," where this symbol was used to denote a sexual and/or romantic relationship between these two characters from *Star Trek: The Original Series*. Early fan studies work by Henry Jenkins, Camille Bacon-Smith, and others considered slash a liberating form that challenged patriarchal and heteronormative understandings of gender, relationships, and sexual identity, and much early work on slash drew from this lead: in "Slashing the Romance Narrative," for example, Anne Kustritz reads slash as "[allowing] women to construct narratives that subvert patriarchy by re-appropriating those prototypical hero characters who usually reproduce women's position of social disempowerment" (371). While not precisely inaccurate in its identification of slash as an interesting and important fan practice, this initial fan studies work has since been critiqued for its narrow focus on particular aspects of fan production as well as its somewhat uncritical, overly celebratory approach to fandom in general (Gray, Sandvoss, and Harrington 3). The scholarship on slash itself is not exempt from similar criticisms either, although happily, much work since has probed further into the contexts that drive slash production and the issues of race, class, and heteronormativity that still haunt it, as well as the assumption that slash is inherently progressive (see Hunting; Spacey; Fowler).

Although contemporary understandings of slash range from "the subset of fan-fiction which eroticizes the homosocial bonds depicted between media heroes" (Woledge 1) to "male-male sexual fanfiction that appropriates characters from preexisting fictional narratives" (Rambukkana 70), there remain certain areas of common ground. Most definitions today take it that slash features sex and/or romance between male characters, that slash is fanfiction (i.e., written about existing fictional characters from other texts), and that slash deals with subtext (i.e., is written about underlying, wished-for, or hinted-at relationships rather than those explicitly verified in the original text, which were usually heterosexual or M/F relationships to begin with).

The relationship between slash and romance has also been debated hotly. Early on, Patricia Frazer Lamb and Diana Veith argue that slash is a "radical departure" from romance because it suggests "that true love and authentic intimacy can exist only between equals" (238)—which to them meant characters of the same sex—while Constance Penley dismisses reading slash as romance due to its "pornographic force" (167). Catherine Salmon and Donald Symons then argue that "slash fiction is so similar to mainstream genre romances that it could reasonably be classified as a species of that genus" (97), while Sara Gwenllian Jones likewise suggests that slash "emulates" the style of romance (81). Catherine Driscoll sums up a common position as one in which "romance is something against which slash appears and to which slash introduces significance" (80), which dissatisfies her because it both generalizes fanfiction and dismisses romance. Later, Deborah Kaplan contends that conflating slash and romance fails to account for their distinct goals and genre structures, particularly because slash includes such a wide range of story types (123), and more recently, Katherine Morrissey has emphasized that "the importance of play with form and intertextuality" ("Fifty Shades of Remix" 2) is a more productive characterization of both romance and slash than any overtly structural elements they may also share. Moreover, many romance authors have drawn connections between slash and the subgenre of M/M romance specifically, even maintaining that M/M romance grew from slash more than from any other genre, including romance at large (see Fessenden; Meeker).

Somewhere between these two related yet distinct conversations, though, falls the question of "original slash," a phenomenon that has received little scholarly attention. In and of itself, the term troubles previous understandings that slash is fan fiction of existing characters—by this reckoning, "original slash" can be seen as a misnomer, with each half of the term contradicting the other. Authors and readers of original slash, however, tend to use the term in full awareness of this discrepancy, and in fact seem to find it useful precisely because it points to important commonalities. The fan-authored resource Fanlore, for instance, defines "original slash" as "a term used to describe homoerotic original fiction by slash-aware authors [who use] fannish tropes with original characters" (par. 1). This definition emphasizes that authors who write original slash are aware of its fannish precedents and consciously draw from them, even as they also strive to create something that is not explicitly fanfiction. Most other discussions of the term still extant today tend to agree that the defining characteristics of original slash include a fanfiction-like writing style and specific tropes regarding character and/or relationship dynamics (see Khana; Dorothea; Francis; Peterson). Moreover, these reader- and author-driven conversations often point out such characteristics as a way of distinguishing original slash from the genres of "boys' love" (also "BL") and *yaoi*[1] as well as the fanfiction where "slash" itself originated. To its authors and readers, then, original slash is something related to, but also distinct from, a number of terms that might be more recognizable to a reader outside this tradition.

Another point of distinction, too, comes from the way in which original slash faces different challenges than slash historically has, including dissimilar issues of production, distribution, and readership. Fanlore contributors sum up these challenges succinctly: for original slash, "there is no canon" (par. 4). That is, even when slash was an underground phenomenon, it had an audience who wanted to read it because they had stakes in the characters it portrayed, who originated from existing media texts. As a result of this demand, slash had vocal champions even when it was a niche taste, and it would eventually come to be included in fandom community resources such as print zines and online fanfiction archives—and from there, as it became more readily visible and available, its own popularity and prominence only grew. As Fanlore contributors are pointing out, though, original slash does not work from any "canon" of beloved characters from existing texts, and because of this, it could not draw the same kinds of (fan) readership that slash did, and there was much less push for its systematic inclusion in (fandom) community networks and resources. As a result, original slash's venues for publication and distribution were fewer, more sporadic, and ultimately more static than those for slash eventually became. The now-defunct Original Slash Archive attempted to create a central space, and original slash authors often had LiveJournal accounts or self-created websites; webrings also attempted to connect readers with both original slash authors as well as "recs," or recommendations. Few of these resources still exist, though, while the networks and resources that were developed to circulate slash—as well as many of the other genres discussed above—remain incredibly strong.

Between its authors and readers distinguishing original slash from similar writing traditions, and then original slash facing particular circulation challenges, this meant that finding, discussing, and sharing original slash was very much a community-driven enterprise—in some ways, even more so than it was for slash fanfiction, which at least later benefited from specific conventions and structures, such as fanfiction archive tags that made for easy searching. It is also worth noting that, as of writing this essay in 2020, the term "original slash" has largely fallen out of use, in tandem with what Katherine Morrissey calls a "post-slash" moment where fandom content focused on male/male relationships has become so prevalent that fans' preferences are no longer categorized primarily along the lines of slash (M/M), "gen" (no sex), or "het" (heterosexual or M/F relationship), but instead according to particular character pairings ("Death of Slash"). Meanwhile, the commercial publishing categories of "M/M romance" and "LGBT romance" are flourishing, both in self-publishing and mainstream venues, while transnational counterparts such as BL and especially danmei continue to thrive and reach new readers.

For the *Captive Prince* series to be discussed as "original slash," then, is for author C.S. Pacat and her readers to be associating this work with a specific tradition and its conventions, which include its fanfiction-driven or "slash-aware" origins, a particular style of writing, and a certain set of tropes as well as a now-vanishing but once highly-specific context of production and distribution. Where E.L. James was often said to be "filing off the serial numbers" with *Fifty Shades of Grey* (Jamison 262)—i.e., repurposing her fanfiction for commercial publication by removing identifying details taken from existing media, such as character names from *Twilight*—original slash stories such as *Captive Prince* drew from a selection of character types, relationship dynamics, and story arcs, not repurposing them so much as operating under the expectation that readers would recognize them as a part of a "slash-aware" (Fanlore) tradition. And, as I explore next, Pacat's *Captive Prince* series does this while also reaching romance-focused reading communities who could enjoy the erotica, characters, or other aspects of the books without necessarily recognizing or engaging with the various underlying traditions of original slash.

Captive Prince *and Networks of Discussion*

The trajectory of the *Captive Prince* series offers the first hint of its complicated relationship with different communities of readers and their differing expectations. Pacat published the first two installments on LiveJournal from 2008 through 2012 under the pseudonym freece, and the first commercial editions were published by Gatto in February 2013. In May of the same year, Penguin acquired the rights to the entire trilogy before the third book had been published anywhere else, and Pacat wrote this third book, *Kings Rising*, offline before it was released by Penguin in 2016. As of this writing in 2020, the freece LiveJournal is largely inaccessible, and the initial versions of *Captive Prince* published there have been taken down. Moreover, most of the timeline that I have summarized here is preserved mainly through fan-authored resources such as Fanlore (see the page "Captive Prince"), with details such as the freece pseudonym or Pacat's primary beta-reader, fellow LiveJournal user bop_radar, rarely mentioned elsewhere, even in Pacat's own interviews.

The wildly mixed reviews that the *Captive Prince* series drew—and continues to draw today—also reflect this complexity, a disparity that becomes particularly visible with what elements of the text and its production various types of reviews focus on. Three general categories each have common refrains. First, reviews by newspapers and trade publications (*Publishers Weekly*, Australian newspapers, etc.) tend to treat the series as a best-selling romance or else the magnum opus of a hometown hero making it big. Overall, this type of review—itself written for a larger, more general readership—rarely engages more deeply with questions of genre or genre conventions, even when it does identify examples of them. Next, reviews by romance outlets, particularly independent romance bloggers, tend to depict *Captive Prince* as an unpredictable romance with a surprising central plot and relationship, a well-written erotic component, and both scenes and themes that can be difficult to the point of off-putting. Finally, reviews by fans of the series, fanfiction-savvy readers, and other similarly "slash-aware" audiences tend to identify some of the same components that romance reviewers found unpredictable and difficult—but also to engage with those aspects almost immediately.

These three types of reviews are worth noting because each is based on a different understanding of what the *Captive Prince* series is, and consequently, a different set of expectations for what it should be doing. For example, when trade and newspaper reviews mention that it was originally published online, few that I've found even mention LiveJournal as its platform of origin or explain exactly how Pacat interacted with her early readers. This vagueness on the part of most mainstream publications leans into the assumption that online publishing is a monolithic phenomenon, and also overlooks the many considerable differences among platforms, reader communities, and the types of work each one makes possible. More significantly yet, this vagueness also suggests to its general readership that *Captive Prince* became successful in the same way, or for the same reasons, that *Fifty Shades* had just years before, particularly because *Fifty Shades*' commercial success and most sensational qualities remained in the public consciousness long after James had finished publishing it. And although the romance outlets and the "slash-aware" reviews are similar to one another in that they usually come from individuals rather than mainstream media venues, the particular individuals writing these two types of reviews often had wildly disparate levels of knowledge and experience with original slash. Thus, while both tend to pick up on characteristic examples in *Captive Prince*, these often constitute a novelty for the former and a point of critical discussion for the latter.

For example, one of the largest and longest-running controversies surrounding the *Captive Prince* series is its treatment of slavery. Sexual slavery is the main premise of the first book, which leans heavily into Damen's experiences not only as a slave, but also specifically a pleasure slave, of the man who is at once his enemy and his "master." Throughout the first book of the series Laurent instigates, or at least permits, nonconsensual sexual encounters between Damen and other men, including an early scene where Damen would have been raped if he lost a wrestling match and a later one where Damen does not consent to oral sex with another slave. Moreover, Damen is often described as having darker skin than Laurent, and many readers were quick to point out how this evokes discomfiting associations with the transatlantic slave trade in addition to the first book's already polemical focus on sexual slavery.

These items are worth noting in part because they inform so many readers' responses to *Captive Prince*, in part because Pacat has addressed them in paratextual writings, and ultimately because they speak to the series' inception—and later, reception—as original slash. Notably, Pacat has been asked about the *Captive Prince* series' online origins in most interviews with large media outlets (see Bartlett; Von; Romano), but Damen's ethnic heritage tends to come up just on social media, and the series' early focus on sexual slavery mainly comes up in reviews by individual reviewers. While these differences certainly speak to what various media outlets are willing to cover when keeping a general-public readership in mind, they also gesture toward different degrees of knowledge about three distinct questions, which regard the trope of slavery in fanfiction and "slash-aware" fiction (Fanlore), perceived race and/or ethnicity in fiction (including fanfiction), and perceived race in online reader communities (including both fan communities and romance readers).

In a long Twitter thread from August 2016, Pacat asserts that Damen's fantasy ethnicity reflects her own experience as a queer person of Greek heritage in Australia ("As for the influence"), a stance that claims a geographically specific form of real-world marginalization. Moreover, Pacat explains that Damen "carries markers of [this] identity" ("It's intentional") although this is "rarely read from that perspective outside of Australia" ("There's a lot"). Many *Captive Prince* readers have pointed to this thread from Pacat as proof that the *Captive Prince* books "aren't racist," which is simultaneously a valid point about authorial intent while also inadequate as a dismissal of all critique of the series.

Notably absent from Pacat's thread, for instance, is any explicit discussion of intersections between Damen's "markers of identity"—as a man of color, if not specifically a Black man—and his being forced into sexual slavery as the premise for a book-length erotic story. Stitch, a Black scholar who writes extensively on issues of race and racism in online fandom, notes that "stories sexualizing slavery" are common in both romance and fanfiction (par. 7), and in a list of frequent occurrences, includes several descriptions that fit *Captive Prince* quite well: inspiration from ancient Greek or Roman customs, marginalization on the apparent basis of alterity other than race, and a focus on "the experience of white male characters who are oppressed" (para. 7–8). Regardless of such stories' genre or tradition of origin, too, Stitch maintains that any sexualization of slavery is necessarily "coming from a place still influenced by that brutal history" of the transatlantic slave trade (par. 19)—not because this trade is or was the only example of real-world slavery, but because it was the most horrific example and its effects survive in the most visible, intense forms today, all in ways that stories "turning slavery into something sexy for commodification and consumption" cannot ever engage with given their primary focus on readerly and authorial pleasure (par. 24).

While some reviews of the *Captive Prince* series—such as those by *Publisher's Weekly*—simply note the presence of themes that readers might find difficult, others dive right into grappling with the kind of non-engagement or re-direction of these themes that Stitch identifies as inherently problematic. Fantasy author Foz Meadows, for instance, spends much of a comprehensive review delving into how the master/slave romance is undoubtedly a narrative device, and one that must have been widely discussed among Pacat and her early readers in ways that "impacted how and why the story was told as it was" (par. 7), but also considers how "given the historical intersection of racism with both slavery and pornography (both straight and queer), it's impossible to argue that race simply doesn't matter, or insist that the characters be judged wholly on the basis of the setting" (par. 12).

Likewise Mesamm, one of the early readers present when Pacat began posting on LiveJournal, offers another appraisal that notes entanglements among genre, "slash-aware" writing traditions, and the often difficult subject matter of the *Captive Prince* series. In Mesamm's experience, the reader community surrounding Pacat's work at the time was familiar with certain conventions from *yaoi* and fanfiction—an impression that echoes Fanlore contributors' definition of original slash as being "by slash-aware authors [who use] fannish tropes"—which Mesamm reports meant that "Slavefic was a semi-popular genre that wasn't generally questioned from [a social justice] perspective; it was purely an id-satisfying narrative trope that many of us enjoyed" (par. 10), Mesamm also notes that, given the conditions with online platforms circa 2008–2010, Pacat happened to be writing during a period when new iterations of digital culture "challenged narrative conventions, raised awareness of larger social justice issues, and shaped a more critical analysis of many of the common tropes seen in fanfic, fantasy and m/m genres" (par. 10)—or, put differently, generally changed online readers' expectations of their own communities and the fiction they could encounter within them. Drawing from what was then 8 years' personal experience reading the *Captive Prince* series, Mesamm points out that

> I do think this [shift away from slave fiction] reflected [Pacat's] own evolving interests and abilities, at the same time as it more or less synced up with the evolving nature of the genre. And as the years passed, it also brought [Pacat] a new kind of readership—one coming from a different starting point and with a different set of expectations [par. 12].

Thus, while multiple types of reviews might express discomfort with the treatment of slavery in the *Captive Prince* series, it is mainly the "slash-aware" readers (Fanlore) who express this discomfort in terms of sexual slavery as an erotic trope with a specific history, and how this played out in *Captive Prince* specifically.

It is also worth noting here that, much like she discussed Damen's ethnic heritage on Twitter, Pacat has confirmed parts of this narrative about "the evolving nature" (Mesamm) of her chosen genre mainly in paratextual materials. In various places Pacat has attributed inspiration to a range of influences, from Dorothy Dunnett's historical novels *The Lymond Chronicles* and their bisexual hero (Ng) to *yaoi* (Romano); likewise, in places she has actually pushed against the term "slash"—the term connoting a fanfiction element—(see Romano), suggesting that there are parts of this tradition that she felt did not apply to her work. The element of sexual slavery, though, is not one that has come up this directly, to the best of my knowledge.

As the series' continued success suggests, *Captive Prince* can certainly be read with only minimal attention to these questions, and the responses from mainstream media outlets and reviewers more familiar with romance than with original slash and its constellation of related genres—slash fanfiction, *yaoi*, BL—reiterate as much. And yet, the *Captive Prince* series happened to be written, initially published, and then acquired and re-released by a major publishing house during a watershed moment in which there was little else like it—a complex, layered same-sex romance dealing candidly and extensively with trauma, abuse, and consent—on the mainstream market. Thus, the series is at once the product of its moment of writing—a period when slavefic was not interrogated as visibly as it is today, and when original slash as a genre was usually produced for a small, insular community of readers who relied on peers to direct them to new material—and also of its moment of re-release, into a mainstream romance market that had just seen the unexpected runaway success of E.L. James's *Fifty Shades of Grey*, another text whose tradition of origin was familiar to some but often a shock to the system beyond that particular community.

"the reality of who they both were stark between them": From Original Slash to Romance?

Although, as long-time reader Mesamm has noted, the *Captive Prince* series changed as Pacat's interests, platform, and readership did, there still remain highly visible traces of its origins even in the installments that only Penguin published. For example, toward the end of *Kings Rising*, the third and final book of the series, Pacat offers readers an eagerly awaited, seven-page-long sex scene. While this is not the first time in the series that Damen and Laurent have sex, it is their first time together after both men have acknowledged that they know each other's complex, multi-faceted personal and political identities. Until this point, Pacat has set up Damen and Laurent as master and slave, but also as soldier and leader, and as the princes of their respective warring nations; readers have also discovered that Damen killed Laurent's beloved older brother in battle several years prior, that Laurent has known from the beginning that Damen is his brother's killer, and that the death of Laurent's brother had paved the way for Laurent's uncle to both seize power in Vere and to groom and sexually abuse Laurent himself. Thus, while this sex scene in *Kings Rising* is not technically the two characters' "first time" together—a much-beloved trope in romance and in slash fanfiction alike, let alone original slash—it also is their first time, in the more metaphorical sense that they can simply be themselves, rather than performing or inhabiting any of their many other identities and experiences. And Pacat leans into this context throughout the scene, creating a metaphorical "first time" for Damen and Laurent in which half the pleasure for both characters and readers comes from the traditions of original slash.

Damen, from whose point of view all three books are told, has both his own and Laurent's histories—both as individuals and with each other—in mind throughout the entire scene, lending it a degree of introspection and internality that very much reflects the nature of original slash as "homoerotic original fiction by slash-aware authors [who use] fannish tropes with original characters" (Fanlore). As a genre, fanfiction has the option of being driven more by emotion or character than by plot, whereas with romance, certain story beats—including sex scenes, introspection, and intimacy—are expected at certain points, and the *Captive Prince* series, being original slash moved into a romance publishing context, is left to negotiate this difference—a challenge that Pacat manages in particular ways. Thus, readers will find that Damen's anticipation and enjoyment of sex with Laurent is at once sensual and erotic, but also contemplative and reflective. His thoughts and reflections about how far he and Laurent have come in understanding and treating one another drive this sex scene as much as his actions or his verbalizations of these thoughts to Laurent, and readers are led to imagine that something similar is happening with Laurent, whose own reflections are visible mainly through what Damen can observe and deduce of his partner.

Pacat's original slash-inflected approach is visible from the very beginning of the scene, where foreplay begins with "Laurent's breathing shallowed as Damen pushed himself up. He had kissed Laurent as a slave, but never as himself. They both felt the difference of it, the anticipated kiss so real between them it was as if it was already happening" (203). Here, foreplay and its pleasures are not limited to the actual, physical gesture of a kiss, or even to its sexual and romantic connotations: instead, Damen locates a great deal of his own pleasure, and assumes much of Laurent's too, in its historical contexts, or the way in which they have kissed before but "never" while acknowledging each other as social equals with no coercive power imbalance between them. Their history lends a weight to the kiss, such that even its anticipation is charged and almost as perceptible "as it if was already happening" (203). Moreover, beyond the fact that this kiss will be exchanged during a time and place in their relationship where it signifies their full knowledge of and trust in one another, here the sexual pleasure and satisfaction of foreplay also stem from the ways in which "they both felt the difference of it" (203). From Damen's account at least, he and Laurent do not even need to communicate this impression aloud in order for them both to know what a kiss, and later sex, means.

Even when Damen actually says some of this to Laurent, such statements are followed by his internal translation or conferral of meaning beyond what is spoken aloud:

"I'm not your slave," said Damen. "I'm a man."
Don't think, he'd said, because it was easier than saying, *Take me for who I am* [203].

Here their shared history of Laurent as Damen's captor and all the nonconsensual sexual experience that came with this fact become compounded with their newfound acknowledgment that Damen killed Laurent's brother in battle, unknowingly leaving a young Laurent open to political exploitation and sexual abuse by his own uncle. Laurent's personal loss, his experience of abuse, and his abuse of others in turn are all laid out in the open between the two men, providing them with the release of catharsis while also leading up to the release of sexual pleasure, and inviting readers to take pleasure from both angles as well. This duality continues through passages such as:

"It's me," said Damen. "It's me, here with you. Say my name."
"Damianos."

> He felt the sundering in Laurent in that, the name an admission, a statement of truth that came out of him, Laurent open to him with nothing to hide behind. He could hear it in Laurent's voice. *Prince-killer.*
>
> Laurent shuddered against him as they kissed ... [204]

As readers' point of view into this sex scene, Damen continues his interior assignment of meaning to tangible gestures even as he and Laurent continue foreplay through getting on the bed (205), then Laurent undressing (206), and then preparation for anal penetration (207–9). At some points, Damen affixes further meaning from their shared past experiences to observation alone, as when Laurent is finally naked and "for a moment they just looked, caught in each other's eyes. More than skin was exposed" (206); at other times, it is sensation that Damen contextualizes this way, as happens when Laurent straddles him and touches his chest, right on the scar that his late brother had inflicted just before Damen killed him (207). In both cases, though, Pacat continues bringing in two-and-a-half earlier books' worth of background into a single sex scene, letting emotion and character drive to the forefront.

All of this comes to a head with Damen's anticipation and enjoyment of anal penetration, a type of intimacy that he and Laurent have not attempted with each other up to this point. For Damen—and by his narration of the scene, readers—this experience with Laurent is entirely inflected by his recently acquired knowledge that Laurent had previously endured the same sexual act at his uncle's hands, and the resulting realization that his willingness to have sex with Damen in this way now is an unprecedented level of trust for Laurent. Much as with the foreplay and preparation earlier, Damen's internal reflection and contextualization of sex here tie together their shared history with the act of sex itself to drive the scene forward. To manage this, Pacat juxtaposes passages such as

> "Let me in," he said, and Laurent made a new sound, his head dropped between his shoulder blades, his breath ribboning out of him. "Let me inside you."

with their results being:

> He was inside Laurent. It felt raw and unprotected. He had never felt more like himself: Laurent had let him inside, knowing who he was. His body was already moving. Laurent made a helpless sound into the bedding that was the Veretian word, "Yes" [209].

As with Pacat's depiction of foreplay and preparation earlier in the same scene, here sex for Damen and Laurent is inextricable from their history with each other, which also includes both the history of abuse each man has suffered as well as the history between their warring nations. In the passages above, Damen's request for Laurent to "let him in" or to be inside Laurent are simultaneously sexual, and also requests for intimacy and trust despite the difficulty of such emotion given their backgrounds. Likewise, the "raw and unprotected" feeling of Damen penetrating Laurent is at once physical and emotional, as Laurent has had to overcome his anger and grief at losing his brother, his pain and mistrust from being abused by his uncle, and his guilt over abusing Damen at the beginning of their relationship in order for the two of them to arrive at this point. Thus, through the mechanism of Damen's perspective, Damen's penetration of Laurent is at once an erotic act, a gesture of desire, and Laurent's ceding power to Damen for once in their relationship—something that Mesamm reports was so widely anticipated and speculated among early readers that Pacat actually had a poll up on LiveJournal at one point (para. 30–33).

In concrete terms, then, this scene in *Kings Rising* depicts the first time that Damen and Laurent have sexual intercourse in a particular way—a common and much-beloved trope. In equally important terms, though, this scene's particular treatment of sex between the series' two main characters is navigated by Pacat using familiar and recognizable traditions from original slash, even as she also worked to move away from more overt parts of that tradition as the *Captive Prince* series was published in more mainstream contexts.

"a choking pleasure that took him, overwhelming and bright": Parting Thoughts

Romance scholar Deborah Kaplan, writing just a few years before Pacat first began posting *Captive Prince* on LiveJournal, muses that when she began researching slash "it was only possible to speculate about how many of the differences between slash fiction and romance are merely due to the changes inherent in mapping a same-sex pairing onto the heterosexual love story" (128). In other words, Kaplan wonders, is it just the focus on a male/male relationship over a female/male one that distinguishes slash from romance?

From today's vantage point, of course, we have seen more than enough to suggest that it is no "merely" separating the two: potential differences between slash and romance expand beyond sexual orientation and desire to encompass the use of existing or original characters, the range of conventions expected, and the communities circulated in, among others. Moreover, as the subject of this essay has demonstrated, Kaplan's speculation about differences between slash and romance oversimplifies the range of writing traditions available for comparison, leaving out genres and traditions ranging from BL to *danmei* to original slash.

Given all of this, I suggest that there is no "merely" about the differences between slash and romance, let alone original slash and romance.

Although there is no single, universal experience of reading and enjoying fiction in these traditions, one way of grouping common experiences might fall as follows: slash fans seek familiar characters in familiar story types; original slash fans seek familiar character types and relationship dynamics in familiar story types; romance fans seek familiar stories featuring familiar character types. And although C.S. Pacat is hardly the first to treat with themes of power, consent, and evolving intimacy in a romance series, it is certainly worth examining how she maps—and then shares—these using conventions of original slash that were more familiar to some readers than others.

Note

1. Though original slash writers may make this claim as a means of distinguishing their own work from other traditions, the reality is more complicated because there are numerous overlaps here as well as among BL, *yaoi*, and the later *danmei*. Boy's love (BL), "an umbrella term for female-oriented romances between two males" (Zhang 249), originated in Japan around the same time as Kirk/Spock slash fanfiction was on the rise in the U.S., to an extent that "it's unclear whether they arose independently or if one genre influenced the other" (Pagliassotti). BL does predate original slash, though, as does its more explicit, sex-focused subtype *yaoi*, whose name is an acronym of the Japanese *yamanashi, ochinashi, iminashi*, i.e., "no point, no climax, no meaning" (McHarry). Meanwhile *danmei*, a Chinese BL form that often focuses on male beauty and aesthetics over explicit sexual content, has grown more visible and distinct from its predecessors in the last several years, including a rising awareness among Western audiences thanks to live-action adaptations of *danmei* web-novels, such as *Guardian* (2018) and *The Untamed* (2019). Across BL, *yaoi*, and *danmei* alike, examples span genres, and so include web-novels, manga, interactive fiction/visual novels, and more: it is also worth noting that these three terms are sometimes conflated or treated as synonyms. For more, see Jin Feng's *Romancing the Internet: Producing and Consuming Chinese Web Romance* (2013), Chunyu Zhang's "Loving Boys Twice as Much: Chinese Women's Paradoxical Fandom of 'Boys' Love' Fiction" (2016), Mark McLelland et al.'s *Boy's Love Manga and Beyond* (2015), and Antonia Levi et al.'s *Boys' Love Manga: Essays on the Sexual Ambiguity and Cross-Cultural Fandom of the Genre* (2010).

Works Cited

Bartlett, Myke. "C.S. Pacat, Melburnian Author of Captive Prince." *The Weekly Review*, 9 June 2015. https://web.archive.org/web/20161203115108/http://www.theweeklyreview.com.au/meet/c-s-pacat-best-selling-melburnian-author-of-captive-prince.
Dorothea. "Original Slash, Once Again." [transl. from German]. *LiveJournal*, 13 September 2004. https://frogspace.livejournal.com/44477.html.
Driscoll, Catherine. "One True Pairing: The Romance of Pornography and the Pornography of Romance." *Fan Fiction and Fan Communities in the Age of the Internet: New Essays*, edited by Karen Hellekson and Kristina Busse, McFarland, 2006, pp. 79–98.
Fanlore. "Captive Prince." n.d. https://fanlore.org/wiki/Captive_Prince.
_____. "Original Slash." n.d. https://fanlore.org/wiki/Original_Slash.
Fessenden, Jamie. "My Take on Women Writing M/M Romance." *Jamie Fessenden's Blog*, 28 June 2014. https://jamiefessenden.com/2014/06/28/my-take-on-women-writing-mm-romance/.

Francis, Manna. "Original M/M Fiction." Mannazone.org, 30 August 2015. http://www.mannazone.org/zone/index.html.

Gray, Jonathan, Cornel Sandvoss, and C. Lee Harrington. "Introduction: Why Study Fans?" *Fandom: Identities and Communities in a Mediated World*, edited by Jonathan Gray, Cornel Sandvoss, and C. Lee Harrington, NYU Press, 2007, pp. 1–16.

Gwenllian Jones, Sara. "The Sex Lives of Cult Television Characters." *Screen*, vol. 43, no. 1, 2002, pp. 79–90. https://doi.org/10.1093/screen/43.1.79.

Fowler, Charity A. "A Bad Bromance: Betrayal, Violence and Dark Delight in Subverting the Romance Narrative." *The Darker Side of Slash Fan Fiction: Essays on Power, Consent and the Body*, edited by Ashton Spacey, McFarland, 2018, pp. 177–199.

Hunting, Kyra. "Queer as Folk and the Trouble with Slash." *Transformative Works and Cultures*, no. 11, 2012. https://doi.org/10.3983/twc.2012.0415.

Jamison, Anne. "An Interview with Eurydice (Vivean Dean)." *Fic: Why Fanfiction Is Taking Over the World*, edited by Anne Jamison, Smart Pop, 2013, pp. 263–267.

Kaplan, Debra. "'Why Would Any Woman Want to Read Such Stories?': The Distinctions Between Genre Romances and Slash Fiction." *New Approaches to Popular Romance Fiction: Critical Essays*, edited by Sarah S.G. Frantz, and Eric Murphy Selinger, McFarland, 2012, pp. 121–136.

Khana. "Original Slash vs Original Yaoi?" [transl. from German]. *LiveJournal*, 30 April 2008. https://obishi.livejournal.com/4309.html.

Kustritz, Anne. "Slashing the Romance Narrative." *The Journal of American Culture*, vol. 26, no. 3, 2003, pp. 371–384. https://doi.org/10.1111/1542-734X.00098.

Lamb, Patricia Frazier, and Diane L. Veith. "Romantic Myth, Transcendence and Star Trek Zines." *Erotic Universe: Sexuality and Fantastic Literature*, 1st ed., edited by Donald Palumbo, Greenwood Press, 1986. pp 235–255.

McHarry, Mark. "(Un)gendering the Homoerotic Body: Imagining Subjects in Boys' Love and Yaoi." In "Textual Echoes," special issue edited by Cyber Echoes, *Transformative Works and Cultures*, no. 8, 2011. https://doi.org/10.3983/twc.2011.0257.

Meadows, Foz. "Captive Prince Trilogy: Review." Fozmeadows.wordpress.com, 11 June 2016. https://fozmeadows.wordpress.com/2016/06/11/captive-prince-trilogy-review/.

Mesamm. "Captive Prince: Reader Expectations and Preference." *Tumblr*, 26 January 2016. https://mesamm.tumblr.com/post/138093164607/captive-prince-reader-expectations-and.

Morrissey, Katherine. "Fifty Shades of Remix: The Intersecting Pleasures of Commercial and Fan Romances." *Journal of Popular Romance Studies*, vol. 4, no. 1, 2014. https://www.jprstudies.org/2014/02/fifty-shades-of-remix-the-intersecting-pleasures-of-commercial-and-fan-romancesby-katherine-morrissey/.

_____. "The Death of Slash." Paper presented at Fan Studies Network North American (FSNNA) conference, Chicago, IL, October 2019.

Ng, Natalie. "SEXtember: Captive Prince Author C.S. Pacat Talks Importance of Diverse LGBTQ Representation in Fiction." *Meld Magazine*, 9 September 2015. https://www.meldmagazine.com.au/2015/09/interview-captive-prince-author-cs-pacat-lgbt-fiction/.

Pacat, C.S. "As for the influence on Captive Prince." Twitter, 29 August 2016. https://twitter.com/cspacat/status/770153811105030144.

_____. "It's intentional that Akielos is based on Greece." Twitter, 29 August 2016. https://twitter.com/cspacat/status/770154324118806528.

_____. *Kings Rising*. Berkeley/Penguin Random House, 2016.

_____. "There's a lot of wog-politics in the series." Twitter, 29 August 2016. https://twitter.com/cspacat/status/770156112783867904.

Pagliasotti, Dru. "Reading Boys' Love in the West." *Particip@tions*, vol. 5, no. 2 (special issue), 2008, pp. 1–25. https://www.participations.org/Volume 5/Issue 2/5_02_pagliassotti.htm.

Penley, Constance. *NASA/Trek: Popular Science and Sex in America*. Verso, 1997.

Peterson, Dusk. "What Is Original Gen, Original Het, and Original Slash?" Duskpeterson.com, 2008. https://duskpeterson.com/definitionoriginalfic.htm.

Rambukkana, Nathan. "Is Slash an Alternative Medium? 'Queer' Heterotopias and the Role of Autonomous Media Spaces in Radical World Building." *Affinities: A Journal of Radical Theory, Culture and Action*, vol. 1, no. 1 2007, pp. 69–85.

Romano, Aja. "Behind Captive Prince, S.U. Pacat's Bestselling Work of Slave Erotica." *The Daily Dot*, 15 February 2013. https://www.dailydot.com/culture/captive-prince-su-pacat-interview/.

Salmon, Catherine, and Don Symons. "Slash Fiction and Human Mating Psychology." *Journal of Sex Research*, vol. 41, 2004, pp. 94–100.

Spacey, Ashton. "Introduction." *The Darker Side of Slash Fan Fiction: Essays on Power, Consent and the Body*, edited by Ashton Spacey, McFarland, 2018, pp. 5–24.

Stitch. "What Fandom Racism Looks Like: (Not-So) Sexy Slavefic." *Stitch's Media Mix*, 12 July 2018. https://stitchmediamix.com/2018/07/12/what-fandom-racism-looks-like-not-so-sexy-slavefic/.

Von. "A Chat with Captive Prince Author C.S. Pacat." *The Geekiary*, 17 April 2015. https://thegeekiary.com/a-chat-with-captive-prince-author-c-s-pacat/23488.

Williams, Rebecca. *Post-Object Fandom: Television, Identity, and Self-Narrative*. Bloomsbury Academic, 2015.

Willis, Ika. "Writing the Fables of Sexual Difference: Slash Fiction as Technology of Gender." *Parallax*, vol. 22, no. 3, 2016, pp. 290–311. https://doi.org/10.1080/13534645.2016.1201920.

Woledge, Elizabeth. "From Slash to the Mainstream: Female Writers and Gender Blending Men." *Extrapolation*, vol. 46, no. 1, 2005, pp. 50–65.

Wynne. "M/M Genre Books: What About [Them] Is So Addictive?" Literature and Movies. com, 3 May 2018. https://literaturesandmovies.com/2018/05/03/i-love-m-m-romance-books/.

yourlibrarian. "What Does Fanfic Leave Out?" *Dreamwidth*, 12 December 2011. http://yourlibrarian.dreamwidth.org/312298.html.

About the Contributors

Maria **Alberto** is working on a Ph.D. in literature and cultural studies at the University of Utah, where she pursues research interests in fan studies, adaptation, and popular culture. She is especially interested in how adaptations can be produced or reworked with particular audiences in mind, as well as how the term "canon" has come to be used. Time permitting, she's inordinately fond of LGBTQ+ romances or new enemies-to-lovers slow burn fiction.

Camille S. **Alexander** completed a Ph.D. in English at the University of Kent. Her research interests include Caribbean studies and literature; Black British literature; American film; and third-wave feminism. She has been published in *The Journal of Popular Culture* and the edited collection *Voodoo, Hoodoo, and Conjure in African American Literature*. She is also an assistant professor at Tuskegee University.

Jonathan A. **Allan** is the Canada Research Chair in Men and Masculinities and professor of English, drama and creative writing at Brandon University. He is the author of *Reading from Behind: A Cultural Analysis of the Anus* (2016), *Men, Masculinities, and Popular Romance* (2020), and *Men, Masculinities, and Infertilities* (2022), an interdisciplinary study of representations of men's infertility in literature, film, memoirs and popular culture.

Elizabeth Reid **Boyd** is an academic in the School of Arts and Humanities at Edith Cowan University in Western Australia. She has published widely and served as a media commentator on the topics of gender, culture, romance, and etymology. She writes fiction as Eliza Redgold, and her historical romances are published internationally by Harlequin (Harper Collins) London. She is a co-founder of the Love Studies Research Group at Edith Cowan University.

Ellen **Carter** is a senior lecturer in English language and translation at the University of Strasbourg, France, and a member of the Linguistique, Langues, Parole research group. Her doctorate in literary sciences was jointly awarded by the École des Hautes Études en Sciences Sociales, Paris, and the University of Auckland, New Zealand. Her research interests are in popular fiction, queer romance novels and the production, translation, and reception of cross-cultural crime fiction.

Ashley Elizabeth **Christensen** is a postdoctoral fellow at Florida State University, where she also received a Ph.D. in 20th-century Anglophone literature, media, and culture. Her research and teaching interests target interdisciplinary intersections of contemporary Anglophone and women's literature, popular culture and media studies, adaptation theory, and gender/femme studies.

Debra **Dudek** is an associate professor in the English program at Edith Cowan University, Australia. She has published internationally on love and ethics, including in her monograph *The Beloved Does Not Bite: Moral Vampires and the Humans Who Love Them* and in book chapters including "'Are you sure we're Witches and not Puritans?' Sexual Flexibility and Unrealised Desire in Netflix's *Chilling Adventures of Sabrina*."

Susan **Fanetti** is a professor of English at California State University, Sacramento, where she serves as coordinator of the English Education program and teaches courses in teaching English language arts and in American literature, genre literature, composition, and popular culture. Her scholarship tends to explore the intersections of teaching and popular culture. She is also a successful independently published romance novelist, with more than fifty titles to date.

Jin **Feng** is a professor of Chinese and the Orville and Mary Patterson Routt Professor of Literature at Grinnell College. She is the author of *Tasting Paradise on Earth* (2019), *Romancing the Internet* (2013), *The Making of a Family Saga* (2009), and *The New Woman in Early Twentieth-Century Chinese Fiction* (2004), in addition to other publications in English and Chinese. She is writing on the institutionalization of creating writing in China.

Nattie **Golubov** works at the Centro de Investigaciones sobre América de Norte (CISAN), Universidad Nacional Autónoma de México, and teaches in the English Department at the Facultad de Filosofia y Letras (UNAM). Her teaching and research focus on 20th-century and 21st-century literary studies, English literature, and literary theory. Her publications include *El amore en tiempos neoliberals* (2017) as well as the collections *Los placers de la lectura* and *TVficciones* (2019).

Madalena **Grobbelaar** is a lecturer and clinical psychologist in the School of Arts and Humanities at Edith Cowan University. Her research focuses on sexuality, gender, and interpersonal violence. She teaches counseling and psychotherapy at ECU and has a part-time private practice. She is the Western Australia branch president of the Society of Australian Sexologists (SAS).

Lucky **Issar** is a literature graduate with a degree in education. He lives in Berlin and is completing a Ph.D. at Berlin Free University. He is interested in gender studies, Dalit studies, and the work of Indian authors who write in English. Apart from literature, he has studied sociology, political science, and public administration.

Lucy **Sheerman** is working on a series of fan fiction versions of iconic novels including *Rebecca* (Dancing Girl Press) and *Jane Eyre* and a critical book about fan fiction responses to *Jane Eyre*. She co-created a new Evensong for Peterborough Cathedral. She runs the Creative Writing Centre at the Institute of Continuing Education, University of Cambridge.

Ashleigh Taylor **Sullivan** is a Ph.D. candidate within the Department of English Literature and Creative Writing at Swansea University. Her doctoral thesis examines the ways in which Daphne du Maurier (1907–1989) uses the Gothic as a device to explore her own gender identity through fiction. Her research interests also include the romance genre.

About the Contributors

Wendy **Wagner** is professor of English and media and communication studies at Johnson & Wales University, where she also serves as the Director of the Honors Program. She wrote her dissertation on 19th- and early-20th-century African American women's literature. She has published biographical essays on romance authors Jennifer Crusie and Janet Dailey and presented papers on the romance plot in popular fiction and television.

Courtney **Watson** is an associate professor of English at Radford University Carilion, in Roanoke, Virginia. Her areas of expertise include undergraduate and graduate curriculum development for research and writing courses in the health sciences and American literature with a focus on literary travel, tourism, and heritage economies.

Rose **Williams** is academic staff in the Master of Creative Arts Therapies program at Murdoch University. Her roles include Clinic Director for the Creative Arts Therapies student clinic and lecturing in trauma and advanced clinical practice. Her interests include consensuality and intimacy alongside the role of reparative imagination and creativity in developing healthy intimate relationships.

Index

abortion 83–4
Allen, Danielle 17, 22
allyship 27–8
alpha male 21, 31–43, 72
antihero 31, 207–8, 210
Anzieu, Didier 53–4
Austen, Jane 32, 35, 104; *see also Pride and Prejudice*
autism 11, 150–63; *see also* neurodiversity

Backfire 169–84; *see also* Coulter, Catherine
bad boy 10, 31–43
Bait 39
Band Sinister 64
BDSM 5, 6, 17, 34, 41, 42, 43, 71, 216, 217
Bérubé, Michael 151, 155
The Best Man's Baby 139, 144
The Big Bang Theory 150–1
Bildungsroman 103, 109, 202, 205
birth control 83–4, 94
Blindside 169–84; *see also* Coulter, Catherine
bloggers 4, 222
Bly, Mary 2–3
bodice-rippers 7, 111, 122
Brontë, Charlotte 10, 32, 97–116; *see also Jane Eyre*
Brontë, Emily 32, 35, 39; *see also Wuthering Heights*
Burke, Tarana 22, 32
Byronic hero 31, 35, 97, 100, 108

The Captive Prince 11, 216–30; *see also* Pacat, C.S.
caste 187–98
Cixous, Hélène 48, 51, 54
class 11, 35, 55, 57, 98, 101, 104, 111, 132, 152, 157, 160, 161, 168, 170–2, 174, 176, 180, 183, 208, 218
Cleage, Pearl 122
Cole, Alyssa 107, 112; *see also An Extraordinary Union*
Cole, Tillie 146; *see also Sweet Fall*
Collins, Sara 109–10, 112; *see also The Confessions of Frannie Langton*
colonialism 102–5, 106–8, 111–16

Colony of Ants 202–4
community 157–9, 172, 176, 182–4, 191–3, 213; academic 69–70, 74; autistic 152, 163; BDSM 40; ED 143, 145; #MeToo 32; online 203, 201–14, 217–18, 222; romance 7, 12, 42, 62, 64–6, 221
The Confessions of Frannie Langton 109–10, 112; *see also* Collins, Sara
consent 5, 10, 31, 32, 34, 36, 39, 52–60, 62–74, 84–5, 88–9, 155, 156–7, 225, 227, 230
Corrupt 31–43; *see also* Douglas, Penelope
Coulter, Catherine 170–77, 184
The Cove 169–84; *see also* Coulter, Catherine
COVID-19 201–2, 214

dark romance 5, 6, 31–2, 34–5, 41, 42
disability 151, 153–5, 157, 161, 163, 180
diversity 10, 11, 12, 17, 20, 29
The Divorce Party 139, 143, 145–6; *see also* Hayward, Jennifer
Double Take 169–84; *see also* Coulter, Catherine
Douglas, Penelope 32, 39, 40, 42, 43; *see also Corrupt*
du Maurier, Daphne 35, 107

eating disorders 136–47
Elliot, Kendra 170–74, 181–2
Empty Net 139, 146; *see also* Gale, Avon
Enigma 169–84; *see also* Coulter, Catherine
Enticing Benedict Cole 48, 55–9; *see also* Redgold, Eliza
erasure 106–7
escapism 33, 72, 106–7, 146
An Extraordinary Union 112–16; *see also* Cole, Alyssa

family 35, 85, 90, 103, 108, 112, 122, 129, 132, 139, 140, 141, 145, 147, 160, 171–3, 175–6, 178, 182, 183–4, 213
fandom 216–17, 224
fanfiction 3, 6, 11, 99, 106, 216–26
fantasy 1, 3, 7, 18, 31, 33–4, 37, 39, 72, 92, 101, 203, 204–8, 211, 214, 223
Fast Women 139

Fatal Accusation 169–84
Fatal Affair 169–84
Fatal Chaos 169–84
Fatal Invasion 169–84
Fatal Jeopardy 169–84
Fatal Justice 169–84
Fatal Mistake 169–84
Fatal Reckoning 169–84
Fatal Threat 169–84
feminism 22, 26, 27, 32, 33, 49–52, 54–9, 63, 65–6, 69, 71–2, 73, 84, 85–6, 87–90, 93, 99–101, 103, 154–5, 160, 163, 168, 202, 214
Fifty Shades of Grey 6, 8, 20–1, 31–43, 100, 101, 216, 221, 222, 225; see also James, E.L.
Forbidden 112–14, 115, 116; see also Jenkins, Beverly
Force, Marie 170–84
Foxes 139
Frye, Northrop 25, 154

Gabaldon, Diana 80, 87–8, 89, 93; see also *Outlander*
Gale, Avon 146; see also *Empty Net*
game culture 207–10
gaze: female 90–1, 93, 168–9; 173; loving 175; male 58, 91; societal 112; surveillant 174–5
gender 10, 17–18, 20, 27, 28, 34, 37, 39, 41, 52–5, 69, 79, 80, 89, 91, 98, 100, 104, 133, 137, 140, 151, 157, 160, 167–8, 169, 173, 179, 189, 191, 208, 210–11, 218
A Girl Like Her 151, 157–60; see also Hibbert, Talia
The God of Small Things 187, 188, 192, 193–4, 197; see also Roy, Arundhati
gossip 157–60
gothic 35–6, 41, 110
Greer, Germaine 21, 100–1
Guillory, Jasmine 121–34; see also *The Proposal*; *Royal Holiday*; *The Wedding Date*; *The Wedding Party*

happy ending (includes HEA, HFN) 3, 6–7, 28, 34, 38, 69, 73, 105, 107, 110, 112, 113, 121, 143, 150, 183, 194, 206
Harlequin (publisher) 5, 10, 31, 47–52, 55, 68, 104, 111, 145
Hayward, Jennifer 145–6; see also *The Divorce Party*
Heavyweight 138, 141
heteronormativity 188, 189, 218
heterosexuality 188, 191, 192
Hibbert, Talia 151; see also *A Girl Like Her*
Hoang, Helen 151, 155; see also *The Kiss Quotient*
The Hollow of Fear 162–3; see also Thomas, Sherry
Holt, Victoria 107–8
homosexuality 80, 91, 194, 225, 229; see also M/M romance; queer romance; same-sex romance
hooks, bell 27, 65, 66, 168

identification 79–95, 98, 163, 179, 208
identity 22, 35, 41, 51, 93, 98, 114, 127, 156, 157, 160, 163, 176, 179, 193, 202, 206, 211, 214, 218, 223, 226
The Illegitimate Tycoon 143, 144
Illouz, Eva 18, 20, 23, 28
The Impossible Boy 140
independent publishing 4–5, 31–2
Insidious 169–84; see also Coulter, Catherine
International Association for the Study of Popular Romance 1, 70
intersectionality 163, 223, 224
intersex 187–190, 194, 198
Intimate Civility 52–60
Irigaray, Luce 39, 51, 54

James, E.L. 6, 32, 42, 100, 216, 221, 222, 225; see also *Fifty Shades of Grey*
James, Eloisa 2
Jane Eyre 10, 31–43, 97–116; see also Brontë, Charlotte
Journal of Popular Romance Studies 1, 70

Kimmel, Michael 22, 25
Kindle 4, 31–2
The Kiss Quotient 151, 155–7; see also Hoang, Helen
Kristeva, Julia 51–2

literary identification 79–83, 86–95, 99, 111
LiveJournal 11
Locke, Katherine 145
Lorde, Audre 51, 131–2
Love on My Mind 152
Loving with a Vengeance 2, 104; see also Modleski, Tania

MacLean, Sarah 21
The Madness of Lord Ian Mackenzie 152
marginalization 8, 51, 80, 81, 108, 133, 171, 188–9, 193, 196, 208, 223
marketability 3, 4, 8–9, 31, 34, 68, 87, 133, 147, 216, 225
masculinity 19, 21, 169, 176; spectacular 24; toxic 10, 18–29, 32, 34, 38, 72, 125
The Master's New Governess 51–9; see also Redgold, Eliza
The Maze 169–84; see also Coulter, Catherine
mental health 11, 92, 136–47
A Merciful Death 169–84; see also Elliot, Kendra
A Merciful Fate 169–84; see also Elliot, Kendra
A Merciful Promise 169–84; see also Elliot, Kendra

A Merciful Secret 169–84; *see also* Elliot, Kendra
A Merciful Silence 169–84; *see also* Elliot, Kendra
A Merciful Truth 169–84; *see also* Elliot, Kendra
#MeToo 10, 18, 22, 32, 42, 47, 49, 51, 52–3, 55–60, 62, 67, 74, 156, 168
Milan, Courtney 12, 141; see also *Trade Me*
Mills and Boon 31, 42, 47, 101
The Ministry of Utmost Happiness 187–98
misogyny 9, 23, 34, 38, 182
M/M romance 137, 141, 146, 216–30; *see also* homosexuality; queer romance; same-sex romance
Modleski, Tania 2, 88, 104; *see also Loving with a Vengeance*
morality 26, 35, 37, 52–4, 98, 102, 112, 138, 147, 167–70, 174, 176–179, 202, 207–8, 209, 213

A Natural History of the Romance Novel 2, 69, 104–5; *see also* Regis, Pamela
Nemesis 169–84; *see also* Coulter, Catherine
neurodiversity 5, 11, 163; *see also* autism
new adult romance 5, 34, 42, 140, 142, 145, 146

objectification 22, 24, 27, 80, 91, 152, 160, 174–5
operating system fiction 201–214
outcast 187, 195–7
Outlander (print and television series) 10, 79–95
#ownvoices 10, 144–6

Pacat, C.S. 11, 216–30
pandemic 201–2, 204, 214
Paradox 169–84; *see also* Coulter, Catherine
patriarchy 2, 3, 20, 55, 59, 72, 80, 81, 83, 86, 90, 94, 100, 101, 103, 116, 151, 152, 172, 202, 205, 214, 218
Playing the Duke's Mistress 48, 55–9; *see also* Redgold, Eliza
police procedurals 169–84
Power Play 169–84; *see also* Coulter, Catherine
pregnancy 83, 143–4
Pride and Prejudice 32, 34–5, 110; *see also* Austen, Jane
privilege 27, 50, 66, 91, 94, 106, 152, 168, 170, 173, 176, 178, 180, 189
The Proposal 124–7; *see also* Guillory, Jasmine

queer romance 187–98, 209–10, 212–13, 216–30; *see also* homosexuality; M/M romance; same-sex romance

race 11, 80, 94, 104, 108–10, 111–16, 121–34, 157, 160, 167, 170–2, 208, 218, 223–4
racism 12, 106–7, 114, 125–6, 128, 131, 132, 168, 171, 181, 183, 223

Radway, Janice A. 2, 20, 24, 87; *see also Reading the Romance*
rape 7, 31, 32, 39, 43, 50, 67–8, 69, 72, 74, 82, 83–5, 91–2, 95, 147, 179, 223; *see also* sexual assault
Reading the Romance 2; *see also* Radway, Janice A
the realness 121–34
Rebecca 35, 108; *see also* du Maurier, Daphne
Redgold, Eliza 47–60; *see also Enticing Benedict Cole*; *The Master's New Governess*; *Playing the Duke's Mistress*; *The Scandalous Suffragette*
Regis, Pamela 2–3, 4, 6, 21, 23, 25, 27, 59, 71, 73, 104–5, 142, 154; *see also A Natural History of the Romance Novel*
representation 10–11, 121–34, 136–47, 150–63
The Ripped Bodice 12
Roach, Catherine 70–3
Roberts, Nora 73
Romance Writers of America 4, 6–7, 12, 70, 156, 202
Roy, Arundhati 11, 187–98
Royal Holiday 129–33; *see also* Guillory, Jasmie
Ryan, Kennedy 12

A Scandal in Belgravia 161–2
The Scandalous Suffragette 47–51, 55–9; *see also* Redgold, Eliza
Second Position 144–5
self-publishing 3–4, 5, 11, 217, 221
sensorium 53–5, 56
sentimental hero 21, 23, 26
sexism 167, 180, 183
sexual agency 66–7, 69, 71, 74, 83, 88, 94, 191
sexual assault 83–6, 91–2, 227; *see also* rape
sexual orientation 11, 80, 137, 218, 229
Shen, L.J. 32, 36; *see also Vicious*
sista lit 121–34
Sixty Days trilogy 31–42; *see also* West, Jade
slash 11, 216–230
slavery: sexual 31, 105, 217, 223–7; slavefic 224–5; transatlantic 94, 101–3, 106–16
Smart Bitches, Trashy Books 4, 48, 70, 73
social media 3, 4, 7, 11, 12, 125–6, 201–14, 216–30
The Speed of Dark 152
Split Second 169–84; *see also* Coulter, Catherine
A Study in Scarlet Women 151, 160–2
Sweatpants Season 17, 22–9; *see also* Allen, Danielle
Sweet Fall 143, 146; *see also* Cole, Tillie

Teach Me Tonight 70, 73
Three Times the Charm 139
time-travel 10, 79–95, 204–9, 211
#TimesUp 31, 62, 67, 74

Torre, Alessandra 33, 40
Trade Me 141; *see also* Milan, Courtney
trope(s) 11, 32–4, 40–1, 57–8, 69, 88, 116, 156, 172, 173, 187, 189, 195, 202, 216–30
The Truth About Happily Ever After 140
Twilight 6, 20, 216

Unicorns and Rainbow Poop 139

Vicious 31–43; *see also* Shen, L.J.

web romance 201–14

The Wedding Date 123–4; *see also* Guillory, Jasmine
The Wedding Party 127–9, 132–3; *see also* Guillory, Jasmie
West, Jade 32, 39, 41, 42; see also *Sixty Days* trilogy
Whiplash 169–84; *see also* Coulter, Catherine
whiteness 11, 81, 107, 110, 113–15, 167–84
The Wide Sargasso Sea 107, 108, 110
Wuthering Heights 31–43, 99, 110; *see also* Brontë, Emily

www.ingramcontent.com/pod-product-compliance
Ingram Content Group UK Ltd.
Pitfield, Milton Keynes, MK11 3LW, UK
UKHW041941140426
5217IPUK00014B/593